Gender,
Culture,
and
Christianity

Asian Thought and Culture

Charles Wei-hsun Fu
General Editor

Vol. 25

PETER LANG
New York • Washington, D.C./Baltimore • San Francisco
Bern • Frankfurt am Main • Berlin • Vienna • Paris

Gael Graham

Gender, Culture, and Christianity

American Protestant Mission Schools in China 1880—1930

PETER LANG
New York • Washington, D.C./Baltimore • San Francisco
Bern • Frankfurt am Main • Berlin • Vienna • Paris

Library of Congress Cataloging-in-Publication Data

Graham, Gael.
Gender, culture, and Christianity: American Protestant
mission schools in China, 1880–1930/Gael Graham.
p.   cm. — (Asian thought and culture; vol. 25)
Includes bibliographical references and index.
1. Protestant churches—Education—China—History—19th century.
2. Protestant churches—Education—China—History—20th century.
3. Missions—China—Educational work—History—19th century.
4. Missions—China—Educational work—History—20th century. 5. Sex
differences in education—China—History—19th century. 6. Sex differences
in education—China—History—20th century. 7. Women
missionaries—China. I. Title. II. Series.
LC626.C5G73   377'.84'0951—dc20   94-47552
ISBN 0-8204-2767-5
ISSN 0893-6870

Die Deutsche Bibliothek-CIP-Einheitsaufnahme

Graham, Gael:
Gender, culture, and Christianity: American protestant mission schools in
China, 1880-1930/Gael Graham. – New York; Washington, D.C./Baltimore;
San Francisco; Bern; Frankfurt am Main; Berlin; Vienna; Paris: Lang.
(Asian thought and culture; Vol. 25)
ISBN 0-8204-2767-5
NE: GT

The paper in this book meets the guidelines for permanence and durability of
the Committee on Production Guidelines for Book Longevity of the Council of
Library Resources.

© 1995 Peter Lang Publishing, Inc., New York

Printed in the United States of America.

Contents

ABBREVIATIONS IN ENDNOTES

ABCFM   American Board of Commissioners for Foreign Missions, United Church Board for World Ministries (successor to the ABCFM), located at the Houghton Library, Harvard University, Cambridge, MA.

BWM   Board of World Missions, Presbyterian Church, U.S., at Presbyterian Church (U.S.A.), Department of History, Montreat, NC.

ECMC   East Carolina Manuscript Collection, Special Collections, Joyner Library, East Carolina University, Greenville, NC.

ELCA   Evangelical Lutheran Church in America, Region 3 Archives, St. Paul, MN.

GBGM   General Board of Global Missions of The United Methodist Church, General Commission on Archives and History, Drew University, Madison, NJ.

MCOHP   Midwest China Oral History Project [ELCA]

HIA   Hoover Institution Archives, Hoover Institution on War, Revolution and Peace, Stanford, CA.

PC (USA)   Presbyterian Church, (U.S.A.), Department of History and Records Management Services, Philadelphia, PA.

RG   Record Group

UBCHEA   United Board For Christian Higher Education in Asia [YDSL]

UOSC   University of Oregon Special Collections, University of Oregon, Eugene, OR.

YDSL   Yale Divinity School Library, Yale University, New Haven, CT.

Introduction

In 1904, Arthur J. Brown, an American missionary in China, asked rhetorically, "What is civilization without the gospel?" He might as easily have inverted the question and asked "What is the gospel without civilization?" for the impulse to civilize as well as Christianize the Chinese was a driving force in the American Protestant missionary movement. In China, missionaries undertook four types of extra-evangelical work designed to help "civilize" the country: medical and educational work beginning in the 1830s, urban social work in the 1920s, and rural reconstruction in the 1930s. In addition to their civilizing functions these works had both charitable and tutelary aspects; the intention was to convey Christian benevolence while simultaneously demonstrating the superiority of Western culture.[1]

Coupling Christianity and civilization—by which American missionaries meant Western culture—was a fundamental characteristic of their work in China until the 1920s, when the missionaries made a belated and lukewarm attempt to Sinify the Christian church in China. Throughout the missionary movement in China there were periods of conflict between those Americans who believed in pure evangelism without a concerted effort at cultural renovation and those who sought a broader mandate. Even those missionaries who argued in favor of simple evangelism, however, were not prepared to countenance such Chinese customs as footbinding or plural marriage. Although they opposed these practices on religious grounds, stating that footbinding, polygamy, and other Chinese customs were incompatible with Christianity, their "pure" evangelism had clear cultural implications. All missionaries therefore expected that their work would bring about basic changes in Chinese society. In the course of the American Protestant missionary movement in China (1830–1950), moreover, those who worked to civilize as well as evangelize were most often in the ascendency.

My initial research question centered on the issue of cultural imperialism in the American China mission. It thus seemed logical to study mission schools as likely sites of American efforts to impose their own culture on the Chinese. As the study progressed, however, the story that unfolded was one of cultural exchange and interaction, of borrowings back and forth across a selectively permeable cultural border. From the missionary perspective, their relationship with the Chinese was not an equal one, for they always conceived of their work in China as a gift bestowed by a superior civilization on a backward one. The missionary enterprise in China was thus intrinsically pedagogical, with the missionaries as teachers and the Chinese as their pupils. Casting the power dynamics in this fashion allowed missionaries to disregard the significant ways in which they altered their own educational project to make it acceptable to the Chinese.

My intention of "adding women missionaries" to my study likewise underwent modification as my pile of research notes grew thicker. Historians have noted the preponderance of women in the Protestant missionary movement (60 per cent by 1900), but the significance of women's presence has not been addressed in the majority of works on missionaries in China.[2] What historians have not understood is that gender ideology—missionaries' deeply held beliefs about sex roles and the relations between the sexes—was a central part of the missionaries' critique of Chinese society. The status of Chinese women, the roles they played within their families and in society, and practices such as female infanticide, footbinding, and polygamy, not only proved to missionaries the inferiority of Chinese culture but also the wickedness of "heathen" religions. Only non-Christian religions sanctioned the abysmal treatment of women in China (and elsewhere on the map of pagandom); the high status of women in Western countries was a direct consequence, missionaries believed, of Christian influence. Only Christianity was capable of saving the women of China. In addition, missionaries believed that converting the women of China was the shortest path to a self-perpetuating Christian church in China. A church of Chinese men, they argued, would last but one generation; if the women were Christian, they would ensure that the next generation was raised in that faith.[3]

Protestant missionaries in China thus had a dual goal: to convert the Chinese to Christianity and to alter their gender patterns. These goals were not easily separable, for the missionaries were convinced that if the Chinese adopted Christianity they would necessarily change their ideas about gender. The missionaries pursued both aims in their schools. Mission schools not only attempted to convert the students by teaching them Christian doctrine, making them attend worship services, and setting them a good example of the Christian life, but they also made determined efforts to eradicate footbinding, modify marriage practices, and enhance the status of Chinese girls and women within Chinese society. In the Christian boys' schools, boys were taught that girls as well as boys were worthy of God's love, that they were responsible for ending the practice of footbinding, and that Christian men respected women.

Education was the first extra-evangelical work that American missionaries undertook in China, and it remained a vital part of their work until the early 1950s, when the American Protestant mission in China ended. For sheer numbers, American missionary educators came to outnumber the educational workers of every other nationality in China.[4] Far surpassing the statistical significance of the American missionary educational movement was the fact that in establishing schools the missionaries had touched the nerve center of Chinese civilization. Not only were teachers and educated people greatly esteemed in Chinese society, but education was the mainstay of the civil bureaucracy that supported the dynastic system. Through a series of imperial examinations educated men were drawn into the ranks of this bureaucracy. Those who failed the examinations were still honored as learned men. Because men from most walks of life were permitted to sit for these examinations, education held the possibility of upward mobility for the Chinese masses. At the same time, by ensuring that successful candidates for public office had thoroughly imbibed, through a standard course of study, the ideology of the ruling class, education enhanced social stability.[5]

Both American missionaries and the Chinese had faith in the power of education to shape what both viewed as essentially malleable human beings. As historian Jessie Lutz has noted, "ethical indoctrination" was at the core of traditional Chinese and Protestant mission education.[6] Rather than complementing or reinforcing each other, however, these two educational systems were in competition. By introducing Christian teachings, the missionaries labored to undermine Confucianism, which was both the ethical base of Chinese society and the main staple of Chinese education. By introducing the so-called "Western subjects" in their schools, they shook China's conception of what constituted education and circumvented the government's power to control it and determine its purposes. By establishing schools for girls and insisting on their right to an education, the missionaries articulated a critique of the Chinese gender system and helped to weaken traditional social relations. In conjunction with military and diplomatic pressure from foreign powers, missionary education was a factor in the decline in the authority of the Chinese ruling elite. Even after the 1911 Revolution, when this elite was increasingly drawn from the ranks of Western-educated Chinese, the presence of a system of education beyond the control of the Chinese government was a threat to the sovereignty, even the legitimacy of the various groups contending to replace the defunct dynasty. Many Chinese believed that autonomous mission schools were an obstacle to the formation of a stable and unified China.

This book advances three arguments. The first is that American teaching missionaries made substantial concessions to Chinese beliefs and practices in the schools they established, even as they sought to undermine many of those same beliefs and practices. Perhaps more surprising is the fact that in their eagerness to provide a quality education and to attract Chinese students to their schools, missionaries acquiesced in the steady dilution of the evangelical component of their enterprise over time. A second argument is that American missionaries attempted to use their schools as vehicles for reforming the Chinese gender system. By "gender system" I refer to ideologies of sexual difference and how these were concretized in the assignment and maintainence of sex roles. Mission schools used a variety of means to induce Chinese students—and their parents—to conform to foreign beliefs about gender. Third, as the pace of revolutionary change in China quickened in the early twentieth century, teaching missionaries revised their earlier assessments of the relative merits of Chinese and American culture. Profoundly threatened by radical Chinese experiments with new gender practices as well as by the rising demands of the Chinese to control education within their own country, and shaken by the emergence of a secular, consumerist youth culture in the United States, American teaching missionaries in China came to see value in Confucian traditions just at the moment when many of their students rebelled against such traditions. The fear that they had contributed to the dissolution of an ideology that was necessary for social control in China led teaching missionaries to question, to some degree, their reformist program.

Rather than focus on one specific missionary society or one region of China in which missionaries worked, I have chosen to make a more general survey. Although there were dozens of American Protestant missionary societies in China, I concentrate primarily on the largest of the mainstream denominations: Congregationalists, Methodists, Presbyterians, Baptists, and, to a lesser degree, Lutherans and Episcopalians. I do not address American Catholics in China because the first American Catholic missionary society to send missionaries to China was not founded until 1911 and they were even slower to become involved in education.[7] In downplaying denominational and regional differences, there are undoubtedly subtleties I am disregarding, but by the 1890s educational missionaries in China were compelled, both by their own increasingly professional outlook as educators and by competition from Chinese government schools, to draw together in organizations that de-emphasized denominational differences in the greater interest of perpetuating and improving Christian schools in China. By the twentieth century, a Baptist mission teacher had more in common with a Congregationalist mission teacher than a Baptist preacher had with his Congregationalist counterpart. (Gender, for one thing; preachers were men, while women dominated mission school teaching.)[8]

The bulk of this study centers on the years 1880 to 1930. Although I will discuss the foundations of American mission education, the years 1880 to 1930 represent the heyday of Christian education in China. Before that time, mission schools were institutionally and academically weak. After 1930, the missionaries were forced to share power with the Chinese in administering their schools and had to abide by regulations laid down by the Chinese government.

In the first chapter, I examine the origins of the educational arm of the American Protestant China mission, the compromises these missionaries felt compelled to make to attract Chinese students into the schools, and the importance of gender among American missionaries. The second chapter discusses the expansion of mission education, both in terms of the number of schools and the broadened curriculum they adopted. Gender played a role in many of the new subjects that missionaries introduced into their school curriculum. Chapter three focuses on the missionary critique of the Chinese gender system and how they used both their boys' and girls' schools to effect its reform. I also discuss the missionary reaction to the "New Woman" of China, who began to emerge in the early twentieth century. In the fourth chapter, I look at the student nationalist movement, how it affected the mission schools and missionary education in general, and the gendered nationalism missionaries observed within their schools. Chapter five is about the missionary reaction to efforts by Chinese

Christians to increase their power within the schools, and the government's insistence that all private schools in China be registered.

In negotiating the transition from the Wade-Giles to the *pinyin* system of transliterating Chinese words, I have retained the older Wade-Giles spelling for the names of mission schools in China and the Chinese who either worked at or attended these schools. I use *pinyin* for places and for well-known people and institutions, whose *pinyin* names are generally familiar. For example, I use "Guomindang" [GMD] and "Jiang Jieshi" rather than "Kuomintang" and "Chiang Kai-shek." Thus the reader will find references to Nanking University, a Methodist institution, in the city of Nanjing. In keeping with common practice, however, I refer to "Sun Yatsen," rather than the Mandarinized "Sun Chongshan."

I would like to thank the archivists and librarians of the following institutions: Yale Divinity School Library, the Archives of the United Methodist Church at Drew University in Madison, New Jersey, the University of Oregon Special Collections in Eugene, the Presbyterian Church (U.S.A.) Department of History and Records Management Services in Philadelphia, the East Carolina Manuscript Collection at East Carolina University in Greenville, the Presbyterian Church (U.S.A.) Department of History in Montreat, North Carolina, the Evangelical Lutheran Church in America, Region Three Archives, at Luther Northwestern Seminary in St. Paul, and Houghton Library at Harvard University. They gave invaluable help in accessing manuscript collections, asked insightful questions, and helped to make the months spent in research pleasurable. Thanks to the United Church Board for World Ministries for permission to cite the ABCFM material housed at Harvard's Houghton Library, and to the General Board of Global Missions for permission to use and cite material from the Archives of the United Methodist Church.

Thanks to the editors of *Signs: Journal of Women in Culture and Society*, published by the University of Chicago Press, for permitting me to reproduce here (in somewhat altered form) my article "Exercising Control: Sports and Physical Education in American Protestant Mission Schools in China, 1880–1930," copyright 1994 by The University of Chicago. All rights reserved. Similarly, I thank the editors of the *Journal of Women's History*, published by the University of Indiana Press, for allowing an abbreviated version of my article "The *Cumberland* Incident of 1928: Gender, Nationalism, and Social Change in American Mission

Schools in China" to be reproduced in this book. Copyright 1994 Journal of Women's History, Vol. 6 No. 3 (Fall).

I would also like to thank my doctoral committee at the University of Michigan for struggling through countless drafts and offering useful criticism: Sidney Fine, Ernest Young, Carol Karlsen, and Martin Whyte. Thanks too to friends and collegues whose support carried me over many a rocky place: Laura Wendorff, Karen Mason, Liao Da-chi, Joel Nigg, Laura Sines, Mark Byers, Andy Rutrough, Barbara Walls, Jamey Wells, Max Williams and Curtis Wood. Thanks to Merry Woodard for her invaluable help with the formatting of the manuscript.

Finally, with the deepest love and gratitude, I thank my family. This book is dedicated to the memory of my grandfathers, Kenneth William Graham, Sr. and Jesse Marion Stevenson, who died while I was in graduate school.

ENDNOTES

1 Arthur J. Brown, *New Forces in Old China: An Unwelcome but Inevitable Awakening* (New York: Fleming H. Revell Co, 1904), p. 127.

2 Jane Hunter, *The Gospel of Gentility: American Women Missionaries in Turn-of-the-Century China* (New Haven: Yale University Press, 1984), p. xiii. Most works have at least managed to mention women, and there are a number of denominational histories that focus on women's missionary societies, but it is only relatively recently that historians have begun to consider gender as a category for analysis. Such works include: R. Pierce Beaver, *American Protestant Women in World Mission: The History of the First Feminist Movement* (Grand Rapids, Mich.: William B. Eerdmans Publishing Co., 1968); Leslie A. Flemming, ed., *Women's Work for Women* (Boulder, Colo.: Westview Press, 1989); Patricia R. Hill, *The World Their Household: The American Woman's Foreign Mission Movement and Cultural Transformation, 1870–1920* (Ann Arbor: University of Michigan Press, 1985); Hunter, *The Gospel of Gentility*; Irwin T. Hyatt, Jr., *Our Ordered Lives Confess: Three Nineteenth-Century American Missionaries in East Shantung* (Cambridge: Harvard University Press, 1976); and Ruth Tucker, *Guardians of the Great Commission: The Story of Women in Modern Missions* (Grand Rapids, Mich.: Zondervan Publishing House, 1988).

3 See, for example, Mary Ninde Gamewell, *New Life Currents in China* (New York: Missionary Education Movement of the United States and Canada, Methodist Book Concern, 1919), p. 144.

4 As early as 1877, Americans had more schools in China than any other Protestant nationality: there were 202 American schools, 123 British schools, and 22 schools run by Continental Protestant missionaries. This trend continued into the twentieth century so that in 1916 there were 2,278 American schools with 67, 394 students, 1,686 British schools with 40,055 students, and 176 German schools with 5,385 students. One should keep in mind, however, that mission statistics are notoriously inaccurate; all statistics used here should be regarded as indicative of general tendencies only. Alice H. Gregg, *China and*

8

Educational Autonomy: The Changing Role of the Protestant Educational Missionary in China, 1807–1937 (Syracuse, N.Y.: Syracuse University Press, 1946), p. 16, and James Bashford, *China, An Interpretation* (New York: Abingdon Press, 1919), p. 115.

5 Robert Dernberger, *et. al.*, *The Chinese: Adapting the Past, Building the Future* (Ann Arbor: Center for Chinese Studies, 1986), p. 141. In practice, the protracted period of study required to prepare for the examinations meant that the gentry generally monopolized the state bureaucratic positions. The lower classes could always hope that their sons, by dint of their brilliance, would prove the exceptions; the fact that poor men sometimes succeeded in the examinations bolstered this dream.

6 Jessie G. Lutz, *China and the Christian Colleges, 1850–1950* (Ithaca: Cornell University Press, 1971), p. 23.

7 Thomas A. Breslin, *China, American Catholicism and the Missionary* (University Park: Pennsylvania State University Press, 1980), p. 23.

8 By 1918, for example, one male missionary estimated that there were five foreign women to every three foreign men teaching in the mission schools; the ratio was two women for every man in the mission normal schools. *Chinese Recorder* 49 (April 1918): 215.

Chapter 1:
A Modest Beginning: American Protestant Education in Nineteenth-Century China

The American Protestant educational enterprise in China began in a quiet way in the port city of Guangzhou in 1833, just three years after Elijah Bridgman and David Abeel arrived in China. Bridgman and Abeel represented the Congregationalist American Board of Commissioners for Foreign Missions (ABCFM). Both men were interested in education, but it was Bridgman who established the first American mission school for Chinese boys. The little school was not Bridgman's sole concern; in addition to street preaching and direct evangelism, he worked on a new translation of the Bible and published a periodical called the *Chinese Recorder*.[1] From this casual beginning, it would have been difficult to foresee the important role education would come to play in the American missionary movement. Although Catholic and Protestant missionaries of other nationalities also engaged in educational work, American Protestants came to dominate foreign education in China.

American Protestant mission schools in China flourished for over one hundred years. In that time, teaching missionaries came to think of themselves as a breed apart from colleagues who limited their work to evangelism: they established organizations that cut across denominational and sometimes national lines; they set professional standards for themselves and their schools, and they created a school system that the Chinese government saw as both a model to emulate and a threat to be controlled. Within these schools, American missionaries not only provided students with both religious and secular instruction but also introduced Western conceptions of gender and citizenship.

These Americans came to China to instruct the Chinese and to change them; like other missionaries, they perceived themselves, initially, as emissaries of a superior culture. Despite American arrogance, their teaching of the Chinese is not simply a story of a one-sided imposition of foreign ideas and institutions. Instead, American teaching missionaries found themselves involved in complex and on-going negotiations with the Chinese, in which each side attempted to shape the mission schools to best serve their own interests. In this chapter, I examine the origins of the missionary educational movement in China, why missionaries decided to open schools there, the nature of the earliest schools, and the importance of gender to the missionary educators.

Purposes of Christian Schools

By 1860, after losing a series of wars to various Western powers, China had been forced to sign a number of agreements known collectively as the "Unequal Treaties." The impact of these treaties on the success of Christian missionary work was considerable: reversing previous prohibitions, foreign missionaries' presence in China was now officially sanctioned, and they were permitted to erect churches, hospitals, schools, and residences, first only in the treaty ports, and later anywhere they chose.[2] The treaties allowed existing missions to expand into China proper and drew new missionary groups into the field.[3] The Unequal Treaties did not, however, compel the Chinese to accept Christianity, so missionaries still had to devise ways to make their message appealing to the Chinese. Some American Protestant missionaries thought education might be a means of attracting Chinese to the missions and ultimately to Christianity.

When the American foreign missionary movement began in 1810, mission boards did not explicitly direct missionaries to establish schools. However, missionaries realized that making converts would necessarily involve some form of education, since converts would have to be taught Christian doctrine and church history. American Protestants wanted converts sufficiently literate to be able to read their Bibles, for unlike Roman Catholicism, Protestantism centered on the authority of the Bible, and so literacy was essential, especially for native pastors and lay assistants. To facilitate literacy among their converts in China, missionaries not only established schools and seminaries but also worked out a system of Romanized writing that allowed Chinese to read transliterated texts after four months of training.[4]

The low social status of their earliest converts made education even more important to American missionaries. Missionaries originally hoped to convert literate Chinese of the "better classes," believing that if the literati adopted Christianity, the great mass of the Chinese population would follow suit. Most Chinese literati, however, regarded the missionaries as uncouth and barely educated, since few missionaries were conversant with the Confucian classics. Worse still, few educated Chinese were impressed with the Bible when they compared it to these classics. Failing to convert the rich and influential, American missionaries were forced to follow Christian teaching and historical precedent by evangelizing among the poor.[5] Thus their first converts were usually mission servants—people of low social status and limited or no education.[6] Later, a twentieth-century Chinese would scorn the earliest Chinese pastors as "coolies with shoes and stockings on." However, at the time, American missionaries hoped education would alter popular Chinese perceptions of the low status of Christian converts.[7]

The dauntingly slow pace of Chinese conversions also helped push missionaries into educational work. American Methodists in Fuzhou, for example, worked for ten years before making a single convert, and by 1853 there were only 350 Chinese Protestants in the entire country. In 1922, after more than a hundred years of Protestant mission work, less than 1 per cent of the Chinese were Christians of any sort.[8] Working with children seemed likely to speed the process. Many missionaries agreed with Electa Butler, who ran a Presbyterian boys' school in China around the turn of the century, that mission schools could be powerful tools of evangelism. "All who are engaged in training children will, I think, agree that they are more easily led to Christ than adults," Butler wrote. "Many...could testify to their stability. They hold fast to their profession. They have more years of service before them, and they do not have to unlearn so much evil as the man who has grown gray in the service of Satan."[9] Moreover, through students, missionaries gained access to their homes, which otherwise might have been closed to them. A report from a Baptist mission station exulted when the Chinese began "patronizing the schools and then attending services," and added, "We now have a point of contact with the heathen and a ground of appeal as well."[10] Because the Chinese regarded the founding of schools as a "good work," missionaries also seem to have hoped that their schools would impress the Chinese as examples of Christian benevolence.[11]

The importance of education in Chinese culture also drew the missionaries into this work. However, until the establishment of the modern educational system in 1903, the sole purpose of formal Chinese education was to prepare boys and men to pass government-sponsored examinations. The civil service that governed the country was staffed from the ranks of successful candidates for these tests. The examination system originated in the Han dynasty (202 B. C. E.–220 C. E.), although the system used by the Qing had evolved during the Ming dynasty (1368–1644).[12]

The Chinese government operated academies (*shuyuan*) for those who passed the prefectural, or lowest-level examinations. The bulk of Chinese education, however, especially elementary education, was privately financed and operated. These private schools, or *sishu,* were managed in several ways. The simplest but most expensive method was for a family to hire a tutor, sometimes allowing the children of neighbors or relatives to share in the lessons. If Chinese girls received any literary education at all, it was through tutors in the home, because it was considered improper for them, especially those girls from wealthier families, to appear on the public streets as they neared puberty. Girls were occasionally educated alongside their brothers until their teens; at that point the girls' education shifted to domestic skills while the boys prepared to sit for the first government examination. Women were not allowed to take the imperial examinations, so there was no reason to educate them further.[13] As an alternative to private tutoring, a lineage might rent space in a local temple and hire a teacher to educate the children of that clan. In other instances, children were sent to schools established by teachers with reputations for preparing successful examination candidates.[14]

Although most education was in private hands, the Chinese curriculum was uniform because the government prescribed the books that were tested in the official examinations. Elementary education was based on character recognition and rote memorization of these texts, which, unlike Western primers, were not written for children. Moreover, they were not written in the vernacular but in a dense, formal language that was incomprehensible to those without classical training. Chinese students were expected to memorize the sounds and characters in the classical texts without knowing what they meant. When a boy was twelve or thirteen, he completed the memorization of the classics. Only then did he begin to interpret the texts, practice calligraphy, and compose essays in a highly formal style, skills that were tested in the imperial examinations. As historians of Chinese education have pointed out, the system did not reward independent thinking or creative genius. It did, however, provide the state with an ample pool of potential servants, all of whom had been thoroughly indoctrinated in the ideology of the ruling class. There were few class restrictions on taking the examinations, but as we shall see, the cost of education was an obstacle for most boys.[15]

Although education was often inexpensive by Western standards, even the trifling cost of books, paper, and brushes was beyond many poor Chinese families. Furthermore, many families could not afford to forego the labor of a son for the years required by a classical education. Hence, although education was highly valued by Chinese at all socioeconomic levels, few Chinese men, and even fewer women, were educated.[16] Many Chinese hungered for education just as American Protestant missionaries were coming to China in larger numbers. If mission schools could rival the traditional schools or provide an acceptable alternative education, they could serve the interests of the Chinese as well as those of the foreigners.

In the nineteenth-century United States, Americans were elevating education to an article of faith; the belief that education was the key to both the development of a successful democracy and the maintenance of social control became widespread as the common school movement gathered force (except in the South) in the 1830s and 1840s.[17] Americans and Chinese shared a belief in the instrumental value of education; in both countries elites perceived it as effective in molding personality and behavior, while non-elites saw it as the key to social advancement. It was upon this patch of common ground that teaching missionaries found a foothold in the inhospitable climate of nineteenth-century China.

Early Mission Schools

American Protestants had good reasons to establish schools, but Christian education would only succeed if Chinese parents could be persuaded to allow their children to attend. Wishing to cast their nets as widely as possible and believing firmly in the attractive power of their Gospel, teaching missionaries made two momentous decisions at the outset: first, they would not limit enrollment to the children of already converted parents, and second, they would offer training in the classics in addition to Christian teaching.[18] The promise that their sons would be taught the classics, traditionally the path that could lead a boy into government service and raise the status of his entire family, prompted many poor parents whose sons would not otherwise have been educated to risk sending them to a mission school. Thus mission students were drawn first from the ranks of the urban poor, and their education was completely subsidized by the missionaries, who paid for their books, paper, food, and often their clothing.[19]

In addition to teaching Christian doctrine and the Confucian classics, American mission schools focused on the "Three R's" (reading, writing, and arithmetic) that formed the backbone of American elementary education. The curriculum of the mission schools did not expand much beyond these subjects until the 1870s and 1880s. In terms of the traditional Chinese curriculum, teaching Christianity was the most important innovation in the mission boys' schools. In terms of pedagogy, at first the missionaries taught as Chinese teachers did and emphasized rote memorization and recitation, but they gradually began to make some changes in traditional Chinese pedagogical methods. They made a determined effort, for instance, to have their Chinese assistants explain the classics to the children, rather than have them struggle along in ignorance of what they were memorizing. Rote memorization was important in Western pedagogy in the nineteenth century, but missionaries believed that Chinese students ought to have some understanding of what they recited. Chanting their lessons aloud also was part of Chinese tradition, but again, missionaries worked to introduce their own practice of silent studying.[20]

The hiring of Chinese assistants, necessary to the schools because few missionaries were adequately trained in the Chinese classics, was often problematic for missionaries. Finding classically trained men who were both willing to teach in a foreign school and acceptable to the missionaries was not always easy. Missionaries sometimes discovered that the man they had hired was, in their eyes, a moral delinquent. This problem plagued the mission schools well into the twentieth century. In 1920, Presbyterian missionary Mary Margaret Moninger wrote to her family that the first Chinese man her school had hired had been caught telling fortunes on the side and the second man had two wives. Both had been dismissed, she said, for "we do not care to hire such men." By Moninger's time, however, there was a larger pool of educated Chinese Christians for missionaries to draw upon in staffing their schools.[21]

A problem more serious for missionaries than the morality of their Chinese assistants was the fear that the latter, by ridiculing Christian teachings and extolling Confucius, might jeopardize what the missionaries saw as the school's purpose. Since the mission schools were intended to create a body of Christian believers rather than to prepare candidates for government examinations, teaching the Confucian classics, although necessary to attract students, was at cross-purposes with the missionaries' primary goal of winning converts. This "built-in contradiction," as historian Irwin Hyatt calls it, created tensions within the early schools and provided ammunition for those missionaries who believed schools detracted from evangelism.[22] One solution was foreign supervision of the Chinese assistants.[23] This, however, was difficult in schools that the missionaries did not actually run themselves but merely subsidized. (Sometimes local missionaries hired a Chinese teacher, and made him responsible for finding a building, enrolling students, and teaching.) Although missionaries did visit these schools, they worried about what the Chinese teacher might teach when no missionaries were present. In one school, the missionary in charge was horrified to discover upon paying a surprise visit that the Chinese teacher was showing the children how to gamble.[24]

The earliest American Christian schools in China were not established in any systematic way but sprang up any place missionaries perceived a need for them. Most of the schools were located near mission stations in treaty ports and large cities, but slowly American missionaries brought schools to the surrounding countryside.[25] Often the schools were not established with the prior approval of the mission board, although missionaries informed the boards in due time that a school had been started. "Now don't ask me 'Did the Board give you permission to start another school?'" wrote Grace Newton to the Presbyterian Board in 1900. "I decided to support this school with money sent by friends from home."[26]

There were no uniform standards for enrollment or for determining when a student had mastered a course and could be graduated. Schools offered variable years of instruction, which tended to increase as the school became more established in the locality. In the early days, few missionaries had training either as teachers or school administrators, and the schools were rarely equipped with more than a few tables and benches, and perhaps a blackboard or a few colored pictures on the walls.[27] Sometimes classes were held in the home of a missionary or in a room rented elsewhere. Few schools had their own buildings before 1880 and many, lacking textbooks, had to produce their own. Turnover in missionaries due to furlough, transfer, or removal from the field had an adverse effect on the stability of many of these early schools, some of which simply disappeared once their founder returned to the United States. American Protestant mission schools in China before 1880 may be characterized as short-lived and primitive, although there were a handful of exceptional schools that survived into the twentieth century.[28]

Gender and Teaching Missionaries

Although American teaching missionaries showed flexibility in admitting non-Christian students to their schools and permitting the Confucian classics to be taught, their ultimate purpose was to win China for Christ. To this end, there was one realm in which they steadfastly refused to compromise: education for Chinese girls. To understand why American missionaries insisted on opening schools for Chinese girls, thereby deliberately challenging Chinese beliefs about gender, it is necessary to understand the roles American women played in the Protestant missionary movement, the gender ideology of American Protestants, and their interpretation of the Chinese gender system.

Initially male mission leaders in the United States had not planned to send women overseas as missionaries, but they soon found three compelling reasons to do so. First, mission boards expected male missionaries to devote their lives to serving overseas, but they also feared miscegenation; as an alternative to marriage, life-long celibacy was considered Popish and could not be seriously advocated. Missionary men thus had to be permitted to take wives with them.[29] Second, the presence of wives and children helped American missionaries meet Chinese cultural expectations. In China, marriage was essential to ensure the continuance of the male lineage; unmarried men were regarded as not fully adult and as failures, since it took money to acquire a wife. Unmarried Chinese women were extremely rare. There is little evidence that missionaries worried about seeming appropriate in the Chinese setting, but American women and men alike believed that the example of Christian homelife would have a salutary effect on the Chinese.[30] Third, American women had no intention of being left at home. Some of them married missionary men (often men they barely knew) and sailed to China as "missionary wives."[31] Others organized women's missionary boards to recruit, send out, and support single women as missionaries; by 1900 there were 41 women's mission boards in the United States. Eventually, women came to outnumber men in the American Protestant mission and Americans outnumbered missionaries of other nationalities in China.[32]

These motives for sending women missionaries to China might not have sufficed if nineteenth-century American gender ideology had not opened social space for women in the missionary field. According to this ideology, women were naturally more religious than men, who were materialistic rather than spiritual in nature. Furthermore, women were considered naturally compassionate, so American society understood and applauded their eagerness to become missionaries and help their "heathen sisters." The doctrine of "separate spheres" also provided American women with an entree into missionary work. American gender ideology posited that the gendered categories of "woman" and "man" were fixed, immutable, and complementary. That being the case, each sex had a role to play in its own set sphere, with the woman's sphere corresponding to the private world of home and family, where her influence was held to predominate.[33] Yet nineteenth-century American women were rarely confined as strictly to the domestic world as this ideology suggests that they should have been. Deftly manipulating the ideology of sexual difference, American women parleyed their posited compassionate and nurturant qualities into public roles as teachers, reformers, and missionaries.[34]

In China, the strict traditional segregation of the sexes also worked to the advantage of aspiring American missionary women. According to the Confucian classics, even brothers and sisters should not eat together or sit on the same mat. Prohibitions against contact between unrelated men and women were even stronger.[35] If Protestant women could not be missionaries, who would reach the women of China? If Chinese women were not converted, how could Christian homes be established there? Without Christian homes, how could a stable Chinese church develop?[36]

Christian theology could also serve missionary women. They argued that since women had been the first sinners in the Garden of Eden, they had greater reason than men to feel grateful to Jesus, whose death had liberated them from a crushing burden of guilt and restored them to a position of equality with men.[37] When American Protestant women observed the lives of non-Christian women, they convinced themselves that their lot was infinitely better and that the influence of Christianity was responsible for their uplifted position. It was thus easy for American Protestant women to agree that they had a particular duty to evangelize among non-Christian women, to share with them the blessings missionary women had already received. "Having ourselves been freed we seek to free others," wrote Lutheran missionary Elma Thorson.[38] This specific call to "free" Chinese women continued to be a factor in drawing new women missionaries into the China field in the twentieth century.

Ideas about proper sex roles and relations between the sexes were part of the ideological baggage that American missionaries carried with them. Missionaries believed that gender categories were eternally fixed rather than being historical, cultural phenomena. In attempting to account for the different gender systems they encountered in foreign lands, missionaries argued that American gender ideology was rooted in Christianity (a universal religion), while foreign gender systems sprang from "heathenism." If non-Christian gender practices were linked to non-Christian religious beliefs, then missionary evangelism had to target both these religions and their accompanying gender systems. Hence, missionary women believed that they had a dual role to play in China: to save Chinese women from their own sins but also to liberate them from a degrading social system.[39] Moreover, because American gender ideology conceded great moral influence to women, especially within their own homes, Protestant missionaries unquestioningly attributed similar powers to Chinese women. They therefore believed that if these women were not converted, Christianity could not take root in China, for the non-Christian women would undo all of the missionaries' hard work. "Notwithstanding their many limitations Chinese women exercised large influence in the home," wrote one missionary woman. "A Christian woman wedded to a non-Christian man was bad enough, but hardly so deplorable as a Christian man with a non-Christian wife, which meant almost certainly a pagan home and a second generation of idolators."[40]

Missionaries were probably correct in assuming that Chinese mothers had great influence over their children, for filial piety was a key social value in China. Chinese grandmothers, by virtue of their age, had a good deal of influence within their homes, particularly if there were no senior males in the household. Individual women of strong personality doubtless also exerted considerable influence over their husbands, but this was not socially legitimate since women were supposed to be subordinate to men in the Chinese hierarchy. Irwin Hyatt has argued that "[c]lassic woman's work seems to have been based on a series of flawed understandings of the nature and role of women in traditional Chinese society."[41]

Not only did American missionary women misunderstand the roles played by Chinese women but their portrayal of the power dynamics within Chinese homes was often inconsistent. Even as they criticized what they perceived as the lowly status of Chinese women, missionary women asserted that Chinese women could subvert the entire missionary enterprise if they were not converted. Clearly, missionary women emphasized the power or powerlessness of Chinese women so as to serve their own purposes. In the same way that American missionary women used alternating interpretations of Chinese home life to justify their presence in the mission field, they also seized upon the superstitions of Chinese women (which seemed greater than those of Chinese men) as proof of these women's spirituality. This showed, they argued, that women were universally more inclined than men to be religious, and that Chinese women would be easy to convert; they were superstitious simply because they had not been taught about Jesus.[42]

By agreeing to limit themselves to working solely with Chinese women and children, American missionary women calmed male fears that women's interest in missions was part of an insidious movement to gain power within the church. Missionary work originated with and was controlled by men; it thus belonged to the public sphere. On the home base, women's mission boards fit American gender ideology because they were auxiliary and in varying degrees subordinate to the male general boards. In the mission field, although men and women missionaries often performed identical tasks, they generally addressed themselves to a sexually segregated clientele. Moreover, within the missions there were significant differences between men and women in terms of voting, salary and marital rights.[43] There was occasional territorial conflict between female and male missionaries but because women's missionary work, both at home and abroad, did not overtly contradict nineteenth-century American rhetoric about appropriate gender roles, men generally welcomed women as partners. Most American men would have agreed with Methodist William Brewster that the foreign missionary movement would be a "broken-winged eagle" without women's participation.[44]

Schools for Chinese Girls

Believing that Chinese gender ideology was part of a heathen culture that needed to be Christianized, American Protestant missionaries spent a good deal of energy attempting to alter the gender beliefs and practices of the Chinese. Although some of these efforts were centered around preaching and evangelism, the most direct efforts to reshape the Chinese gender system were located in the mission schools. Women missionaries popularized female education in China and eventually helped open career options for Chinese women. Mrs. Henrietta Shuck, a Baptist, is credited with establishing the first American school for Chinese girls. She opened her school in Macao in 1836, and moved it to Hong Kong after the Unequal Treaty system was in place. The ABCFM organized a girls' school in Guangzhou in 1846, the Northern Baptists established one in Hong Kong in 1851, and the Presbyterians in Guangzhou in 1853. The Methodists opened the first girls' boarding school in Fuzhou in 1859. In the twentieth century this school evolved into Hwa Nan College, one of the three Christian women's colleges in China.[45] A later chapter will examine the American missionary critique of the Chinese gender system and the concrete ways in which the schools were used as vehicles of reform. Here let us examine the missionaries' rationales for opening schools for girls, and some of the difficulties they faced in trying to induce Chinese parents to permit their daughters to enroll.

The value of education for girls was widely accepted among white, middle-class, nineteenth-century Americans, from whose ranks the vast majority of China missionaries came. By the 1830s and 1840s, higher education for middle-class white women was gaining acceptance and public school teaching opened up as a respectable career for larger numbers of women.[46] This departure from strict domesticity was justified, according to the prevailing gender ideology, as an extension of women's domestic functions. Since teaching was done by single women, it did not interfere with the duties of a wife and mother but substituted for them.[47] This opened up the possibility of missionary women being permitted to teach; it certainly supported the notion of Christian schools for Chinese girls.

Missionary men shared American beliefs about the worth of women teachers and the need to educate girls. As early as 1836 the head of the ABCFM, Rufus Anderson, suggested that all missionary wives prepare themselves to teach. "Education is becoming a science, an art, a profession," he said, "and they [missionary wives] must study the science, practice the art and become interested in the profession." David Abeel, one of the first American missionaries to enter the China field, urged British and American women to establish their own missionary societies and to work for the education of Chinese women, which he claimed was desperately needed.[48]

In China, as in America, the educational movement was shaped by considerations of gender, some of which are apparent in the arguments missionaries put forward in favor of establishing schools for Chinese girls and women. In part, these arguments paralleled those advanced to justify education for Chinese boys: education would give the missionaries access to the homes and hence the families of their students, children were easier to convert than adults, and a literate church was imperative. The missionaries also argued that education would make girls into good wives and mothers.[49] There was no point in educating Chinese Christian boys, the missionaries argued, if they had no choice but to marry uneducated, non-Christian girls. Irritated by the Presbyterian Board's hesitancy in supporting girls' schools, missionary Harriet Noyes wrote in 1896: "I can hardly believe that you wish the daughters of the 1,442 members of the Presbyterian church here—the wives of the assistants—young women who are preparing themselves for service—should be without opportunity of obtaining an education."[50]

Although missionaries believed that Christian men made better husbands (and presumably fathers) than non-Christian men, they rarely suggested that the purpose of educating boys was to train good partners for Christian girls. On the other hand, even in the twentieth century proponents of girls' education frequently had to fend off criticism of their work from both Chinese and American critics, by denying that it made the girls less feminine, unwilling to do domestic work, or less inclined to marry.[51] Rather, they argued, the education of women enhanced their understanding of and willingness to comply with their social role as women. As one pamphlet from the Methodist Mary Porter Gamewell School in Beijing stated in 1899: "Care is taken not to spoil them with luxuries, but to train them for model Chinese homes."[52]

Not only did American missionaries have to answer the fears of their U.S. supporters that they might be spoiling Chinese girls for domestic life, but they had to surmount the indifference of Chinese parents, who saw no practical purpose in educating their daughters. The lure of a classical education held no appeal here; girls were excluded from taking the civil service exam. As one parent put it, "Will it [education] bring a girl more to eat, more to wear, increase her dowry or secure a rich mother-in-law? If not, what use can it be?"[53] Margaret Burton, writing about women's education in China in 1911, stated: "In many places, if anything was to be done toward educating girls it was necessary to go out and scour the highways and byways for possible pupils; children who had no homes, or those from homes so poor that their parents were willing to run the risk of sending them to the strange-looking foreigners, since they would thus be relieved of their support."[54]

The difficulties in attracting Chinese girls meant that all of the early mission girls' schools had to provide full support for their students, and some, unlike the boys' schools, even paid the students a tiny sum in cash for every day they attended school. The first boarding school for girls in Fuzhou met the problem of finding students by enrolling girls from a nearby missionary-run orphanage.[55] Henrietta Shuck found still another solution. "When I first mentioned to the Chinese here that I intended to open a school," she wrote, "they brought boys in number, but not one girl. At last I refused to take any more, unless for every boy they would bring a girl."[56]

Part of the problem missionaries faced in attempting to enroll children in their schools was that the Chinese were often deeply suspicious of foreigners, fearing that missionaries boiled the children to make opium, dug out their eyes to make telescopes, or exported them to foreign countries for a variety of nefarious purposes.[57] Presbyterian missionary Helen Nevius wrote in 1895 that Chinese men stood on a mound overlooking her school "to see in what suspicious performances I might be engaged."[58] The 1909 Foochow [Fuzhou] Girls' School Catalogue related that in the nineteenth century when the school first opened, one village had feared the worst for one of its girls until "after three years she returned

home, having been well fed, clothed, instructed, and been given more extra clothing besides."[59] The potential material and social rewards of a classical education for Chinese boys may have outweighed the physical risks that their parents associated with the mission schools. This was not true in the girls' schools; although there was a set of "Girls' Classics," which the missionaries duly offered in their girls' schools, few Chinese parents found these necessary or desirable for their daughters.[60]

Missionaries also had difficulties staffing their girls' schools. This problem was compounded by the fact that before the advent of Christian education in China, educated Chinese women were a rarity. Those who were educated were from well-to-do families and were therefore bound by Chinese notions of propriety, which forbade women to leave their own courtyards. Poorer Chinese women were less subject than the wealthy to this prohibition, but they could not be used as teachers because they were not educated. As a consequence, mission girls' schools frequently had no choice but to hire Chinese men to assist in these schools. These men had to be at least thirty-five years old (Methodists preferred them to be over fifty), married, and respectable in both Chinese and American eyes. If a woman missionary was not available to chaperone the girls during their classes with the male teacher, they hired a Chinese matron to fill this role.[61] Chaperonage continued into the twentieth century.[62]

Chinese propriety affected female students as well as teachers. Because the Chinese did not believe it was proper for unmarried girls above the age of ten or twelve to be seen on the public streets, most mission schools for girls that offered higher than a fourth grade education were boarding schools. This alleviated the need for girls to travel back and forth between home and school.

Solving the problem of physical access to education also provided Chinese parents with positive incentives to send a daughter to school, for during her stay in a boarding school, her parents were freed entirely from having to support her. It was China's grinding poverty, therefore, that gave missionaries the opportunity to promote education for girls successfully. Chinese parents only accepted the idea that it was *worthwhile* to educate girls at a later time, when their daughters could earn money as teachers, when nationalists demanded women's education as a means of strengthening the country, and when some Chinese young men began to prefer educated women as brides. There was substantial indifference in some areas to educating girls, in fact, even in the twentieth century.

Missionaries were often frustrated that few girls stayed in school long enough to acquire much education, in spite of the pecuniary benefits to a Chinese family from enrolling their daughters in a Christian school. Sometimes Chinese parents took their daughters home as soon as the missionaries had distributed new suits of clothing.[63] More commonly, girls left the school after completing only one or two years of work. Lida Ashmore, a Baptist missionary working in Shantou, wrote in 1882 that her mission station's girls' school had just inaugurated the practice of summer vacation for the girls. Previously they had been kept in school all year long. "The principal reason for this," Ashmore said, "was the fact that when the missionary had once succeeded in getting the girl to come to the school, it was safer to keep her there, than to risk the danger of her not coming back." Now, however, "there was a faint but increasing desire by parents to have their children educated."[64]

Early betrothal and marriage also contributed to the continual difficulties missionaries found in keeping girls in their schools. "You know," Methodist Julia Bonafield wrote in 1904, "the parents and relatives of a Chinese girl think only of getting her married early in life, and we have a constant fight to keep them until twenty or twenty-two."[65] To the Chinese, arranging a marriage was the natal family's most important duty towards its daughters and sons alike. While the parents of sons were eager to acquire a daughter-in-law to help with the heaviest domestic work and to bear sons for their lineage, parents of daughters wanted to have their daughter's future settled as soon as possible. Infant betrothal was common, and betrothal was as binding as marriage in Chinese society. Daughters were often married off when they were quite young to save their families the expense of rearing them. Sometimes infant girls were raised by their mothers-in-law until they were considered old enough to consummate a marriage.[66]

These were all eminently practical arrangements, given the poverty of many Chinese families and the cultural emphasis on the continuance of ancestral lines. But American missionaries were harsh critics of Chinese betrothal and marriage customs, which not only interfered with missionaries' educational ambitions for Chinese girls but also, more importantly, formed part of the gender system that missionaries hoped to destroy. As late as 1919, Methodist missionary Monona Cheney wrote:

> There is no one thing, I think, that is more sickening than the low, low ideals of marriage and family life; and there is such a long, *long* distance to go before even the majority of our Christians reach the ideals which with us are very ordinary. Of course, more than one wife is not tolerated for one minute among the church membership; but in other things the ideals are so little above the animal plane.[67]

We can see here missionaries' commitment to gender reform. They tried to use their girls' schools as agencies for altering Chinese marriage practices. This will be discussed at length in a future chapter; for the moment let us note that before 1900 missionaries' prime weapon against early marriage and betrothal was the "indenture." Parents were required to sign a promise to allow their daughter to complete as many years of school work as the mission offered, at the missionaries' expense, without forcing her to marry before that time. Some indentures further stipulated that the girl was not to be betrothed to a non-Christian or as a second wife and that the missionaries in charge must consent to any betrothal before it was arranged. If these conditions were not observed, the parents had to pay back the cost of the girl's education to the missionaries. Boys' schools rarely used indentures; when they did, it was to keep the boys in school rather than control or prevent their marriage, for boys' parents generally permitted them to attend school even after marriage, as was not the case with girls.[68]

Coercive measures to reform Chinese marriage practices could not be successfully implemented until there was, in Lida Ashmore's words, "a faint but increasing desire" among the Chinese for girls' education. When they first opened their schools, the missionaries were in no position to impose their marital beliefs on the Chinese and could do nothing as their students were claimed by marriage. Students who enjoyed school and wanted to remain there may have been able to exert some pressure on their parents to delay a marriage, but it was not until the parents and parents-in-law came to value education for girls that they were willing to comply with missionary marital regulations. It is true that missionaries offered otherwise unavailable incentives for the Chinese to abide by mission rules; this must nevertheless be balanced against deep Chinese cultural disincentives to have anything to do with the missionaries. With regard to Christian education, the missionaries could hope to entice students into their schools; they could not compel them. Within their schools, missionaries likewise had no leverage to enforce their marital ideals except on a *quid pro quo* basis.

The curriculum in the girls' schools differed from that of the boys' schools. Most of the early girls' schools taught sewing, embroidery, and various household skills, including making clothing and shoes and sometimes cooking (which required special equipment and therefore was less common). Chinese and missionary gender beliefs reinforced each other at this point, since both parties believed that girls needed to be taught domestic skills. In 1898, a Chinese official visited the Methodist school that Miranda Croucher ran, and was pleased to learn that the girls were being instructed in cooking and sewing. Croucher remarked that the official's concern that girls be taught the feminine arts gave her "a glimpse of common masculine humanity," because she recognized that American men, too, had an interest in seeing that women learned these skills.[69]

Except for these gendered subjects, girls in American mission schools studied what boys studied, at least on the primary school level. At a public examination in the Methodist Girls' School in Beijing in 1877, the girls were examined in Bible history, the Harmony of the Gospels, arithmetic, Romanized characters, and the Chinese classics. They also recited portions of the Bible.[70] Students in Gertrude Howe's school in Fuzhou (Methodist) could read and write in Chinese, recite the works of Confucius from beginning to end and explain their meaning. They had a good grasp of Bible and church history and knew some geography and arithmetic.[71] Although Catholic missionaries began schools for Chinese girls in 1835, Protestant mission schools were the first to give girls an education paralleling that given to boys. Catholic missionaries focused on religious training, not education, for their schools were only open to Catholic children, and the girls were taught nothing more than needlework and catechism.[72] By teaching girls the Chinese classics, American Protestant missionaries gave them limited access to the status Chinese society accorded to educated people, which previously had been reserved for a few men and fewer exceptional women.

The congruence between missionary and Chinese gender beliefs on the subject of domestic skills helped reconcile Chinese parents to the break with tradition entailed in sending a daughter to school. Seeing girls mastering the same subjects as boys removed Chinese doubts that girls were capable of learning, made parents less dubious about the value of educating their daughters, and reduced early opposition to the mission girls' schools—just as missionaries had hoped. Parents swelled with pride as they watched their daughters perform in public examinations, and villagers were awestruck when a girl returned from a mission school able to read. Chinese parents and in-laws were perhaps even more impressed by the possibility that a girl with education could find employment as a teacher and, ultimately, be in great demand as a wife. However, this did not happen often in the nineteenth century.[73]

Vindication of the Teaching Missionaries

In the nineteenth century, missionary arguments for educating Chinese girls and boys did not convince all Americans, either in the field or at the home base. The controversy over the role of schools in the missionary movement became sharper in the 1880s, when the educational arm of missionary work expanded dramatically, in terms of the number of schools and teaching missionaries, and the time and money that missions spent on education. Originally, medical workers were the only "specialists" sent to China, the other missionaries being primarily ministers and their wives.[74] However, some ministers and their wives became permanently involved in education; toward the end of the nineteenth century they began to perceive themselves as specialists and to request that only trained missionary teachers be assigned to their schools. This caused tension between educational missionaries and those who remained in direct evangelistic work, for the latter sometimes saw education as competing with their own work and feared that an increasingly secular education might one day come into opposition with the gospel they were preaching. To counter these fears, educators claimed that education was both supplemental to regular evangelism and essential to the victory of Christianity in China. They further argued that even secular education could help to loosen the bonds of tradition on Chinese minds and so enable converts to defend Christianity more intelligently.[75]

The home boards worried that schools might divert money and energy away from direct evangelism. They also feared that if church-going supporters of missions believed that mission schools were secular institutions more involved in imparting worldly knowledge than in saving souls, this might adversely affect the rest of the missionary movement. The debate over missionary education persisted throughout the nineteenth century, both at home and in the field.[76]

Missionaries in China discussed the role of education at their first general conference in Shanghai in 1877. Presbyterian missionary Calvin Mateer praised the educational achievements of his boys' school in Dengzhou, denied that schools robbed evangelism of its strength, and urged his co-workers to broaden their vision of what constituted missionary work. Mateer's speech was not greeted with tremendous enthusiasm by other missionaries, but a small group of like-minded missionary educators formed a School and Textbook Series Committee. The committee both translated textbooks for mission schools and published translations of philosophy and natural science for educated Chinese who were interested in learning about Western thought.[77]

By the time of the second missionary conference in 1890, most American Protestant missionaries agreed that education was a necessary part of their work in China. The educational work of the missions had already substantially enlarged from a total of 5,917 students in Protestant schools in 1876 to 16,836 in 1889.[78] At the 1890 conference educational missionaries no longer needed to defend their work. Instead, they presented papers focused on practical questions such as whether to teach English, whether to hire non-Christian teachers, and to what degree the schools ought to be self-supporting. Missionary teachers Harriet Noyes (Presbyterian) and Laura Haygood (Methodist) read papers on schools for girls, which were appreciatively received. Among the resolutions passed at the conference, one stated that although the mission schools should provide physical and intellectual training, religious instruction should be their primary emphasis. Another resolution encouraged the establishment of more Christian schools for girls.[79]

In spite of the difficulties and frustrations missionaries encountered while establishing their schools in China, the fledgling schools sprang up wherever the missionaries built a mission station. Early correspondence between missionaries in the field and the home boards shows the missionaries planting schools with seemingly casual abandon while the boards alternated between anxiety and approval.[80] It was clear by 1890, however, that the schools could thrive on Chinese soil and there was no thought then of turning back. Education had gained legitimacy as a feature of the missionary movement, and this legitimacy was not seriously questioned in the field until the 1920s, when the Chinese began to attack the mission schools and Christian education. However, there was a continuing debate within the educational movement over the purposes and content of Christian education, who should be received into mission schools, and, as the schools became more popular, what sort of relationship the schools should strive for with non-Christian Chinese and with the Chinese government.

Two initial compromises—the teaching of the Chinese classics and the admission of non-Christian students—established a pattern of accommodation to Chinese demands that was to have great influence on the future development of missionary education in China. At the same time, missionaries' actions to improve the welfare and social status of Chinese girls and women gave American missionaries a significant role in the development of what was called the "emancipation" of Chinese women in the twentieth century. From the earliest date, the missionaries used their schools not only to propagate Christianity but also to effect reform of the Chinese gender system. Thus American missionaries interjected as many of their own cultural and religious ideals into their schools as they could persuade the Chinese to accept. The Chinese, conversely, did what they could to reshape the Christian schools into institutions that would serve their own purposes. This pattern continued into the late nineteenth century when the mission schools became both more secular and more popular with the Chinese.

ENDNOTES

1 Kenneth Latourette, *A History of Christian Missions in China* (New York: MacMillan, 1929), pp. 217–218.
2 *Ibid.*, p. 230.
3 William Purviance Fenn, *Christian Higher Education in Changing China, 1880–1950* (Grand Rapids, Mich.: William B. Eerdmans Publishing Co., 1976), p. 29; Latourette, *Christian Missions in China*, pp. 244–251; Mary Raleigh Anderson, *A Cycle in the*

Celestial Kingdom or Protestant Mission Schools for Girls in South China (1887 to the Japanese Invasion) (Mobile, Ala.: Heiter-Starke Printing Co. 1943), pp. xix–xxii; Lucerne H. Knowlton, "One Hundred Years of Methodism in China," p. 2, Lucerne H. Knowlton Papers, Box 1, HIA.

4 *Chinese Recorder* 47 (February 1916): 118; William N. Brewster, *The Evolution of New China* (Cincinnati: Jennings and Graham; New York: Eaton and Mains, 1907), pp. 105–109, 112. Being able to read a Romanized text was not quite the same as being literate because one was limited to reading Romanized texts published by the missionaries and could not read Chinese characters.

5 *Records of the Second Triennial Meeting of the Educational Association of China* (Shanghai: American Presbyterian Mission Press, 1896), p. 50.

6 Latourette, *Christian Missions in China*, p. 226

7 Lida Ashmore to family, Nov. 8, 1925, William and Lida Ashmore Papers, RG Ax 564, Box 1, UOSC.

8 Knowlton, "One Hundred Years of Methodism," p. 2, Lucerne H. Knowlton Papers, Box 1, HIA; *Christian Education in China: A Study Made by an Educational Commission Representing the Mission Boards and Societies Conducting Work in China* (New York: Committee of Reference and Counsel for the Foreign Missions Conference of North America, 1922), p. 31.

9 Electa Butler, "Historical Sketch of the Pui-Kei Boys' School," booklet, 1904, NT6.3 B976hp, PC (USA).

10 "Report of the Chaoyang Station," n.d., Adam and Clara Groesbeck Papers, RG Ax 818, Box 1, UOSC.

11 S. A. Hunter to the Presbyterian Board of Foreign Missions, July 25, 1890, Presbyterian Letterbook (a ledger containing copies of incoming and outgoing correspondence between missionaries and the Board), 1890, PC (USA); Irwin Hyatt, "Protestant Missions in China, 1877–1890: The Institutionalization of Good Works," pp. 93–126 in Kwang-Ching Liu, *American Missionaries in China, Papers from Harvard Seminars* (Cambridge, East Asian Research Center: Harvard University Press, 1970); Evelyn Rawski, "Elementary Education in the Mission Enterprise," pp. 135–151 in Suzanne Wilson Barnett and John K. Fairbank, eds., *Christianity in China: Early Protestant Writings* (Cambridge: Harvard University Press, 1985).

12 Frederic Wakeman, Jr., *The Fall of Imperial China* (New York: Free Press, 1975), pp. 20–21.

13 Sally Borthwick, *Education and Social Change in China: The Beginnings of the Modern Era* (Stanford: Hoover Institution Press, 1983), chapters one and two. According to Borthwick (p. 114), there were a handful of public schools for girls in South China before the arrival of the missionaries, although the latter are generally credited with initiating girls' education in China.

14 Evelyn Rawski, *Education and Popular Literacy in Ch'ing China* (Ann Arbor: University of Michigan Press, 1979), pp. 29–38.

15 Marianne Bastid, trans. Paul J. Bailly, *Educational Reform in Early Twentieth-Century China* (Ann Arbor: Center for Chinese Studies, 1988), p. 31; Kiang Kang-hu, *On Chinese Studies* (Shanghai: Commercial Press, Ltd., 1934), pp. 196–197.

16 Rawski, *Education and Popular Literacy*, pp. 8–9. Rawski estimates that between 30 and 45 per cent of Chinese men had rudimentary literacy skills; her figure is between 2 and 10 per cent for Chinese women. What Rawski means by "rudimentary" skills is that a significant number of men could write their own names and workers in some areas knew a few key characters that permitted them to deal with shipping orders, receipts, and the like.

17 Joel Spring, *The American School, 1642–1985* (New York: Longman, 1986), ch. 4.

18 Rawski, "Elementary Education," p. 135. American teaching missionaries continued to argue that the Christian Bible outshone the Confucian classics well into the twentieth century. See William C. Cummings to home church, May 24, 1925, Microfilm # 102, BWM.

19 Lucius Eddy Ford, "The History of the Educational Work of the Methodist Episcopal Church in China: A Study of its Development and Present Trends" (Ph.D. diss., Northwestern University, 1936), p. 119.

20 *Ibid.*, pp. 75, 120; Monona Cheney to family, Dec. 26, 1918, Monona Cheney Papers, RG Ax 275, Box 1, Folder 1, UOSC.

21 Mary Margaret Moninger to family, March 13, 1920, Mary Margaret Moninger Papers, RG 230, Box 1, Folder 15, PC (USA).

22 Irwin T. Hyatt, *Our Ordered Lives Confess: Three Nineteenth-Century American Missionaries in East Shantung* (Cambridge: Harvard University Press, 1976), p. 161. In 1878, Presbyterian missionary Harriet Noyes commented that it was an "unspeakable blessing" to have a Christian teacher in a mission school. *Woman's Work for Woman* 8: 4 (April, 1878): 96.

23 *China Centenary Missionary Conference, Records* (Shanghai: Centenary Conference Committee, 1907), pp. 174–175.

24 *Chinese Recorder* 28 (January 1897): 3; Ford, "History of the Educational Work," p. 75.

25 Ida Belle Lewis, *The Education of Girls in China* (New York: Teachers' College, Columbia University, 1919), p. 39.

26 Grace Newton to the Presbyterian Board of Foreign Missions, Feb. 14, 1900, Presbyterian letterbook, PC (USA).

27 Mary Isham, *Valorous Ventures: A Record of Sixty and Six Years of the Woman's Foreign Missionary Society of the Methodist Episcopal Church* (Boston: Woman's Foreign Missionary Society, Methodist Episcopal Church, 1936), p. 197. While most of the junior middle, senior middle, and higher-level schools were better equipped in the late nineteenth century, many of the elementary-level day schools were extremely ill-equipped even in the twentieth century. Methodist missionary Elsie Reik described day schools in the Nanjing area in 1925: "You would hardly recognize some of these places as schools....just an ordinary room in an ordinary house, mud walls and a mud floor. One with only a door, no windows at all, had the most pictures up." Elsie Reik to family, Feb. 28, 1925, Elsie Reik Papers, UOSC.

28 Anderson, *A Cycle,* chapters 11 and 12; Fenn, *Christian Higher Education in Changing China,* p. 27. Colleges and universities were not the only institutions to survive over a long period of time; some high schools and higher elementary schools founded in the nineteenth century were still going strong in the twentieth century. Among Methodist schools, for example, the Foochow Girls' Boarding School (1859), Marguerite Stewart Girls' School (1895), Kutien Girls' Boarding School (1893), Carolyn Johnson Memorial Boys' School (1891), Rulison-Fish Memorial High School (1873), Lucy Alderman Memorial Girls' Boarding School (1889), Mary Porter Gamewell School (1870), Wiley Institute (1888), and Tsunhua Boys' School (1886) were among the longest-lived institutions. See 79-16: 1459-4-2: 11 through 5-1: 14, GBGM.

29 A third option—sex outside of marriage for male missionaries—was apparently unthinkable. R. Pierce Beaver, *American Protestant Women in World Mission: The History of the First Feminist Movement* (Grand Rapids, Mich.: William B. Eerdmans Publishing Co., 1968), p. 35. This issue seems not to have arisen in later discussions of the possibility of sending single women as missionaries overseas, probably because the subject was too fraught with anxieties to be openly discussed.

30 See, for example, Samuel Colcord Bartlett, *Historical Sketches of the Mission of the American Board* (New York: American Board of Commissioners for Foreign Missions, 1872), p. 134; and John L. Nevius, *China and the Chinese: A General Description of the Country and its Inhabitants; its Civilization and Form of Government; its Religion and Social Institutions; its Intercourse with other Nations and its Present Condition and Prospects* (New York: Harper and Brothers, 1869), p. 323.

31 Hyatt, *Our Ordered Lives Confess,* pp. 3–62.

32 Helen Barrett Montgomery, *Western Women in Eastern Lands: An Outline Study of Fifty Years of Woman's Work in Foreign Missions* (New York: The MacMillan Co., 1910), pp. 25–35; Beaver, *American Protestant Women*, ch. 4.

33 Linda Kerber, "Separate Spheres, Female Worlds, Woman's Place: The Rhetoric of Women's History," *Journal of American History* 75 (June 1988): 9–39.

34 Carroll Smith-Rosenberg, "Beauty, the Beast, and the Militant Woman: A Case Study of Sex roles and Social Stress in Jacksonian America," pp. 197–221 in Nancy Cott and Elizabeth Pleck, eds., *A Heritage of Her Own* (New York: Simon and Schuster, 1979); Patricia Hill, *The World Their Household: The American Woman's Foreign Mission Movement and Cultural Transformation, 1870–1920* (Ann Arbor: University of Michigan Press, 1985), p. 3.

35 Kiang, *On Chinese Studies*, p. 194.

36 This was a commonly used justification for women's work in missions. See *Woman's Work for Woman* 8: 1 (January, 1878): 10. A 1909 open letter stated "They [Chinese women] must be taught by women *and only by women*." Oct. 12, 1909, recipient and author unknown, 79-16: 1459-4-3:11, GBGM. Emphasis in original.

37 *Woman's Work for Woman* 8: 5 (May 1878): 139.

38 Elma Thorson, "The Emancipation of a Chinese Woman," pamphlet, n.d., in the folder labeled "I Kwang/Lena Dahl School," ELCA; Joan Jacobs Brumberg, "Zenanas and Girlless Villages: The Ethnology of American Evangelical Women, 1870–1910," *Journal of American History* 69 (Sept. 1982): 347–371.

39 See, for example, *Woman's Work for Woman* 16: 5 (June 1886): 126. This concept also continued into the twentieth century. Writing to her family in 1921, Presbyterian missionary Harriet Stroh praised the familial relations in a Chinese Christian home she had recently visited, contrasting it to what she assumed to be the norm in non-Christian Chinese homes. Harriet Stroh to family, April 22, 1921, Harriet Stroh Papers, RG 187, Box 1, Folder 4, PC (USA).

40 Mary Ninde Gamewell, *Ming Kwong, "City of the Morning Light"* (West Medford, Mass.: Central Committee on the United Study of Foreign Missions, 1924), p. 119. Accustomed to American churches where the majority of active members were women, missionaries believed that the difficulties they had in persuading Chinese women to join the church proved how oppressed those women were. Even in the twentieth century, the Chinese Christian Church was predominantly masculine. See Murray Scott Frame to family, March 28, 1914, Murray Scott Frame Papers, RG Ax 421, Box 2, UOSC.

41 Hyatt, *Our Ordered Lives Confess*, p. 92; Martin C. Yang, *A Chinese Village: Taitou, Shantung Province* (New York: Columbia University Press, 1945), p. 57.

42 Adrian Bennett and Kwang-ching Liu, "Christianity in the Chinese Idiom: Young J. Allen and the Early *Chiao-hui hsin pao, 1868–1870*," pp. 159–96, see p. 168, in John K. Fairbank, ed., *The Missionary Enterprise in China and America* (Cambridge: Harvard University Press, 1974); Francis L. K. Hsu, *Under the Ancestors' Shadow: Kinship, Personality, and Social Mobility in China* (Stanford: Stanford University Press, 1971), pp. 171–176, 203.

43 Jane Hunter, *The Gospel of Gentility: American Women Missionaries in Turn-of-the-Century China* (New Haven: Yale University Press, 1984), pp. 12–13, 83–85.

44 William Brewster, circular letter, Apr. 18, 1914, 73-43: 1183-6-2:06, GBGM. Some male missionaries, however, were uneasy about women's going "beyond their sphere." See the *Chinese Recorder* 27 (October 1896): 472.

45 Anderson, *A Cycle*, pp. xix–xxi; Knowlton, "One Hundred Years of Methodism," p. 2, Lucerne H. Knowlton Papers, HIA; Ethel L. Wallace, *Hwa Nan College, the Woman's College of South China* (New York: The United Board for Christian Higher Education in Asia, 1956), p. 1.

46 Thomas Woody, *A History of Women's Education in the United States*, Vol. I (New York: Octagon Books, 1966), ch. nine.

47 Carl F. Kaestle, *Pillars of the Republic: Common Schools and American Society, 1780–1860* (New York: Hill and Wang, 1983), pp. 84–87, 124.

48 Quoted in Clifton Jackson Phillips, *Protestant America and the Pagan World: The First Half-Century of the ABCFM, 1810–1860* (Cambridge: East Asian Research Center, Harvard University Press, 1969), p. 311; Mrs. W. I. Chamberlain, *Fifty Years in Foreign Fields—China, Japan, India, Arabia: A History of Five Decades of the Woman's Board of Foreign Missions, Reformed Church in America* (New York: Woman's Board of Foreign Missions, Reformed Church in America, 1925), pp. 4–5.

49 *Records of the Third Triennial Meeting of the Educational Association of China* (Shanghai, American Presbyterian Mission Press, 1899), p. 162.

50 Harriet Noyes to the Presbyterian Board of Foreign Missions, Sept. 18, 1896, Presbyterian Letterbook, PC (USA).

51 Lida Ashmore, for example, said that girls in Christian schools were often accused of being haughty and making poor wives and daughters-in-law. Lida Ashmore, "My Life Story," p. 53. William and Lida Ashmore Papers, RG Ax 564, Box 1, UOSC. Similar criticisms accompanied the development of women's higher education in the United States.

52 Mary Porter Gamewell School, pamphlet, 1899, 79-16: 1459-4-3:50, GBGM.

53 Mrs. John R. Mott, "China's Daughters and Their Education," *The Evangel* 11: 109 (May 1899): 6–9, RG 46, Box 219, Folder 668, YDSL.

54 Margaret Burton, *The Education of Women in China* (New York: Fleming H. Revell Co., 1911), p. 48.

55 Ford, "History of the Educational Work," p. 55.

56 Quoted in Anderson, *A Cycle,* p. 62.

57 Burton, *The Education of Women in China*, p. 47.

58 Helen S. Coan Nevius, *The Life of John Livingstone Nevius, Forty Years a Missionary in China* (New York: Fleming H. Revell Co., 1895), p. 244.

59 Foochow Girls' School Catalogue, 1909, 79-16: 1459-4-2:11, GBGM.

60 I assume that many of the girls' schools did teach the classics, although they do not always specify that they did. The Methodist Keen School in Tianjin and other Methodist girls' schools in West China made a point of mentioning it. See Frances J. Baker, *The Story of the Woman's Foreign Missionary Society of the Methodist Episcopal Church, 1869–1895* (Cincinnati: Cranston and Curtis, 1896), pp. 277–278.

61 *Centenary Conference,* p. 174; "Day Schools in Western China," *Woman's Missionary Friend* 42 (July 1910): 249.

62 Lily Woods to home church, Nov. 29, 1920, Microfilm #117, BWM; Anderson, *A Cycle,* p. 166. Anderson makes a tantalizing reference to a special group of women who she claims made a substantial contribution to mission teaching in girls' schools in south China. These were the "combed-up hair women," women who, having received permission from their relatives not to marry, combed their hair in the style worn by married women. Anderson claims that these women gave invaluable service to the mission schools in south China, but she does not name her source and her claim is not corroborated in other writings about mission schools or in letters of the missionaries themselves. Janice Stockard, writing about these women as well as others in south China who delayed moving to their husband's house after marriage, says nothing about any of them working as teachers in mission schools. Janice E. Stockard, *Daughters of the Canton Delta: Marriage Patterns and Economic Strategies in South China, 1860–1930* (Stanford: Stanford University Press, 1989).

63 Mary Porter Gamewell School, pamphlet, 1899, 79-16: 1459-4-3:50, GBGM.

64 Lida Ashmore, "My Life Story," p. 50, William and Lida Ashmore Papers, RG Ax 564, Box 1, UOSC.

65 *Woman's Missionary Friend* 36 (September 1904): 340. Chinese girls did not usually enroll in a mission school until they were more than ten years old, so a twenty-two-year-old might well have had no more than an eighth-grade education.

66 Marion J. Levy, Jr., *The Family Revolution in Modern China* (Cambridge: Harvard University Press, 1949), pp. 94–96.

67 Monona Cheney to family, Oct. 23, 1919, Monona Cheney Papers, RG Ax 275, Box 1, UOSC. Emphasis in original.

68 *Second Triennial of the EAC*, 1896, p. 208; Elsa Felland, "Sinyang Girls' School, Before and Now," pamphlet, n. d., in folder titled "I Kwang/Lena Dahl School," ELCA. For boys' indentures, see Jessie G. Lutz, *China and the Christian Colleges, 1850–1950* (Ithaca: Cornell University Press, 1971), p. 75.

69 *Woman's Missionary Friend* 30 (May 1898): 354.

70 Burton, *The Education of Women in China*, p. 66.

71 Ford, "History of the Educational Work," p. 63. It is not clear what "the works of Confucius" encompassed in this reference.

72 Marianne Bastid, "Servitude or Liberation? The Introduction of Foreign Educational Practices and Systems to China from 1840 to the Present," pp. 3–20, see p. 5, in Ruth Hayhoe and Marianne Bastid, eds., *China's Education and the Industrialized World: Studies in Cultural Transfer* (Armonk, N.Y.: M. E. Sharpe, Inc., 1987).

73 Lida Ashmore, "My Life Story," p. 53, William and Lida Ashmore Papers, RG Ax 564, Box 1, UOSC. Not all girls' schools gave public examinations since the Chinese looked askance on such exhibitions by girls.

74 The first American medical missionary, Peter Parker, went to China in 1834, representing the ABCFM. See Latourette, *Christian Missions in China*, p. 218.

75 Ford, "History of the Educational Work," p. 71.

76 For a description of the debate within the ABCFM, see Phillips, *Protestant America and the Pagan World*, pp. 43–45, 53, 98–100, 195. Because the ABCFM began overseas missions in 1812, but did not launch its China mission until 1830, much of the discussion of the role of education occurred in connection with missions other than the China mission, but the effects on overall policy naturally affected China as well. For the educational debate within the Baptist church, see Robert Torbet, *Venture of Faith: The Story of the American Baptist Foreign Mission Society and the Woman's American Baptist Foreign Mission Society, 1814–1954* (Philadelphia: Judson Press, 1955), chapter six.

77 Hyatt, *Our Ordered Lives Confess*, pp. 179–181.

78 Latourette, *Christian Missions in China*, p. 442. These figures include students in all Protestant schools, not merely those in American mission schools.

79 *Report of the Missionary Conference* (Shanghai: American Presbyterian Mission Press, 1890), pp. 52–53.

80 This was true even in the last decade of the nineteenth century. See the correspondence between missionaries and board members in the Presbyterian letterbook, 1890–1900, PC (USA). The ambivalent attitude of the boards toward the establishment of schools was also related to the intermittent debate within the various boards over the appropriateness of missionaries founding schools overseas. Missionaries and their Christian Chinese colleagues continued to establish schools without heeding financial considerations in the twentieth century. Chinese and American Methodists in Jinjiang in 1917, for example, opened a school with no appropriation for it. "We have faith to believe that the money will come from somewhere," they asserted confidently. *Woman's Missionary Friend* 49 (May 1917): 173.

Chapter 2:
A Measure of Success: Compromise, Continuity, and the Expansion of Missionary Education

During the first fifty years of American missionary education in China, mission schools were tiny, struggling adjuncts to the evangelical endeavor. The shaky foundation of Christian education began to stabilize, however, by the 1880s. Individual schools were filled to capacity and more missionaries were assigned to do educational work. In part, the enlargement of the educational movement was due to the increased number of Chinese Protestants, of whom there were more than 37,000 by 1889.[1] A more significant cause was the awakening of interest in Western learning among those non-Christian Chinese who began to see Western knowledge as a source of power that could not be entirely scorned. These Chinese, often treaty port merchants, began to take advantage of the schooling missionaries offered.

American missionaries were pleased to draw greater numbers of Chinese into their schools. But paradoxically, the enhanced standing of the mission schools did not give the missionaries a free hand to promote their educational and evangelical agendas. Instead, loathe to undercut their newfound popularity, teaching missionaries found themselves even more responsive to the demands of the Chinese than they had been before. As missionaries built new schools and offered courses extending from kindergarten to college, they broadened the school curriculum and increased its secular content at the expense of both the Chinese classics and Christian teaching. The Educational Association of China (EAC), established at the Shanghai Missionary Conference in 1890, announced in 1896 that Christian schools no longer existed for the sole purpose of making converts or training a native clergy. Instead, they should give students a good secular education. That this startling claim stirred no controversy shows the degree to which education had been accepted within the missionary movement.[2] Moreover, the arguments teaching missionaries developed to justify this change—that schools did not have to concentrate solely on religious instruction in order to impart a Christian education, that the nurturing of a Christian character in the students was nearly as good as promoting conversions, and that the study of Western secular subjects could aid evangelism—were to become standard defenses for the steady weakening of overt evangelism in their schools. Educational missionaries were still using these defenses when the missionary enterprise was cut off in the early 1950s.

The reader will recognize this as the same opportunism that prompted the early missionaries to teach the Chinese classics in order to attract students. Missionaries' willingness to adapt their schools to the demands of the Chinese, however, should not be construed as an abdication of their primary goals; they continued to assume that Western education was superior to that of China, to promote changes in Chinese gender practices, and to teach Christianity in the schools. They acquiesced in the Chinese desire to reshape the schools by calculating that this would be the entering wedge for the missionaries' religious and social concerns. They believed that this strategy would prove effective both in converting the Chinese and reforming their gender practices.

Three curricular changes are particularly important indicators of the relationship between missionaries and Chinese in the realm of Christian education: the introduction of physical education, new developments in domestic education, and the beginnings of English language instruction. Missionaries' attention to gender issues is clearly visible in the first two innovations, less so in the last. Moreover, an examination of these new additions to mission school education makes quite evident the fact that the missionary relationship with the Chinese was characterized by interaction rather than by a unilateral imposition of ideas and practices. While the missionaries manipulated the Chinese desire to educate their children in order to proselytize among the students, the Chinese also made use of the schools and the missionaries for reasons of their own.

The Expansion of Missionary Education

In the late nineteenth century a series of revivals led by Dwight Moody and other Protestant evangelists swept the United States, resulting in a flood of volunteers for China, the largest American mission field. There were 513 American Protestant missionaries in China in 1890; within ten years there were more than a thousand, over half of whom were women. Simultaneously, increasing numbers of missionaries, particularly women, were assigned to educational work.[3] China missionaries were delighted. In 1891, a missionary journal, the *Chinese Recorder*, crowed: "China missionaries, have we not profound reason to thank God and to take courage?"[4]

The growth of the missionary educational movement in China that accompanied the influx of new missionaries did not slow until after the first World War.[5] This growth created both difficulties and opportunities for teaching missionaries. One difficulty was that educational missionaries became overworked and overextended. Baptist missionary G. H. Waters wrote to a co-worker in 1911 that "the demands of the local teaching work has advanced so rapidly [*sic*] that now the churches and field get only the by-ends of our time and strength snatched at the week-ends from school preparation...."[6] More missionaries gave up direct evangelism and devoted themselves exclusively to teaching.

Some mission schools were seriously overcrowded. The Congregationalist Girls' High School in Fuzhou, for example, was so over-enrolled by 1895 that classrooms had to be converted into dormitories, and in one room the beds had to be removed every day so that the table could be set for breakfast. In South China, where the climate was temperate, some schools housed students in bamboo matsheds (lean-tos) until more permanent structures could be erected. This was hardly conducive to high quality education, but having toiled for years to draw students into their schools American missionaries were now reluctant to turn any applicants away.[7]

Although it could not keep pace with demand, school construction proceeded at a feverish rate, momentarily halted by the Boxer Rebellion in 1900, but then regaining momentum until World War I.[8] Unfortunately, primary schools were generally neglected in this upsurge of building and improvement unless they were connected to a higher-level or boarding school. "Money has been freely spent on buildings for boarding schools," Reverend R. T. Bryan noted critically in 1899, "but the day schools have to put up with small, rented, dark, poorly-ventilated houses which were neither built for schools nor altered as to be suitable for that purpose." Rather than upgrade existing primary day schools, missionaries founded new schools or put the money into higher education.[9] In part, this was done because American missionaries were haunted by the number of Chinese children who wanted to attend school but could not be accommodated.

Perhaps more importantly, the trend toward foreign administration and Chinese teaching in mission schools had already begun, particularly in the primary day schools; because missionaries were less involved in these schools and did not have much faith in the education and training of the Chinese teachers, they did not want to waste precious resources on the day schools.[10]

The missionary building program was quite expensive. Since few of the schools were totally self-supporting before the turn of the century, they were a drain on mission board finances. Teaching missionaries also tended to have ambitions for their schools that exceeded the funds of the home boards. Baptist missionary Adam Groesbeck and his colleagues in Guangzhou, for example, wanted to establish a college preparatory school for Chinese boys in 1904. Groesbeck wrote the Baptist board that they would need at least $33,000 for this undertaking. The Baptist Board, however, had long been plagued by debt and rejected Groesbeck's plan.[11] In the long run, a more serious monetary problem than the limitations of the home boards was the fact that the schools were beyond the ability of the Chinese Christians to run and finance themselves, although this did not become manifest until the Chinese actually attempted to run the schools after 1927.[12]

To American missionaries, however, the widened opportunities beckoning them far outweighed the difficulties that came in their wake. They were delighted to note that Chinese parents were now often eager to enroll their daughters in a Christian school. When Methodist missionary Frances Wheeler opened the first girls' school in Chongqing on October 1, 1883, forty girls enrolled on the first day. This was a far cry from the days when four or five pupils were considered sufficient to justify opening a school. Boys' schools were developing faster, but the expansion of girls' schools seemed to indicate that Chinese gender ideology was changing in a most promising way.[13]

Another positive new development was the establishment of Christian higher education. Before the establishment of Christian and government colleges in China, Chinese students who were interested in Western-style higher education had to go overseas to get it, sometimes with missionary help.[14] American missionaries, however, were not enthusiastic about Chinese students studying abroad. Some were displeased when returned students failed to repay the missionary loans that had financed their overseas study. Others regarded returning students as "denationalized": half-Chinese, half-American hybrids, with the least attractive features of both cultures. Worse yet from the missionary perspective, in the twentieth century some students became infected with religious skepticism in American colleges and universities and returned to China carrying this virus with them. [15]

American missionaries therefore refused as a general policy to promote overseas study for their students, turning their energies instead toward developing Christian colleges in China. They were motivated not only by fears of what students might learn in the institutions of the West but also by the practical consideration that a foreign education was a lengthy and expensive process that very few mission students could afford. Both generosity and anxiety underlay the missionaries' desire for higher education under their own auspices in China. Methodist Monona Cheney, reflecting in 1919 on the importance of her own college days, showed typical ambivalence. "I *ache* at the realization that such a tiny handful of Chinese girls are knowing the same privileges," she wrote. But she added that she hoped Christian colleges in China would prosper, because "[g]oing to America is not a very good thing for [Chinese students]."[16]

By 1900 there were six Christian colleges in China. All were for men, had evolved from mission boys' high schools, and were primarily intended to train ministers. At first they were only equivalent to American high schools. By the late nineteenth century, however, all of these institutions were attempting to raise their standards by setting more stringent criteria for matriculation, requiring entrance examinations, refusing to provide remedial work for students whose preparation was inadequate, and by improving their books, equipment, and faculty.[17] In 1890, the Regents of the State of New York granted a charter to Peking University (a Methodist institution, not to be confused with the government university of the same name), authorizing it to confer American degrees. This initiated a trend toward foreign accreditation by most American mission colleges in China, in what one historian has called "a curious extension of extraterritoriality."[18]

As a number of existing secondary schools grew into colleges, these colleges simultaneously stimulated the growth and improvement of other secondary schools. The secondary schools then served as feeders for the colleges. In the twentieth century, some colleges even had their own attached middle schools or preparatory departments to ensure a supply of adequately prepared students.[19] Missionary Henry Graybill hoped the establishment of a women's college with attached lower schools at Canton Christian College would accomplish three things: feed the higher school, give the college students opportunities for practice teaching in the lower schools, and spur the establishment of other schools throughout Guangdong province.[20]

At the lower end of Christian education, the first kindergarten in China was established by missionaries in 1894. Kindergartens, like the colleges that mimicked American institutions, were an obvious import from the United States. American reformers promoted kindergartens in the U.S. to give immigrant and poor children the moral training that, according to the reformers, their families were failing to provide. Children were also expected to take this moral training back into their homes and reform their parents.[21] American missionaries in China agreed with these reformers that it was a good idea to expose their students to Christian influences from a very young age. John Fryer, addressing the Second Triennial of the EAC, urged educational missionaries to found more kindergartens, saying that this would "save much time, trouble and expense in after years."[22]

Practically speaking, kindergartens served to draw students into the mission system of schools by "creating in them a thirst for knowledge." Missionaries also found that kindergartens were an excellent way of reaching Chinese families, especially the mothers, who often sat in the classroom watching the proceedings. In 1924, a missionary teacher at a kindergarten training school described a mother who sat just outside the circle of children. Day by day she drew her chair closer to the teacher until she finally approached the missionary and shyly asked how to become a church member.[23]

Toward a More Secular Curriculum in the Mission Schools

More significant than the increase in the number of schools and their expansion to the kindergarten and collegiate levels was their shift away from Bible-centered education to a liberal, largely secular curriculum. Since secular education made the schools attractive to those Chinese who wanted a secular, Western education (rather than a Confucian one), greater numbers of non-Christian students were drawn into the mission schools. This permitted missionaries to begin charging tuition in some of their schools. Tuition, in turn, had three consequences: it altered the class background of the students; it released mission board funds that otherwise would have been earmarked for these increasingly self-supporting schools, permitting the establishment of new schools; and it gave the schools that charged tuition the means to upgrade their plants and equipment and to raise their academic standards. As the educational quality improved within the mission system, schools that were not up to the standard were under considerable pressure to upgrade their plants, organization, and curricula from the numerous missionary educational associations and commissions that formed in the late nineteenth and early twentieth centuries.[24]

Events in both the United States and China contributed to the secularization of the mission school curricula in China. In the United States, education was increasingly controlled by the state rather than by local denominational churches or private schoolmasters, with the result that religious instruction became diffuse and generalized.[25] It was in fact more often taught as "natural theology" or "Evidences of Christianity," with less recourse to the Bible as the prime source of authority.[26] Although American missionaries with advanced education were often graduates of denominational colleges, they were familiar with a model of primary and secondary education that did not center on religious teaching and shaped their schools in China accordingly.[27]

In China, increasing numbers of Chinese were coming to believe that there must be a special quality to Western knowledge and education that gave the Western countries their power. While some Chinese pressured the Qing government to establish centers for foreign learning, others turned to the missionaries and urged them to liberalize their school curriculum. Because the Chinese demand for secular education coincided with new emphases in American education as well as with missionary ambitions to make Christian schools in China equivalent to those at home, in most instances the missionaries were happy to accede. The fact that progressive non-Christian Chinese wanted their children to have what was coming to be thought of in China as a "modern" education, with an emphasis on Western learning, struck the missionaries as both a tremendous evangelical and educational opportunity. A *de facto* bargain was struck: in return for access to modern learning, non-Christian Chinese understood that their children would be required to learn the rudiments of the Christian religion, study the Bible, and attend chapel and Sunday worship services. Chinese parents consented, but often warned their children against the religious proselytization of their missionary teachers. For their part, missionaries asked only that the children not be overtly hostile to Christianity. Methodist missionary Laura Haygood wrote that although no "undue influence" would be brought to bear on girls in her McTyeire School in Shanghai to make them convert, they would be taught Christian doctrine and expected to go to church. "No girls are desired as pupils whose parents object to this," Haygood wrote firmly.[28] In this way, missionaries were able to convince themselves and, more importantly, their financial supporters at home, that the schools still served an evangelistic purpose.

Missionaries further justified the secular changes in their schools by developing a specific rationale for each new subject introduced into the curriculum. Tying each to some putative flaw in the Chinese allowed teaching missionaries to claim to be advancing the Christian cause in China. They argued, for instance, that the study of astronomy "helped correct many superstitious beliefs." Mathematics taught "the faculties of reasoning and analysis in which the Chinese are so deficient." According to Methodist missionary Elsie Clark, "The Chinese have no native music of their own that is worthy [of] the name," and thus needed to learn Western choral singing. Music was deemed particularly suitable for girls because it somehow made them more "refined." History offered "moral lessons" and helped show China "what has been and is now her real position amongst the nations of the earth."[29]

Geography was important for the same reasons as history: it showed "what a small space China occupied on the map of the world and what other countries have achieved in comparison." Chinese students, according to missionaries, "became very humble and their conceit left them" when these lessons were impressed upon them.[30] Historian Fred Drake gives a fascinating account of the way in which ABCFM missionary Elijah Bridgman used geography to impart other lessons. Bridgman's tracts on geography were written in the form of letters from a fictive Chinese living in the West to his (equally fictive) relatives back home. Among other things, these tracts emphasized that in Western countries there was no female infanticide and that women were educated and did not have bound feet. Bridgman's aim was both to convince the Chinese of the superiority of the West and to induce them to enact the reforms, particularly reforms concerning women, that missionaries argued were necessary before China could join the modern world as an equal.[31]

Teaching science was more problematic than some of the other subjects that constituted the secular elements of mission school education. A 1902 catalogue from the Methodist Anglo-Chinese College noted anxiously, "It seems to be the desire of the leading men in China to want to show that China needs Western education without what is called the Western religion."[32] Missionaries were consequently often uneasy about the teaching of science in their schools. They hoped that teaching science would disprove Chinese superstitions and demonstrate the superiority of Western culture, which would in turn open Chinese minds to Christian truths. Many missionaries discovered to their dismay that, on the contrary, when educated Chinese began to discard their traditional understanding of the natural world, they did not necessarily become Christians. In fact, in the twentieth century Chinese students often equated Christianity with superstition and rejected both.[33]

In spite of their misgivings, American missionaries could not refuse to teach science in their schools. They believed that the scientific accomplishments of their culture, along with their religious beliefs, gender system, and form of government, proved their superiority over the non-Western world. Moreover, progressive Chinese demanded that the subject be offered. Missionaries believed that it would be best for the Chinese to enter this new field under the auspices of Christian education. As one missionary remarked in 1896, "Whether [science] is to be a power for good or a power for evil depends on how and by whom it is taught. If the Church is wise she will seize the occasion and not let Satan run this mighty engine in China."[34] Here, too, American missionaries argued that Christian influence could permeate secular education, but their anxiety about the teaching of science suggests that their faith in this doctrine was not unwavering.[35]

Three additional subjects had considerable impact on the missionary educational movement and on students in mission schools and thus require a closer examination below. The first, physical education, was not initially welcomed by the Chinese but was energetically promoted by the missionaries, largely as a means of cultivating gender reform in their schools. The second, domestic work, was not new but underwent some interesting changes and provoked controversy in the late nineteenth century. The third subject, the English language, was reluctantly added to the mission schools' curriculum because the Chinese clamored for it. Among missionaries, it was the focal point of heated debate throughout the late nineteenth century.

Physical Education in Mission Schools

The earliest mission schools had done little along the lines of physical education, but by the 1880s both boys' and girls' schools began to include some form of exercise, whether it was games, sports, or simply drills. In part, this was to improve student health, for missionaries regarded their students as sickly and believed that exercise could help build them up. Their perception of their students' vulnerability to disease was somewhat accurate, for trachoma, malaria, smallpox, the plague and tuberculosis were rampant in late-nineteenth-century China, often forcing mission schools to shut down temporarily.[36] Missionary concern with the health of Chinese students also reflected trends in American schools, where medical experts exerted control over students, particularly girls, through physical examinations and a passion for bodily measurements.[37]

How missionaries perceived their students, especially the boys, was also a key component in their physical training agenda. In missionary eyes, their students were frail and prone to wasting illnesses—that is, unmanly. This image took on greater significance as the missionaries applied it to their diagnosis of China's political and national health. As China was seen as "the sick man of Asia," American missionaries projected this pejorative assessment of China's health back onto the bodies of their students and in so doing reconfirmed their superiority over the Chinese. The desire to conquer disease was less significant than the missionaries' determination to transform gender conventions in Chinese society and to literally reshape their male and female students to embody the appropriate American gender standards.[38]

American missionaries also believed that physical education could overturn Chinese class conventions, particularly among boys. Wealthy and educated Chinese men did no physical work; their long fingernails and flowing gowns were signs of status and privilege that marked their social distance from the lower classes. Education was the key to social mobility in China; wishing to join the elite, mission schoolboys, who were drawn from the urban poor and, increasingly, the merchant class, were sensitive to issues of class identity. In the Kutien [boys'] School, for example, the students petitioned the Board of Trustees to assign servants to carry their Bibles and hymnals to church for them "lest the populace get the wrong idea that they were day laborers."[39]

American missionaries criticized this elitism, based upon their own ideological construction of "Christian manhood." Physical strength, stamina, and muscular development formed half of this image; the other half was character—possessing personal virtues such as courage, courtesy, honesty, self-discipline, diligence, and sportsmanship.[40] Missionaries regarded their male students, and Chinese men in general, as deficient in both physique and character.[41] A report from the Methodist Boys' School in Chongqing noted that initially the boys "just could see no fun" in physical education, seeing it as a form of labor that was degrading to students. The report continued by disparaging the boys: "They tossed the ball like a lot of schoolgirls and used the skirts of their padded gowns for a basket in which to catch the ball. It took them a good while to get over being afraid of it."[42]

Physical education in the mission boys' schools was thus intended to mold Chinese boys after American gender patterns. Missionaries were therefore pleased and proud when "their [Chinese boys'] hollow chests, stooping shoulders, shuffling gaits, and flabby muscles" were replaced by "an erect carriage, firm step, and toughened muscles."[43] Missionaries also wanted Chinese boys to act like their American counterparts—boisterous, active, and energetic. Martha Wiley, a Congregationalist teaching in Fuzhou, wrote that one of her male students, whom she saw yelling wildly while galloping on horseback, later asked if she was ashamed of him. "No indeed!" she hastened to reassure him, "Ride as often as you can. It will build you up and make a real man of you."[44] What Wiley and other missionaries failed to understand was that in the context of Chinese culture, male students were expected to adopt a sober, scholarly mien, in keeping with their class status.

It is likely that mission schools introduced sports for Chinese girls because this was a familiar part of American education. By the turn of the century, public schools in the United States included physical training for both sexes, and most women's colleges encouraged their students to engage in such activities as bicycling, basketball, softball, golf and tennis. The American "New Woman" of the late nineteenth century was physically active.[45]

Since it was not in keeping with missionary ideals of appropriate gender roles, the muscular development of their girl students was not an issue for missionaries. Missionaries, however, did believe that Chinese girls could benefit from physical education. As Harriet Stroh, a Presbyterian missionary, remarked, "Athletics are good for the Chinese character." Stroh meant that sports and drill would teach students discipline, competition, and sportsmanship. An emphasis on teaching "character" became yet another component of the missionary justification of Christian education after the turn of the century.[46]

Teaching physical education also had a practical value, for, like English, it was something that neophyte missionaries could teach while they were acquiring the language skills they needed to teach academic subjects. For example, Frida Nilsen, a Lutheran, taught physical education at a Congregationalist girls' school in Beijing while she was attending the Beijing language school for missionaries.[47]

Given the prevailing Chinese attitude that physical exertion was demeaning, missionaries who first introduced exercise into their schools met with incredulity and resistance. Lau Sing Hiong, who worked for 33 years in the Anglo-Chinese College in Fuzhou (later Foochow University), wrote in 1920: "One of the foreign innovations which seemed very strange to our Chinese people was the calisthenics [sic] introduced by Mrs. Smith....[These were considered] a highly interesting, almost ludicrous form of entertainment. Every time Mrs. Smith conducted the drill people came flocking in to watch it, for they considered it more amusing than a theatre."[48] One can only imagine the mortification of Chinese students and how bizarre they must have found these drills, which necessitated such a loss of personal dignity. Mission students offered to hire coolies to exercise for them and pled injury and illness, but missionaries, both entertained and irritated by such excuses, continued to insist on mandatory physical training.[49]

When they tried to instill the values of competition and sportsmanship in their students, American missionaries encountered opposing cultural ideals: i.e., the Chinese concept of "face" and a preference for cooperation over competition. Describing traditional Chinese games in 1926, Gunsun Hoh mentioned only one in which the score was kept with one team winning the game; in all of the others mentioned, "losing" meant simply switching roles and allowing the game to continue. Other games were cooperative and did not involve winning or losing.[50] Erwin Hertz recalled that when he taught his students to play basketball in the mid-1920s, they refused to keep score because losing the game meant losing face and aroused too many hard feelings among the players. Chinese students preferred to play the game for its own sake rather than compete.[51]

Missionaries perceived this reluctance to compete as cowardice and students' chagrin upon losing as poor sportsmanship—proof that these students lacked character. Few missionaries attempted to understand the Chinese view. Instead, they shamed, ridiculed and coerced students into participating in athletic contests. Missionary Chester Fuson reported that it was only after "considerable straight talk...about the cowardice of not trying" that he was able to convince Canton Christian College boys to take part in a track meet. Missionaries also expected Chinese girls to be good sports. When Methodist missionary Elsie Reik's junior class at Hwa Nan Girls' Middle School moped for several days after losing a basketball game, the missionaries told the girls unsympathetically that they were "making fools of themselves."[52]

Physical education developed more slowly in mission girls' schools than in boys' schools for several reasons. One was that both missionary and Chinese beliefs about gender roles rendered some forms of exercise inappropriate for girls. Soon after her arrival at the Methodist Foochow Girls' School in 1888, Julia Bonafield was told by her Chinese assistants that only the younger students should do calisthenics because, for unspecified reasons, the exercises were immodest for older girls.[53] American notions of feminine propriety also restricted some forms of exercise. "After the track was completed," wrote Chester Fuson of Canton Christian College, "Mr. Chung took [the girls] while the boys were drilling, to run races on it but Mrs. Wisner and I thought that was a little too 'modern' so I am now teaching them how to swing [Indian] clubs, which they seem to like." In the first decade of the twentieth century American schoolgirls did not usually participate in track events; Fuson and

Wisner shared a belief that such activities were not suitable for Chinese girls.[54]

The most obvious obstacle to athletics for girls was the practice of footbinding.[55] Girls with bound feet could scarcely walk, let alone run or jump. The systematic crippling of Chinese women was one of the Chinese gender practices that most appalled the missionaries, bolstering their belief that the women of China needed Christ. Because they were unable to agree to make unbound feet a condition of church membership, however, missionaries initially made little headway in changing the custom among their converts.[56] It was in the mission schools that the first breaches were made in the practice of footbinding. The tactic eventually adopted by most mission schools was introduced by Methodists Mary Porter Gamewell and Maria Brown Davis, who made unbound feet a condition of entrance into their Peking School, which opened in 1872. They also helped arrange marriages for their students, which may have made it easier for the girls and their parents to accept this stricture since small feet were usually a factor in a Chinese girl's desirability as a wife. Although the Peking School did have difficulty retaining students for the first few years, in time it became one of the strongest mission schools in the city, and by 1900 Gamewell wrote, "The entire school now breathes an atmosphere unfavorable to foot-binding."[57]

Gradually, other mission girls' schools barred girls with bound feet, unless the girls were willing to remove their bindings and let their feet spread to a more normal size. In the end, however, it was Chinese, not missionary leadership, that succeeded in turning the tide of educated Chinese opinion against the custom.[58] When government schools for girls were established in 1907, Chinese officials, reflecting new sentiments about footbinding, ruled that girls with bound feet could not be admitted to these schools.[59]

In spite of increasing pressure by educated Chinese to end footbinding, the practice persisted in many areas, particularly in the countryside, to the annoyance of missionaries in those places. "I've talked myself hoarse to these freakish, foggish, old-time, undatable, unbendable Yuhsien women," complained Bertha Magness to her sister in 1919, "and I simply can't cajole them into the unbinding of their pesky daughters [sic] blooming bound feet."[60] But girls who did unbind their feet were able to begin enjoying athletics. Even as Bertha Magness bemoaned the conservatism of women in rural Hunan, ABCFM missionary Alice Reed wrote to her family from Sichuan, "Although the bound-footed girls hate to unbind, I think the large-footed ones never regret their comfortable state with the added liberty and fun they can have. They do love to play basketball."[61]

Basketball was not deemed proper for girls in the mission schools until the twentieth century; before that time most girls' schools taught calisthenics rather than team sports. Mission school reports rarely specified what forms of exercise were being offered, but it appears that calisthenics, track events and basketball were the most common, probably because none of these required much in the way of space or equipment.[62] After the turn of the century, both boys' and girls' schools began to hold field meets and other athletic competitions. These events often attracted large crowds, provided the mission schools with valuable publicity, and gave them friendly contacts with other schools, including government schools.[63] Girls' field meets were often restricted to an audience of parents and specially invited guests in order to exclude what missionary Harriet Stroh called "a masculine rabble for whose eyes such an affair was not meet." However, mission school girls did participate in the Far Eastern Olympics in Shanghai in 1921 and again in Manila in 1925.[64]

The participation of male and female students in international athletic competition indicated clearly the profound cultural changes that were altering China's class and gender ideology by the early twentieth century. When the Qing government launched its first modern national educational system in 1905, physical training was included in the curriculum.[65] Although missionaries credited themselves with having inspired these reforms, in fact the new national system of education in China was borrowed from the Japanese, who had modeled their system after that of Germany. German/Japanese education emphasized physical training as a way to inculcate habits of obedience, glorify the military, and promote nationalistic ideals. These goals were primary to most Chinese reformers, smarting as they were under their inability to prevent foreigners from seizing special privileges in China and by Chinese defeat in the Sino-Japanese War of 1895.[66]

The mechanized brutality of the first World War, however, turned some liberal Chinese educational officials against the concept of "military citizenship" and they abolished military training in government-run schools. Games and calisthenics replaced military drills, with an emphasis on health, teamwork, and all-around fitness. Even before the war, regional amateur athletic associations sprang up across China and each region held its own competitions. Many sports clubs were sponsored by the YMCA, although these foreign associations were generally dominated by Chinese leaders.[67]

The rise of student nationalism led Chinese students in government schools to demand in 1925 that military training and drills be reinstated in the schools; the Guomindang [GMD] government, eager to assert its nationalistic credentials and win student support, did so in 1928. The GMD's essential social conservatism meant that Chinese girls were offered courses in first aid rather than military drill.[68] Mission school students clamored for military drills as well. Missionaries gave in, both because they feared student protests if they did not do so and because, by that period, mission schools generally followed the curriculum laid down by the Chinese government.[69] Thus the missionary promotion of physical culture principally to shape the class and gender identities of their Chinese students was ultimately transformed by those students into an expression of nationalism. As later chapters will detail, missionaries in the 1920s were taken aback by the fierceness of Chinese student nationalism and disturbed by alterations in the traditional gender system.

Chores, Industrial Arts, and Domestic Science

As the American mission school curriculum broadened and advanced levels of education became more common, missionaries introduced three new categories of practical training: household chores, which were performed by both boys and girls in mission boarding schools, outside of class hours; industrial arts, also performed by both sexes, often for money or in partial payment of school fees and which might be done during or after school; and domestic science or "home economics," taught only in girls' schools as an academic requirement. The reasons for including these new activities in the mission schools had to do with missionary gender ideology, their determination to build character in their students, and the continuing evolution of their vision of the purpose of Christian education in China.

Requiring Chinese students in Christian boarding schools to help out with chores was practically universal, beginning in the nineteenth century and continuing into the twentieth, although the chores varied from school to school. Mary Margaret Moninger, principal of the Presbyterian Kachek Gospel Girls' School on Hainan Island, described the jobs assigned to her students in 1916:

> Every girl in our school has to work. They change work every week. One big girl and two middle-sized ones cook for a week....for about fifty people. Others sweep the schoolrooms, dust things, keep the yard and garden in order, and inspect the work. Every pupil washes his or her [sic] own dishes, but they only have a bowl and a pair of chopsticks....The girls make their own clothes too and they do all their own washing.[70]

Although some schools demanded less work from their students, Moninger's list is by no means unique. Missionaries took it to be their duty to prepare girls for their future roles in the home. Boarding school teachers felt this responsibility especially keenly for their students were away from home during the years in which girls were customarily instructed in home-making by their mothers. Missionaries believed, however, that the training they offered was superior to anything a Chinese girl might learn in her own home. The dirt and lack of charm missionaries claimed characterized non-Christian Chinese homes were important elements of the missionary critique of the Chinese home.[71]

American missionaries also worried that education, particularly secondary or college education, might make Chinese young women dissatisfied with home life, which missionaries assumed was the destiny of the great majority of their female students.[72] At the 1907 China Centenary Missionary Conference, one woman explained that a "share in the cooking and cleaning is absolutely essential for middle-class girls to prevent them from being unfitted for their future life."[73] In both China and the United States, schools for girls and women commonly included some form of domestic work as a means of silencing critics and proving that female students were not being encouraged to rebel against the limits placed on them by contemporary gender ideology.[74]

Mission school boys were often given the same chores as girls, including supervising the kitchen. They did not sew, however, and rarely washed their own clothes. They were often given heavy work, such as fetching water and raking the schoolyard, from which girls were generally exempt.[75] There was no suggestion among missionary teachers that this would benefit the boys in later roles as husband and father. Instead, the principal argument in favor of boys' doing these tasks was that it would show them the value of manual labor and develop their characters. As missionaries at the Methodist Chungking Boys' High School stated in 1908, the boys disliked manual work "for this is considered coolie work, but it is sort of a test of their worth."[76]

Chores in boys' schools, then, were another way in which missionaries attempted to break down Chinese beliefs about physical exertion, scholarly dignity, and class status. Girls could learn the value of labor as well; Presbyterians in Hangzhou lauded chores as a means of preventing girls from "forming habits of sloth and indolence."[77] Missionaries stressed the importance of promoting a work ethic among girls, however, less often than they did the primacy of domesticity. Chinese and American beliefs that girls ought to be trained to be good wives and mothers intersected; consequently there was little resistance to mandatory chores for girls. It seems likely that in the boys' schools, manual labor was promoted successfully only because Chinese habits of obedience to their teachers compelled students to submit to their rules. By the 1920s, when Chinese students began to rebel against their teachers (especially foreign ones), traditional opposition to physical labor had already declined.[78]

The advent of tuition charges in the mission schools, which developed faster in boys' than in girls' schools, altered the justification for students' doing chores in some of the schools, for missionaries now encouraged chores as a form of work-study for poor students who could not afford to pay for their own room, board, or tuition. This was crucial to the mission schools' sense of identity, for although the inauguration of fees drew in new classes of students, often students from the merchant class, it also threatened to separate the schools from their Christian constituency, the vast majority of whom were exceedingly poor until the twentieth century. Although the schools had never operated exclusively for the children of native Christians, most missionaries agreed that they could not now abandon their converts in favor of the "better classes" of non-Christians who were taking advantage of the expanded curriculum and were willing and able to pay for the privilege.[79] Thus mission schools had to find a way to continue providing education for the children of converts once they began to charge for their services; paying students for doing chores was one way of accomplishing this. Mission schools saved some money by making students responsible for custodial work since it meant that fewer servants were needed.[80]

Even with the initiation of school fees, however, most schools continued to insist that the students do their share of the chores. Although some missionaries argued that students paying for their education should not be made to work, others responded that requiring students to work regardless of their financial standing would promote a spirit of democracy. Speaking of her school at the China Centenary Conference in 1907, Sara Dodson asserted proudly, "rich and poor, Christian and heathen, all were treated alike, and all performed the same duties." Others justified chores by stating that students "will prize more highly the privileges that are theirs if they do something in return."[81]

The same desire to teach the value of labor and make the schools more self-supporting without squeezing out the poor students underlay the creation of "industrial arts" departments in some of the Christian schools. In the girls' schools, industrial work nearly always took the form of needlework. Through missionary connections with their home churches Chinese girl students sold fancy embroidery, cross-stitch, and lace in the United States. This practice, like school chores, began in the nineteenth century and continued into the twentieth. Girls in the Lucy Alderman Memorial School, for example, spent their Saturdays doing drawn-work, making lace, and cutting out paper dolls for sale. The Mary Stevens Memorial Girls' School had a rule that students were not eligible for financial aid from the missionaries unless they paid half of their tuition and board with proceeds from their needlework.[82]

In addition to helping a girl pay for her education, missionaries foresaw that industrial skills might be useful after she left school. The Presbyterian Nanking Girls' Boarding School reported in 1902, "Sewing, mending and embroidery form a regular part of the curriculum. Spinning, knitting and lacemaking have been taught that the girls might in future [sic] be able to earn their own living or supplement that of the family."[83] Missionaries also believed, probably correctly, that an educated girl who could earn money through handicrafts would be attractive to prospective mothers-in-law and that this might reconcile families to postponing a girl's marriage until she had completed her education. Baptist Lida Ashmore recalled in her autobiography that mission school girls were perceived by Chinese mothers-in-law as haughty because the girls were of an independent cast of mind and were not used to taking orders from "ignorant" mothers-in-law. Ashmore hoped that teaching the girls to weave and thus earn money for the family would help ease acceptance of educated Chinese girls by their in-laws.[84]

None of the industrial arts taught in mission girls' schools contradicted Chinese ideas about proper activities for women. Nor was it uncommon for a Chinese woman to sell the products of her labor. Indeed, some unmarried women, notably in south China, were able to maintain an existence independent of their families, without ever marrying.[85] Among Chinese women, mission school girls were unique because they could use their earnings for education. While this did not make them independent of their families or in-laws, their earning power undoubtedly enhanced their position within both their natal and marital families and became a factor in altering traditional configurations of power within the Chinese family.

Not every girls' school had an industrial department; even fewer boys' schools had them. There were several reasons for this. First, since Chinese parents were more eager to have sons educated than daughters, it was easier for missionaries to collect fees in the boys' schools. Second, an educated boy had career possibilities open to him that made it less important to learn practical skills. Since American missionaries hoped that many of their boy students would enter the ministry or some other area of Christian service, missionaries themselves were ambivalent about teaching boys extraneous skills. Third, while teaching needlework was a simple matter, boys required more expensive equipment and materials as well as a greater investment in training to produce saleable goods. Furthermore, the articles produced in boys' schools were sold in China, not the United States, and had to compete with native goods and with the native guilds in each industry.[86]

Instead of attaching an industrial school to a regular mission school, missionaries generally established separate industrial schools for their male students. Although some academic and religious courses were offered, the primary focus in these schools was on training poor boys in a mechanical skill. An example is the Methodist Chinkiang Industrial School, which was founded in 1896 for "the training of Christian mechanics." The school operated for only a few years before it merged with another industrial school. According to mission historian Eddy Lucius Ford, "The vocational work did not become a permanent feature." The school was soon transformed into a regular academic institution.[87]

There were sharp gender distinctions between industrial subjects offered to girls and boys. Girls most frequently learned needlework, while boys were taught wood-working. Some missionaries hoped boys might be taught match-making, glass-blowing, shoe-making or watch-making, but it is unclear that any of these ambitious schemes was ever realized.[88] In the early twentieth century, influenced both by the trend toward vocational education in U.S. schools and by the missionaries' conviction that their students needed more practical training, American mission schools offered a broader range of training courses. For girls, the options were teacher training or domestic science, which as we shall see, included more than mere needlework. For boys, the emergence of "rural reconstruction" as a pressing social concern prodded the missionaries to offer courses on agriculture, soils, and animal husbandry, as well as normal [teacher] training.[89] Missionaries also established a number of professional schools. By 1876, there were twenty Protestant theological schools in China. This increased to 68 by 1906, reflecting both the missionaries' desire to train a Chinese ministry and the enhanced popularity of mission schools. Medical education began informally, with some thirty students studying medicine by 1877. The Peking Union Medical College (PUMC), which was taken over by the Rockefeller Foundation in 1915 and came to dominate foreign medical training in China, was founded in 1906. Many of the Christian colleges developed their own medical or nursing training departments.[90]

Throughout the nineteenth century, girls in American mission schools were taught only the most basic of domestic arts as part of the regular curriculum. After the turn of the century, however, influence from the American home economics movement began to affect many mission schools in China. As a result, a wide range of subjects was taught under the rubric of "domestic science." This was particularly true in the three Christian women's colleges that existed by 1915. In 1919 the North China Union Women's College in Beijing described its domestic science offering as "a course covering the theory and practice of dietetics, home nursing, sewing, keeping accounts, etc., adapted to the Chinese environment, instruction in fine Chinese and foreign cooking." A related course in the same department was "Household and City Sanitation."[91]

While the American home economics movement influenced the missionaries, there is some evidence of two other motivations for the emphasis on domestic science: to disarm critics who insisted that girls' education must prepare them for domestic roles after leaving school and to permit schools to offer Chinese girls instruction in the "hard" sciences. In many Christian girls' schools, scientific instruction was neglected because it was difficult to square the teaching of science with an ideology that justified education for girls primarily for its value in training good wives and mothers. Alice Parker made an impassioned plea to her colleagues in 1896 to offer science to Chinese girls:

> In most of our boys' schools there is a great effort being made to have a well-supplied lab, but what about our girls' schools? We see in most of them nothing of the kind. They have a few maps and perhaps a globe to help in the teaching of geography, but nothing to show the girls the wonders of electricity, light, sound, etc....It is considered necessary to teach our Western girls these things, why not our Chinese girls?[92]

Her arguments that Chinese girls ought to have a grounding in science simply because Western girls did and her implication that what was necessary for Chinese boys was also important for girls were not the arguments generally used by missionaries who urged the teaching of science in girls' schools. "Practicality" was most often the litmus test for teaching science and mathematics in mission schools for girls. The more common tack was that taken in 1916 by Matilda Thurston, president of the newly-established Ginling Women's College in Nanjing. Thurston defended her decision to offer chemistry, biology, botany, and zoology by stating that these subjects were "important both as preparation for teaching and for medicine. Both have very practical uses in everyday life which China very much needs."[93] Criticized for teaching "impractical" solid geometry, missionaries at Hangchow Union Girls' School replaced that course with one on domestic science in 1916. It would be interesting to know what precisely was included in this new course, for chemistry, physics, physiology and psychology, especially child psychology, were sometimes subsumed under the heading "domestic science."[94]

It is important to note that both Alice Parker and Matilda Thurston defended the idea of teaching science in girls' schools not to Chinese patrons of the schools but to their own missionary colleagues. Thurston's reference to teaching and medicine demonstrated the broadened view of appropriate roles for Chinese women that American missionaries promoted in the twentieth century. But the fact that she invoked these roles as a defense of her decision to include the hard sciences in Ginling College's curriculum shows that, even in that era, education for girls and young women had to be justified in ways that distinguished it from male education. Teaching domestic science was thus a graceful way to accede to American gender ideology while making a subtle shift in the ideology itself. American Protestant missionary women, who self-consciously set out to remake the gender system of the Chinese, were simultaneously remaking their own.

English in the Mission Schools

Perhaps the most critical addition to the mission school curriculum was the teaching of English. Missionaries were caught off guard when a demand for this subject emerged both within and without the Chinese Christian community. It had not occurred to American missionaries that the Chinese would be interested in learning their language or that there could be any conceivable use for such training, other than as preparation for the few students who would study in American colleges. The opening of the treaty ports that began with the 1842 Treaty of Nanjing, however, spawned a number of foreign enclaves along China's coast where businessmen, diplomats, and adventurers settled. These foreign settlements offered job opportunities for enterprising Chinese men as translators, interpreters, clerks, and secretaries. Working in such capacities conferred none of the social status that government service did, but it was fairly lucrative and did not require years of study to pass an imperial examination.[95]

The Qing government had attempted to fill its need for trained linguists by establishing several language schools called *Tongwenguan* in the early 1860s. To enroll, however, a young man had to have passed the lowest level civil service examination. So young men who lacked a classical education but were interested in treaty port work turned to the mission schools for instruction. Men of the Chinese merchant class were highly interested in learning foreign languages because they had the closest ties to foreigners. Due to the political and military pressures Western countries exerted on China in the late nineteenth century, some Chinese began to think it necessary to learn from the West in order to stave off national ruin. Merchants were among this group, but they were not its sole constituents. A desire to study English, then, went beyond pecuniary considerations; it showed one's desire to be able to communicate with foreigners, to be conversant with their ideas, and to be willing to move past the narrow confines of Chinese cultural provincialism in order to strengthen the Chinese nation. In short, the study of English, like physical training, came to be regarded by many Chinese as modern, progressive, and patriotic.

China's military defeat by Japan in 1895 heightened the sense of crisis among politically conscious Chinese, as missionaries were well aware. Soochow University evolved out of an English class begun by Methodists at the behest of six Chinese students shamed by "this great defeat."[96] In the welcoming address of the Second Triennial meeting of the EAC in 1896, missionary John Fryer commented, "The belief is now very widespread that only by adopting Western learning and methods as Japan has done can China hold her own. The better classes of mission colleges are almost overwhelmed with applications for admission, especially where English is taught."[97] Once again, teaching missionaries sensed an opportunity and pursued it.

It is impossible to determine exactly when the Chinese first expressed interest in learning English, but even before the Sino-Japanese War some mission schools had already begun to teach it. In 1881 St. John's College (Episcopalian, later St. John's University) in Shanghai introduced the subject. The same year, the Methodist Wiley Institute announced the formation of two parallel courses of study: the Chinese classics and Western mathematics and science or an English language course along with the Confucian classics.[98] At the same time, missionaries founded a number of "Anglo-Chinese institutes," often with the financial support of local Chinese. Like the Wiley Institute, these Anglo-Chinese schools taught a course that was half Chinese, including the Confucian classics, and half English, usually including "foreign" subjects such as math and science, which were taught in English. The Methodist Anglo-Chinese College which later became Foochow University, was built in 1881, thanks to a gift of $10,000 from a wealthy Chinese merchant. The Presbyterian Anglo-Chinese College in Zhefu was built by Chinese merchants with the understanding that the buildings would become the property of the Presbyterian mission if the missionaries would teach English.[99]

Some Chinese parents wanted their daughters as well as their sons to be instructed in English. Girls, of course, did not take jobs in treaty ports, but in some instances knowledge of English seems to have been an indicator of class status. Mission girls' schools that sought to attract the daughters of the rich placed a heavy emphasis on English in their coursework. Two examples of this type of school are the Methodist McTyeire School in Shanghai, which opened in 1862, and the Tianjin Keen School, also Methodist, which opened in 1909. Both schools taught "Western" subjects in English, which was unusual in mission girls' schools. Both schools also emphasized music, another obviously ornamental and therefore status-denoting feature. McTyeire students even studied Latin.[100]

Chinese fathers who had been exposed to Western learning, including English, often wanted the same for their daughters. Grace Liang Yapp's father had been a member of the "Yung Wing Mission," a group of 120 Chinese boys who were sent to school in Hartford, Connecticut, between the years 1872 and 1875. Grace's father sent her to the Keen School to get a Western education and influenced several other Chinese officials to enroll their daughters as well.[101] Moreover, the girls themselves sometimes asked to be taught English, often because the boys to whom they were betrothed spoke English. In 1905 Methodist bishop James Bashford recommended that English be taught in all girls' schools under the direction of the Methodist Women's Foreign Missionary Society, but it is not clear whether or not his suggestion was adopted. According to Reverend J. A. Silsby, editor of the *Chinese Recorder*, "nearly all" mission boys' boarding schools and many day schools taught English by 1902. He added that "the girls' schools are rapidly following suit."[102]

The demand for English put the missionaries in a quandary. Teaching mathematics and science could be justified by linking the subjects to Christianity or by arguing that they broadened students' minds and empowered them to defend Christianity intelligently.[103] Teaching the Confucian classics alongside Christian doctrine, many missionaries argued, revealed which of the two was superior. No one ever suggested, however, that studying English could lead one to Christianity or make one a better Christian. The Bible had already been translated into Chinese in 1819, and missionaries knew that Chinese ministers would have to address their congregations in their mother tongue. One missionary did suggest that if the Chinese were interested in learning a foreign language, they should be taught Greek so that they could read the New Testament in the original.[104]

Because the teaching of English was not connected in any obvious way to Christianity, mission schools had to develop some other justification for teaching it. Some missionaries, in fact, opposed teaching English, and some schools refused to so do. In the American mission school system as a whole, however, rejecting Chinese demands for English was not seriously considered despite the disquiet some missionaries continued to feel about teaching it. Some missionaries linked it to their gender goals by asserting that teaching English in the girls' schools might make Chinese children regard their mother as the intellectual equal of their father.[105] Generally speaking, however, gratification that the Chinese were seeking out their schools overcame missionaries' qualms about teaching English. In addition, large donations from rich Chinese for the purpose of building schools were difficult to turn down. Missionaries began to regard teaching English in return for money as a reasonable exchange.

School fees and the teaching of English were clearly linked. At the 1890 Shanghai Conference, missionaries lauded English teaching both for attracting students to the mission schools and inducing them to pay tuition. By 1902 the Chiningchow Boys' Boarding School no longer gave financial aid to its students because English now formed part of the curriculum. In the same year, the Clara Linton Memorial School for Boys in Qianfu insisted that all boys pay half of their board; boys taking the English course were required to pay full board. Teaching English thus helped to finance the expansion of the missionary educational movement in China even as it drew larger numbers of students into the schools.[106]

Mission schools were not only interested in Chinese money; they were also interested in the rich Chinese themselves. According to one missionary, "The principal reason for opening a school in the English [sic] is not so much to teach them English as to come in touch with the better class of Chinese."[107] American missionaries had long been preoccupied with converting the "better class of Chinese." English was something well-to-do Chinese increasingly desired; teaching it gave missionaries a point of contact with this class of people. In more than one instance, missionaries used the Bible as an English text, thus neatly combining their evangelistic purposes and the practical concerns of their Chinese patrons.[108]

Debates over teaching English in the mission schools contained echoes of earlier disputes over teaching the Confucian classics. Some American missionaries believed that there were no grounds for including English instruction in a Christian school curriculum. Since the Chinese desired it, however, and were willing to pay for it and even submit to simultaneous religious instruction, most missionaries understood that acceding to the Chinese demand for English could make their schools more popular. Evangelistic success, they argued, would follow.

The establishment of the North China College by missionaries of the ABCFM highlights the contours of the debate over English and competing strategies of promoting Christian education in China. In 1882, Charles A. Stanley wanted to found a Congregationalist Anglo-Chinese College in Tianjin that would emphasize English and science, downplay religious instruction, and be open to any boy who could pay the tuition. His colleague Devello Z. Sheffield was horrified, believing that missionaries had no mandate to initiate what amounted to secular education. His counterproposal was that his own boys' high school be advanced to college grade. This college would accept only Christians, sons of Christians, and local boys, teach only in Chinese, and focus on religious teaching. In 1889 Sheffield's plan, but not Stanley's, was approved by the American Board, and the North China College was founded. The contrast between this institution and its rival, the Methodist University of Peking, thirteen miles away, is instructive; the University conducted classes in English and was able to attract well-off students who paid for their education, while the North China College was forced to provide its students with free room and board.[109]

In the twentieth century, when the Chinese developed their own system of non-classical, secular schools, the teaching of English remained one of the strongest attractions of the mission schools for the Chinese. Missionaries were highly conscious of this fact. "You would have to live here to realize what a craze there is for English," wrote missionary Monona Cheney in 1922, reflecting the ambivalence missionaries continued to feel about the demand for English, "a rather unwholesome one I feel.

But what an opportunity they all represent!" In 1925, in the midst of Chinese student agitation against foreigners in China, Methodist General Secretary of Education Frank Gamewell put it more forcefully: "You will readily appreciate the fact that the heaviest demand in connection with our middle schools is, probably, the teaching of English, and that there will be a tendency to utilize foreigners for this purpose often to such an extent as to make their main service the teaching of the English language."[110]

Although American missionaries were not unreservedly enthusiastic about the "craze" for English among the Chinese, the need to teach the language did help to make the missionary educational endeavor more efficient. Previously, new missionaries had been largely useless around the mission station until they learned to put together a few words of Chinese. In the mid-nineteenth century, for example, Presbyterian missionary John Nevius could not begin his work until after eight or nine months following his arrival. In contrast, ABCFM missionary Alice Reed was teaching English in the Bridgman Academy one month after her arrival in 1916. Because there was a demand for English teachers in the mission schools, new missionaries could simultaneously teach English and study Chinese. Some schools taught subjects such as music, Western history, and science in English, enabling missionaries who were not yet proficient in Chinese to teach these courses as well.[111]

The success and popularity of mission schools in China in the late nineteenth century should not be exaggerated. It was still only relative success and relative popularity. The vast majority of the populace continued to regard the mission schools with suspicion; they were still foreign institutions occupying an awkward and precarious position in the larger framework of Chinese education. Missionaries were delighted now that students no longer had to be dragged in off the streets, even though they realized that secular subjects and English were the chief attraction for the Chinese. The mission schools' focus on providing a good secular education, however, meant that Christianity, rather than being the sole or even primary emphasis, was but one of many messages that students in mission schools received. The evangelistic side of Christian education thus grew weaker as the educational quality of the schools was enhanced.

This development posed a threat to the evangelical aspect of missionary educational work in China. Teaching missionaries were aware of this, but rather than face the issue squarely, they chose to evade it with references to the mysterious and subtle power of Christian influence. "There is always a recognized danger that Christian students will suffer from intimate association for a period of years with other students who are indifferent or opposed to religious thoughts," conceded Reverend Devello Sheffield in 1899, "but against this danger confidence is placed in the power of Christian instruction and in the secret ministry of the Spirit of truth...." This faith in an undefinable but tangible Christian spirit sustained educational missionaries in China through every vicissitude down to their expulsion from China in the early 1950s, and was a stock answer to evangelical critics who opposed the increasing secularity of mission education.[112]

Although by the turn of the century American Protestant mission schools were considerably more secular than they had been fifty years earlier, the commitment of American missionaries to "Christianize," as they put it, the Chinese gender system was unabated. Their fervor to reform their students' attitudes and behavior had to be balanced against meticulous calculations of how much could be demanded without driving Chinese students out of the schools. Within these parameters, however, American teaching missionaries did their best to transfer to their students their own beliefs about the essential natures of men and women, the roles that were appropriate for them in society, and how the sexes should interact with one another. It is to this endeavor that we now turn.

ENDNOTES

1 Albert Feuerwerker, *The Foreign Establishment in China in the Early Twentieth Century* (Ann Arbor: Center for Chinese Studies, 1976), p. 42; Paul Varg, *Missionaries, Chinese and Diplomats: The American Protestant Missionary Movement in China, 1890–1950* (Princeton: Princeton University Press, 1958), p. 13.

2 *Records of the Second Triennial Meeting of the Educational Association of China* (Shanghai: American Presbyterian Mission Press, 1896), p. 54.

3 Irwin Hyatt, "Protestant Missions in China, 1877–1890: The Institutionalization of Good Works," pp. 93–126, see p. 100, in Liu Kwang-ching, ed., *American Missionaries in China, Papers from Harvard Seminars* (Cambridge: East Asian Research Center, Harvard University, 1970). American missionaries represented only 35 per cent of all Protestant missionaries in 1900, but their numbers increased faster than those of non-American Protestants. By 1912, British missionaries, who had previously dominated Protestant ranks, were equaled by the number of American missionaries; by the early 1930s, American Protestants were the dominant group, accounting for 47 per cent of all Protestant missionaries in China. M. Searle Bates, "The Theology of American Missionaries in China, 1900–1950," pp. 135–158, see p. 137, in John K. Fairbank, ed.,

The Missionary Enterprise in China and America (Cambridge: Harvard University Press, 1974).

4 Varg, *Missionaries, Chinese and Diplomats*, pp. 54–62; *Chinese Recorder* 22 (May 1891): 221.

5 Eddy Lucius Ford, "The History of the Educational Work of the Methodist Episcopal Church in China: A Study of its Development and Present Trends" (Ph.D. diss., Northwestern University, 1936), p. 191.

6 G. H. Waters to William Ashmore, March 11, 1911, William and Lida Ashmore Papers, RG Ax 564, Box 1, UOSC.

7 Report of the Foochow Mission of the American Board, 1895–1896, p. 36; *Records of the Third Triennial Meeting of the Educational Association of China* (Shanghai: American Presbyterian Mission Press, 1899), p. 105; Mary Raleigh Anderson, *A Cycle in the Celestial Kingdom or Protestant Mission Schools for Girls in South China (1827 to the Japanese Invasion)* (Mobile, Ala.: Heiter-Starke Printing Co., 1943), p. 108.

8 Ford, "History of the Educational Work," pp. 120–123; Valentin Rabe, *The Home Base of American China Missions, 1880–1920* (Cambridge: Harvard University Press, 1978), chapter seven.

9 *Third Triennial of the EAC*, 1899, p. 104.

10 *Second Triennial of the EAC*, 1896, p. 188; *The Evangel* (May 1899): 9, RG 46, Box 219, Folder 1668, YDSL. By 1916, the *China Mission Handbook* claimed that there were 1,350 missionaries engaged in educational work. They were vastly outnumbered, however, by the Chinese teachers in the mission schools, who numbered around 9,500. From a folder on the United Board for Christian Colleges in China, 1913–1923, 73-43: 1115-3-2: 10, GBGM.

11 Adam Groesbeck to Rev. George Huntingdon, May 5, 1911, Adam and Clara Groesbeck Papers, RG Ax 818, Box 1, UOSC.

12 *Third Triennial of the EAC*, 1899, p. 104.

13 Lucerne H. Knowlton, "One Hundred Years of Methodism in China," p. 6, Lucerne H. Knowlton Papers, Box 1, HIA; Mrs. John Mott, "China's Daughters and Their Education," *The Evangel* 11: 109 (May 1899): 6–9, RG 46, Box 219, Folder 1668, YDSL.

14 Yung Wing, *My Life in China and America* (New York: Henry Holt and Co., 1909), pp. 38–39; Knowlton, "One Hundred Years of Methodism," p. 6, Lucerne H. Knowlton Papers, Box 1, HIA.

15 William Ashmore, Jr., "Some Thoughts and Some Queries with Regard to Oriental Students Returning to their Home Lands," March 13, 1926, William and Lida Ashmore Papers, RG Ax 564, Box 1, UOSC; Assistant Treasurer of the Methodist Board of Foreign Missions to Dr. J. P. MacMillan, March 27, 1928, 73-43: 1047-5-1: 31, GBGM; Report of the Norwegian Lutheran Church of America, 1928, p. 249, ELCA.

16 Monona Cheney to family, May 3, 1919, Monona Cheney Papers, RG Ax 275, Box 1, UOSC. Emphasis in original.

17 Latourette, *A History of Christian Missions in China* (New York: MacMillan Co., 1929), p. 447; W. B. Nance, *Soochow University* (New York: United Board of Christian Colleges in China, 1956), p. 18.

18 Kenneth Latourette, *Christian Missions in China*, p. 627. The Christian colleges include: Fukien Christian University, founded in 1915, chartered in New York, 1931; Ginling Women's College, founded in 1913, chartered in New York, 1915; Hangchow Christian College, founded in 1893, chartered in the District of Columbia, 1920; Hua Chung College, formed in 1924 from the merger of Boone University (1871), Wesley College (1885), Griffith John College (1899), Huping College (1910), and Yale-in-China (1914), with degrees granted by Boone University, which had been chartered in New York in 1909; Hwa Nan College for Women, established in 1914, chartered in New York under the auspices of the University of Nanking in 1922 and rechartered independently in 1933; Lingnan University, founded in 1893 and chartered in New York in 1894; St. John's

University, established in 1879, chartered in the District of Columbia, 1906; Shantung Christian University (also known as Cheeloo University), founded in 1904, chartered in Ontario in 1924 and rechartered in New York, 1946; Soochow University, founded in 1900, chartered in Tennessee the same year; the University of Nanking, founded in 1888 and chartered in New York in 1917; the University of Shanghai, founded in 1906 and chartered in Virginia in 1917; West China Union University, founded in 1910 and chartered in New York, 1922; and Yenching University, established in 1918 and chartered in New York in 1915 (Yenching was formed from the merger of several existing institutions). See John Barrow, "American Institutions of Higher Learning in China, 1845–1925," *Higher Education* 4 (February 1, 1948): 121–124, and William Purviance Fenn, *Christian Higher Education in Changing China, 1880–1950* (Grand Rapids, Mich.: William B. Eerdmans, 1976), pp. 19–70; Mary Lamberton, *St. John's University, Shanghai* (New York: United Board for Christian Colleges in China, 1955), p. 63.

19 The following Christian colleges had attached middle schools: Lingnan University, Shantung Christian University, Hangchow Christian University, St. John's University, and Hwa Nan College for Women. See Charles Hodge Corbett, *Lingnan University* (New York: United Board for Christian Higher Education in Asia, 1963), p. 47; Corbett, *Shantung Christian University (Cheeloo)* (New York: United Board for Christian Colleges in China, 1955), p. 156; Clarence Burton Day, *Hangchow University, A Brief History* (New York: United Board for Christian Colleges in China, 1955), p. 20; Lamberton, *St. John's University*, p. 60; and L. Ethel Wallace, *Hwa Nan College, The Woman's College of South China* (New York: United Board for Christian Colleges in China, 1956), p. 38. Yenching University and Huachung University, both union institutions, did not have middle schools on campus, but were affiliated with middle schools operated by the various denominational missions participating in the union. See Edwards, *Yenching University*, pp. 101–103, and John L. Coe, *Huachung University* (New York: United Board for Christian Higher Education in Asia, 1962), pp. 7–9.

20 Henry Graybill, "Developing a Woman's college," p. 31, 1913, Canton Christian College pamphlet, RG 31, Box 273, Folder 1944, YDSL.

21 Mary Ninde Gamewell, *Ming Kwong, "City of the Morning Light"* (West Medford, Mass.: Central Committee on the United Study of Foreign Missions, 1924), p. 73; Joel Spring, *The American School, 1642–1985* (New York: Longman, 1986), p. 161.

22 *Second Triennial of the EAC*, 1896, p. 23; Alice Reed to family, Excerpts from Letters, 1916-1948, April 15, 1917, pp. 17–18, Alice Reed Papers, RG 8, Box 136, YDSL.

23 *Third Triennial of the EAC*, 1899, p. 99; Bertha St. Clair to family, March 30, 1924, Bertha St. Clair Papers, RG 8, Box 174, YDSL.

24 *Christian Education in China* (New York: Committee of Reference and Counsel of the Foreign Missions Conference of North America, 1922).

25 Spring, *The American School*, p. 71.

26 Thomas Woody, *A History of Women's Education in the United States,* Vol. 1 (New York: Octagon Books, 1966), p. 414.

27 Feuerwerker, *The Foreign Establishment in China*, p. 53.

28 Anna and Oswald Brown, *The Life and Letters of Laura Askew Haygood* (Nashville: Publishing House of the Methodist Episcopal Church, 1904), p. 280; *China Centenary Missionary Conference, Records* (Shanghai: Centenary Conference Committee, 1907), p. 188; Adam Groesbeck, "How the Chinese Boy Finds Christ, or stated Psychologically and less intelligently: the Conversion Experience Among Adolescent Chinese," n. d., Adam and Clara Groesbeck Papers, RG Ax 818, Box 1, UOSC.

29 Margaret Burton, *The Education of Women in China* (New York: Fleming H. Revell Co., 1911), p. 69; *Second Triennial of the EAC*, 1896, p. 52; Elsie Clark to family, March 13, 1913, Elsie Clark [Krug] Papers, RG 8, Box 41, YDSL; 1923 Report of Chengtu Methodist Girls' High School, quoting a letter of May 24, 1911, 79-16: 1459-5-1: 34, GBGM.

30 *Second Triennial of the EAC*, 1896, p. 135; *Third Triennial of the EAC*, 1899, p. 76.

31 Fred W. Drake, "Protestant Geography in China: E. C. Bridgman's Portrayal of the West," pp. 89–106 in Suzanne W. Barnett and John K. Fairbank, *Christianity in China: Early Protestant Writings* (Cambridge: Harvard University Press, 1985).

32 Anglo-Chinese College, catalogue, 1902, 79-16: 1459-4-2: 09, GBGM.

33 *China Centenary Conference,* 1907, p. 62.

34 *Second Triennial of the EAC,* 1896, p. 53.

35 Hangchow Christian College, publicity, p. 9, 1903, RG 11, Box 187, Folder 3308, YDSL.

36 Day, *Hangchow University,* p. 16; Ford, "History of the Educational Work," p. 126; and "Jefferson Academy at Tungchow and its Significance for Christian Education in China," pamphlet, n. d., RG 31, Box 297, Folder 1967, YDSL.

37 Paul Atkinson, "The Feminist Physique: P.E. and the Medicalization of Women's Education," pp. 38–57 in J. A. Mangan and Roberta J. Parks, eds., *From "Fair Sex" to Feminism: Sport and the Socialization of Women in the Industrial and Post-Industrial Eras* (London; Frank Cass & Co., 1987). Mary Margaret Moninger tried to interest her students in calisthenics by rigging a device to measure their lung capacity. Mary Margaret Moninger to family, October 6, 1918, Mary Margaret Moninger Papers, RG 230, PC (USA).

38 Chester Fuson to family, April 28, 1906, Chester Fuson Papers, RG 8, Box 71, YDSL.

39 Arthur Braden Coole, *A Trouble Shooter for God in China* (Kansas: Intercollegiate Press, 1976), p. 28, Arthur and Ella Coole Papers, RG Ax 652, Box 1, UOSC.

40 O. G. Reuman, "Some Suggestions Toward a Progressive Program of Projects for Younger Adolescent Boys in China," pamphlet, 1923, O. G. Reuman Papers, RG 8, Box 164, YDSL.

41 Jane Hunter, *The Gospel of Gentility: American Women Missionaries in Turn-of-the-Century China* (New Haven: Yale University Press, 1984), pp. 204–209.

42 Chungking Methodist Boys' High School, Announcement, 1908–1909, p. 23, 79-16: 1459-5-2:02, GBGM.

43 "The Making of a Christian College in China: discussing boy students of early times," p. 18, Canton Christian College, pamphlet, n. d., RG 31, Box 273, Folder 1946, YDSL.

44 Martha Wiley, Memoirs, p. 2, n. d., Martha Wiley Papers, RG 8, Box 218, YDSL.

45 Christine Simmons, "Companionate Marriage and the Lesbian Threat," *Frontiers* IV: 3 (1979), pp. 54–59; Carroll Smith-Rosenberg, *Disorderly Conduct: Visions of Gender in Victorian America* (Oxford: Oxford University Press, 1985), pp. 176–181, 245–296; Martha Verbrugge, *Able-Bodied Womanhood: Personal Health and Social Change in Nineteenth-Century Boston* (Oxford: Oxford University Press, 1988), p. 149.

46 Harriet Stroh to family, May 23, 1921, Harriet Stroh Papers, RG 187, Box 1, Folder 4, PC (USA).

47 Frida Nilsen interview, p. 3, MCOHP, 1976, ELCA.

48 Lau Sing Hiong, "Reminiscences," p. 5, 1920, 79-16: 1459-4-2:09, GBGM.

49 Coole, *A Trouble Shooter for God,* p. 29, Arthur and Ella Coole Papers, RG 652, Box 1, UOSC; Jeanie McClure to family, Oct. 6, 1918, Robert and Jeanie Graham McClure Papers, RG 8, Box 120, YDSL.

50 Gunsun Hoh, *Physical Education in China* (Shanghai: Commercial Press, Ltd., 1926), pp. 63–89.

51 Clemens Granskou interview, p. 7, MCOHP, 1976, ELCA; Erwin Hertz interview, pp. 24–25, MCOHP, 1980, ELCA.

52 Chester Fuson to family, Jan. 10, 1908, Chester Fuson Papers, RG 8, Box 71, YDSL; Elsie Reik to family, Dec. 19, 1926, Elsie Reik Papers, UOSC.

53 Julia Bonafield, Foochow Girls' School 70th Anniversary pamphlet, 1929, 79-16: 1459-4-2: 11, GBGM.

54 Chester Fuson to family, April 28, 1906, Chester Fuson Papers, RG 8, Box 71, YDSL.

55 Delia Davin, *Woman-Work: Women and the Party in Revolutionary China* (Oxford: Oxford University Press, 1976), p. 11; Adele Field, "Women in China," n. d., RG 8, Box 183, Abbie Sanderson Papers, YDSL.

56 In her dissertation on the women's movement in China, Charlotte Beahan states that American Baptists did make it a condition of membership in their church, but does not say when the rule was adopted. I suspect that it was not until the twentieth century, when footbinding was already greatly in decline among urban, educated Chinese. She also states that in 1878 the Hangchow Presbyterian Synod officially expressed its opposition to footbinding, but does not reveal what actions, if any, the Synod took to put teeth into its disapproval. Charlotte Beahan, "The Women's Movement and Nationalism in Late Ch'ing China" (Ph.D. diss., Columbia University, 1976), p. 56.

57 "A History of the Peking Station of the North China Mission of the Woman's Foreign Missionary Society of the Methodist Episcopal Church," a handwritten history *cum* journal begun by Mary Porter Gamewell in 1899 and continued in the early twentieth century by an unknown missionary, p. 42, RG 8, Box 73, YDSL.

58 George Barbour to family, Nov. 18, 1911, George and Dorothy Barbour Papers, RG 8, Box 13, Folder "1911," YDSL; Alison R. Drucker, "The Influence of Western Women on the Anti-Footbinding Movement, 1840–1911," pp. 191–196, see 199, in Richard W. Guisso and Stanley Johannesen, eds., *Women in China: Current Directions in Historical Scholarship* (Youngstown, N.Y.: Philo Press, 1981).

59 Beahan, "The Women's Movement," p. 341.

60 Bertha Magness to sister, May 2, 1919, Bertha Magness Papers, RG Ax 846, Box 1, UOSC.

61 Alice Reed to family, Excerpts from Letters, 1916–1948, Oct. 19, 1919, p. 50, Alice Reed Papers, RG 8, Box 163, YDSL.

62 Alice Margaret Huggins, Goodrich Girls' School, Jan. 22, 1927, RG 31, Box 276, Folder 1963, YDSL; Venetia Cox to family, November 24, 1918, Venetia Cox Papers, 263. 1a, ECMC.

63 Lida Ashmore to daughter, Nov. 21, 1915, William and Lida Ashmore Papers, RG Ax 564, Box 1, UOSC.

64 Harriet Stroh to family, May 4, 1924, Harriet Stroh Papers, RG 187, Box 1, Folder 7, PC (USA); James Webster, *Christian Education and the National Consciousness in China* (New York: E. P. Dutton and Co., 1923), p. 217; Jean McPherson Pommerenke to family, May 3, 1925, Pommerenke Family Papers, RG 193, Box 1, Folder 9, PC (USA).

65 Theodore Hsiao, *The History of Modern Education in China* (Peiping: Peking University Press, 1932), p. 37.

66 W. Tchishin Tao and C. P. Chen, *Education in China, 1924* (Shanghai: Commercial Press, Ltd., 1925), p. 1.

67 Tsang Chih-sam, *Nationalism in School Education in China Since the Opening of the Twentieth Century* (Hong Kong; South China Morning Press, Ltd., 1933), p. 77; Hoh, *Physical Education*, pp. 92, 102, 138, 162–220.

68 Tsang, *Nationalism in School Education*, p. 77.

69 Nance, *Soochow University*, p. 43.

70 Mary Margaret Moninger to family, March 8, 1916, Mary Margaret Moninger Papers, RG 230, Box 1, Folder 4, PC (USA).

71 Ava R. Milam, Yenching College Newsletter, Dec. 1923, UBCHEA, RG 11, Box 376, Folder 5719, YDSL.

72 Sara Collins, "Presbyterian Schools in China," 1902, NT6.3 C692p, PC (USA); *Centenary Conference*, p. 582.

73 *Centenary Conference*, p. 162.

74 Barbara Solomon, *In the Company of Educated Women: A History of Women and Higher Education in America* (New Haven: Yale University Press, 1985), chapter three; Willystine Goodsell, *Pioneers of Women's Education in the United States: Emma Willard, Catherine Beecher, Mary Lyon* (New York: McGraw-Hill Book Co., 1931); and Sara

Delamont, "The Contradictions in Ladies' Education," pp. 134–161, in Sara Delamont and Lorna Duffin, eds., *The Nineteenth-Century Woman: Her Cultural and Physical World* (London: Croom Helm, 1978).

75 "Tientsin Hui Wen Middle School and Four Year's Growth, 1919–1923," p. 3, pamphlet, 79-16: 1459-5-1: 13, GBGM.

76 Chungking Methodist Boys' High School, Announcement, 1908–1909, 79-16: 1459-5-2: 02, GBGM.

77 Hangchow Girls' Boarding School, Mission Annual Report, 1898, BWM.

78 Nance, *Soochow University*, p. 37.

79 A few missionaries opposed the idea of running "charity schools" and argued that it would be more useful to the Christian cause to win "the souls of the rich and more intelligent," but this was distinctly a minority view. *Second Triennial of the EAC*, 1896, p. 257; Mrs. F. A. Butler, *A History of the Woman's Foreign Missionary Society of the Methodist Episcopal Church, South* (Nashville: Publishing House of the Methodist Episcopal Church, South, 1904), p. 124.

80 Gamewell School Report, 1899, p. 9, 79-16: 1459-4-3: 50, GBGM.

81 *Centenary Conference*, p. 576; *Woman's Missionary Friend* 40 (October 1908): 377.

82 Clara Hess to parents, May 14, 1897, Foster Family Papers, RG 1, Box 5, Folder 87, YDSL; Alderman School Report, 1922, 79-16: 1459-4-3: 44, GBGM; Lois Young to family, 1922, n. d., Lois Young Miscellany, RG 8, Box 224, YDSL.

83 Sara C. Collins, "Presbyterian Schools in China," 1902, NT6.3 C692p, PC (USA).

84 Lida Ashmore, "My Life Story," p. 53, William and Lida Ashmore Papers, RG Ax 564, Box 1, UOSC.

85 Marjorie Topley, "Marriage Resistance in Rural Kwangtung," pp. 67–88, in Margery Wolf and Roxane Witke, eds., *Women in Chinese Society* (Stanford: Stanford University Press, 1975).

86 The subject of boys' industrial work was discussed in some detail at both the First and Second Triennials of the EAC: *Records of the First Triennial Meeting of the Educational Association of China* (Shanghai: American Presbyterian Mission Press, 1893), pp. 38–40; *Second Triennial of the EAC*, 1896, pp. 87–89, 109.

87 Ford, "History of the Educational Work," p. 112.

88 "The Life of Emily Susan Hartwell," autobiography, Emily Susan Hartwell Papers, RG 8, Box 92, Folder 1, YDSL; *First Triennial of the EAC*, 1893, p. 39.

89 Wynn C. Fairfield, "The Foochow Union High School—Cooperation in Training for Christian Rural Service," pamphlet, 1933, 79-16: 1459-4-2: 33, GBGM; Spring, *The American School*, pp. 149, 208–209. Some missionaries, like Joseph Bailey, established rural cooperatives which taught industrial arts and helped the students to market their goods in China. Both the Communists and the GMD approved of these undertakings. See Victoria W. Bailey, *Bailey's Activities in China: An Account of the Life and Work of Professor Joseph Bailey in and for China, 1890–1935* (Palo Alto, Calif.: Pacific Books, 1964); Helen Snow, *China Builds for Democracy: A Story of Cooperative Industry* (New York: New Age Books, 1941); and James C. Thomson, Jr., *While China Faced West: American Reformers in Nationalist China, 1928–1937* (Cambridge: Harvard University Press, 1969).

90 Latourette, *Christian Missions in China*, pp. 427, 638–640.

91 *North China Women's College Bulletin*, # IV, 1919, UBCHEA, RG 11, Box 298, Folder 4639, YDSL; Dolores Hayden, *The Grand Domestic Revolution: A History of Feminist Designs for American Homes, Neighborhoods and Cities* (Cambridge: Massachusetts Institute of Technology Press, 1981), pp. 151–155.

92 *Second Triennial of the EAC*, 1896, p. 117.

93 Matilda Thurston, Typed Excerpts from Letters, May 18, 1916, Ginling College, Correspondence, UBCHEA, RG 11, Box 143, Folder 2842, YDSL.

94 Hangchow Union Girls' High School, Minutes, Board of Directors' Meeting, June, 1916, RG 31, Box 276, Folder 1963, YDSL. At Soochow University, for example, the

home economics course, although not formally a part of the science program, was affiliated with the College of Science. Nance, *Soochow University*, p. 59. At Ginling College, chemistry was taught "with special adaptation to practical problems in domestic science." *Woman's Missionary Friend* 47 (October 1915): 353.

95 *Second Triennial of the EAC*, 1896, p. 58. The missionary perception that treaty port wages were high was probably skewed by the fact that mission wages for Chinese helpers, even Chinese pastors, were notoriously mean. *Chinese Recorder* 28 (March 1897): 131.

96 Quoted in Nance, *Soochow University*, p. 4.

97 *Second Triennial of the EAC*, 1896, pp. 23–24.

98 Lamberton, *St. John's University*, p. 20; Wiley Institute, pamphlet, 1888, 79-16: 1459-4-3: 54, GBGM.

99 Knowlton, "One Hundred Years," p. 6, Lucerne H. Knowlton Papers, HIA; Collins, "Presbyterian Schools in China," 1902, PC (USA). It is not clear what form of currency was in question. In all likelihood, the author meant $10,000 Mexican currency, which amounted to $5,000 in gold.

100 Anna and Oswald Brown, *Laura Askew Haygood*, p. 176; Ida F. Frantz, "The Keen School I Remember," pamphlet, 1972, 79-16: 1459-5-1: 12, GBGM.

101 Frantz, "The Keen School," 1972, 79-16: 1459-5-1: 12, GBGM.

102 *Woman's Missionary Friend* 36 (September 1904): 320, and 37 (November 1905): 394; *Chinese Recorder* 34 (January 1903): 35.

103 Ford, "History of the Educational Work," p. 71.

104 Latourette, *Christian Missions in China*, p. 212; Elsie Clark to family, Oct, 3, 1915, Elsie Clark [Krug] Papers, RG 8, Box 41, Folder 1912, YDSL.

105 *Third Triennial of the EAC*, 1899, p. 162.

106 Shanghai Conference report, p. 38; Collins, "Presbyterian Schools in China," PC (USA).

107 *Our First Decade in China, 1905–1915*, by "Missionaries in the Field" (Minneapolis: China Mission Board of the Augustana Synod, 1915), p. 82, ELCA.

108 Ruth Gilbertson interview, p. 42, MCOHP, 1978, ELCA; Monona Cheney to family, April 13, 1921, Monona Cheney Papers, RG Ax 275, Box 1, UOSC; Caroline Lee to home church, Dec. 15, 1922, microfilm #107, BWM; Nance, *Soochow University*, p. 5.

109 Robert Paterno, "Devello Z. Sheffield and the Founding of North China College," pp. 42–92 in Liu, *Protestant Missionaries in China*.

110 Monona Cheney to family, Oct. 10, 1922, Monona Cheney Papers, RG 275, Box 1, UOSC; Frank D. Gamewell to Reverend Edward Dixon, Sept. 19, 1925, 73-43: 1043-2-3: 44, GBGM.

111 Helen S. Coan Nevius, *The Life of John Livingstone Nevius, Forty Years a Missionary in China* (New York: Fleming H. Revell, 1895), p. 128; Alice Reed, Excerpts from Letters, 1916–1948, p. 8, Alice Reed Papers, RG 8, Box 163, YDSL.

112 *Third Triennial of the EAC*, 1899, p. 22.

Chapter 3:
"The Rising Tide of Emancipation:" Gender Reform in the Mission Schools

As American Protestant educators moved from the nineteenth into the twentieth century, they were forced to adapt to a China that was undergoing deep political and social change. Changes in Chinese gender ideology and practice were among the most striking of the transformations taking place, which eventually compelled the missionaries to rethink some aspects of their long-standing critique of the Chinese gender system. Missionaries were pleased with some of the new developments, but appalled by many others. Ascribing to themselves enormous power, American missionaries guiltily assumed that they—or the West in general—bore responsibility for some of the less desirable social changes that they witnessed. This led, by the mid- and late-1920s, to a fundamental reorientation among American teaching missionaries of their attitude toward traditional China and the modern West.

Before examining this radical change, however, it is necessary to understand the nature of the critique of Chinese gender beliefs that American missionaries articulated and the ways in which they utilized their schools to effect reform of Chinese gender beliefs and customs. Nineteenth-century American missionaries discovered in China a system of gender relations that bore a superficial resemblance to American gender ideology: it divided the world into public and private spheres, confined women to the latter, and, despite protestations that the two spheres were of equal value, clearly denigrated the sphere occupied by women.[1] The way in which this ideology was practiced in China, however, provided a striking contrast with American practices, which allowed missionaries to make exaggerated claims regarding the egalitarian nature of American gender beliefs. The missionary critique of China thus included not only a repudiation of its non-Christian religions but also a stinging indictment of its gender system.

Chinese society was built upon a hierarchy of paired dominant-subordinate relationships: ruler over ruled, elder over younger, and male over female. Social harmony, indeed the entire social order, was predicated on people knowing and accepting their place in the hierarchy. Within this highly integrated system, any attempt to raise the status of women, as missionaries desired to do, had the potential of unraveling the fabric of Chinese society. To the missionaries, however, the low status of Chinese women within this system amounted to degradation. Writing in 1872, ABCFM missionary Samuel Bartlett wrote a characteristic critique of Chinese women's lot: "From the cradle to the grave her life is one long-drawn woe." He criticized female infanticide, the selling of girls as slaves, their lack of education, and the power their husbands wielded over them. In common with other missionaries, Bartlett was confident that the greater esteem accorded women in the Christian religion would attract Chinese women into the church.[2]

Besides criticizing the position allotted to Chinese women in their society, missionaries specifically abhorred certain Chinese customs. Female infanticide, footbinding, plural marriage and concubinage were the key practices that distinguished Chinese from Americans and convinced the missionaries that the Chinese were not fully civilized. Similarly, missionaries opposed the concept of arranged marriages, particularly when a Christian was engaged to a non-Christian against his or her will. They also opposed childhood betrothals, which they stigmatized as "abominable."[3]

Missionaries were also highly critical of Chinese homes. In some instances, missionary judgments were based on physical attributes: non-Christian homes, according to missionaries, were filthy, unsanitary, dark, and crowded. ABCFM missionary Elizabeth Perkins found Chinese homes so unspeakable that she could "hardly wonder" that Chinese women sometimes committed suicide. One of the visible manifestations of conversion to Christianity was that a Christian Chinese home met missionary standards of cleanliness.[4]

But in missionary eyes, "home" was more than simply a physical dwelling; it was men's sanctuary from the public world and the locus of women's power, influence, and happiness. Since American gender ideology focused on the cooperation between husband and wife and the mutual dependence of their roles, the home, missionaries agreed, was the place where the fundamental complementarity of male and female gender roles could be seen.[5] They argued that Christian gender roles were based on harmony, not polarity, and on cooperation, not dominance and submission. Thus although Americans and Chinese both located women in the domestic realm, American missionaries denied that Chinese domesticity was the real thing. Ruth Chester, a teacher of physics and chemistry at Ginling Women's College, hoped that a married couple would be appointed to the Ginling faculty in 1924 because many of the students "come from non-Christian homes...with no opportunity to see real home life.... It must be very difficult," Chester wrote sympathetically, "for a girl who has never seen a Christian home and the kind of fellowship and cooperation that such a home should have, to know how in later years to apply her own Christian ideals to her home life."[6]

The ideal of Christian home life was not solely a woman's issue, according to missionaries, nor was it significant only as the place where Christian gender relations were worked out. Although the home was acknowledged to be separate from the larger society, missionaries knew that it was indisputably linked to public social life. "The home," they argued, "is the foundation of the state." As in the United States, missionaries claimed that public virtue was impossible if the home was corrupt. According to Alice Brethorst, a Congregationalist missionary, educated Christian Chinese women would not only create model homes but they would also "[bring] the men up to a much higher moral standard than they have ever known." This would result in the establishment of "a new social order in this hoary old land."[7]

Building on their perception that their own gender relations were egalitarian and their sex roles complementary, American missionaries also argued that the dynamics of sexual power within the home were skewed in China. The degree to which missionaries actually witnessed what went on within Chinese homes is not clear. Missionary educators of both sexes occasionally visited the homes of their students, but this did not mean that they observed Chinese home and family life in any systematic way. Instead, missionaries seem to have used the existence of certain customs — notably footbinding, arranged marriages, and concubinage — to infer the workings of Chinese homes and the power relations therein.[8]

Missionaries argued, first of all, that rather than being a sphere pervaded by women's moral influence, Chinese homes were "centers of degradation." They failed to provide children with anything missionaries were prepared to recognize as moral training, which was one reason for promoting Christian boarding schools: missionaries claimed that it was necessary to remove children from their own homes and immerse them in the moral environment of the mission school. Moreover, rather than being at the heart of a wholesome religious life, missionaries viewed the Chinese home as "the citadel of heathendom."[9]

All of these judgments are disputable. What power Chinese women wielded was exercised within their homes, although as in the United States, this power was limited to a narrow range of domestic affairs. Children did receive both moral and religious training in Chinese homes. Confucian ceremonies honoring the ancestors were in fact carried out within the home rather than in a temple. From an early age children were taught the significance of these rites, and *li* (right behavior) was a primary focus of parental teachings. Moreover, the idea that the home was the foundation of society was not alien to Chinese philosophy. As Mencius, a contemporary of Confucius, expressed it, the man who would rule the country must first regulate his own home.[10]

Missionaries seemed unaware of this congruence between American and Chinese beliefs about the centrality of the home in much the same way that they apparently saw no similarities in the patriarchal ideology of the two countries. The Confucian basis of Chinese patriarchy was partly responsible for missionaries' blind spot, since in the nineteenth century, few American missionaries accepted Confucius as a legitimate source of moral authority.

American missionaries also objected to some of the marital and sexual practices that took place within the home. For reasons never entirely clear, they disapproved of the custom of several generations living together. "I thoroughly believe," wrote Methodist missionary Elsie Reik in 1925, "that we can never have anything approximating decent home life until each family has its own establishment." In alluding to "decency," Reik may be referring to the fact that in poor homes entire families shared sleeping space.[11] In general, however, missionary assertions that Chinese homes were "centers of degradation" had to do with their belief that the home was the site of such appalling practices as female infanticide, foot-binding, child marriages, wife-beating, and especially concubinage.[12]

Although both Chinese and American gender ideology relegated women to the constricted world of home and family, by the late nineteenth century, American women had substantially enlarged the range of activities deemed appropriate for their sex. They justified this by employing a loose interpretation of what constituted the private sphere, and by arguing that their inherent traits of nurturance, morality and compassion made them uniquely fit to serve in this expanded sphere. Writing about women's work in 1919, Margaret Burton noted that the traditional feminine sphere "has burst all bounds within the past years and can never again be forced within the old limits....We must recognize," she added in a revelatory comment, "that no task which contributes to human welfare can be justly designated as 'unwomanly.'"[13]

Contemplating their own relative freedom of movement, American missionary women agreed that Chinese women were too strictly confined to their homes. Chinese women needed to be freed to attend church services, to pursue education—even college education—to take up careers as teachers, nurses and doctors, and to be active in philanthropy and reform efforts. Missionaries similarly found the sexual segregation of Confucian China to be an obstacle to the new relations between the sexes they were trying to encourage and so worked to undermine it.

As missionaries recounted with shock and horror the treatment of women in China, their appreciation of their own gender practices increased. Missionaries interpreted and judged Chinese gender practices on moral and religious grounds, not in terms of sexual power. They failed to see, therefore, any latent similarities between male domination in the United States and China. Instead, missionaries emphasized the differences in the way male power over women was exercised in China and the United States and were self-congratulatory about their own gender system. Even when some missionaries admitted that the position of women in the United States fell short of equality, they insisted that the flaw lay in human imperfection, not in the Christian ideology that ostensibly formed the basis of the American gender system. As mission board executive Helen Barrett Montgomery put it, the "wrongs against women" in the West ran counter to the precepts of Christianity, unlike in China, where women's inferior status was "buttressed behind the sanctions of Chinese religion."[14] Christian gender ideology was what missionaries believed was needed in China, with mission schools as the key vehicles for their reform agenda.

Gender Reform in the Mission Schools

Mission schools attacked Chinese gender practices in five areas: foot-binding, infanticide, marriage customs, low social esteem of women, and rigid sexual segregation. We have noted in the previous chapter how the schools made unbound feet a condition of enrollment and thus contributed to the elimination of that custom. The fight against infanticide was less strictly a matter for educational missionaries than it was for the Christian church as a whole. Nevertheless, infant girls who had been saved from death were automatically enrolled in mission schools when they were old enough to attend. Some of these girls were cared for by mission orphanages, while others were adopted by missionary teachers.[15]

Marriage practices also concerned the missionaries. Nineteenth-century missionaries, as we have seen, sometimes used indentures to keep the girls in school, prevent betrothal or marriage at too young an age, and avoid engagement to non-Christian men. As education for girls became more popular, the practice of indentures declined. Missionaries still utilized pecuniary incentives to induce parental compliance with school rules concerning marriage and betrothal, but now, instead of offering to pay for a girl's education if she was not betrothed, the missionaries threatened to increase her fees if she was.

It is not clear how widespread this practice was, nor how effective. In the Methodist McTyeire School, a school for wealthy girls in Shanghai, missionaries charged double fees for married students from the time the school opened. Of the ninety-nine students in the school in 1903, only six were married. Although this might imply that the policy was effective, it could also signify that few Chinese bothered to educate their married daughters-in-law.[16]

Missionaries in schools without wealthy patrons had to move more slowly in reforming marriage customs. It was not until 1921 that Methodist Myrtle Smith and her colleagues in Gutian concluded that their school was so firmly established that they could begin making rules about marriage and betrothal. In that year, Smith informed the parents that all betrothed girls, including those who, as "little daughters-in-laws," lived with their in-laws, would be required to pay their full board. "There were several who wanted to enter but could not pay the full amount," Smith reported, "but I would not make any exceptions. A few will be martyrs to the cause but it is the best method we can use to eradicate early betrothals."[17]

Some American teaching missionaries were more sympathetic than Smith to the hardships their marital policies might cause for Chinese girls.

Others feared that encouraging their students to delay betrothal and marriage might be interpreted as a critique of marriage itself. Since nearly half of American missionary women were single by 1900, missionaries might well worry about the message they were conveying to their students. Gertrude Howe, a Methodist, suggested that missionaries "keep on the side of conservatism and...hold before the Chinese the ideal woman, the wife and mother."[18]

Although missionaries disapproved of early betrothals and marriages, their condemnation of Christian girls being engaged or wed against their wills to non-Christian boys was more pronounced. At the 1890 Shanghai Missionary Conference, one missionary urged that Christian schools work to discourage Christian girls from marrying non-Christian husbands. Eight years later, Baptist missionary Lida Ashmore wrote to her daughter that girls in her school who were betrothed to non-Christians had to pay for their education, for it was against mission rules to support them.[19]

Not only did Christian schools charge higher fees for girls engaged to non-Christians, but missionaries also intervened in betrothals between their students and non-Christians. ABCFM missionary Miss Woodhull reported that when one of their nine-year-old students was betrothed in 1895, the missionaries interfered and "the affair was stopped."[20] Similarly, Monona Cheney wrote to her family that the Methodist missionaries had paid $300 to a Chinese man to induce him to release one of the schoolgirls from her engagement to him. "Didn't know we were in the girl-buying business, did you?" Cheney asked flippantly.[21]

Parents of children in the mission schools sometimes asked the missionaries to help break an engagement. In Chinese society, ending a betrothal was a very serious step, as serious as divorce in the United States. Seeing that missionaries apparently had few qualms about such action and perhaps also believing that missionaries had more influence with the local authorities, some parents took advantage of missionary sympathy to accomplish what their own society did not condone. More often, the young people themselves asked for missionary intercession.[22]

Missionaries rarely questioned their marital meddling. One might plausibly argue that missionaries were within their rights to set the rules for enrollment in their schools and to attempt to control student marriages. It was quite another matter, however, for missionaries to hide daughters from their families, threaten their parents, or bribe proposed husbands to withdraw their suits. With these actions, missionaries established themselves as an authority to whom students could appeal over the heads of their parents in a kind of domestic extraterritoriality. By breaking down traditional filiality in families with links to the Christian schools, the missionaries may have fostered a social change they were later to regret.

Although few missionaries hesitated to break student betrothals, they were much more wary about coming between husband and wife, even in a polygamous marriage. Presbyterian missionary Mary Margaret Moninger refused to take an unhappy second wife into her school without the husband's consent. "This is not a home for runaway wives," Moninger stated.[23] Reluctance to take action on behalf of married Chinese women stemmed less from missionaries' scruples about meddling than it did from cultural differences. Marriage and betrothal were equally binding to the Chinese. Missionaries, on the other hand, believed that betrothals could be broken at will but that marriages were indissoluble. Only in extreme and rare cases, such as when a non-Christian man abandoned his Christian wife, were missionaries willing to sanction divorce.[24] President Matilda Thurston of Ginling Women's College, for example, was at a loss to know what to do about a Ginling student who had run away from an arranged marriage and enrolled in the college. Thurston did not want to surrender the girl to her husband's family, but she felt stymied by the marriage tie. Seeking a loophole, she wondered if the girl was really married "in any Christian sense of the word."[25]

In addition to breaking up engagements, which missionaries did more often on behalf of Chinese girls than boys, missionaries also arranged marriages for their students of both sexes. As early as 1852, the Presbyterian Ningpo Boys' School had a rule that indentured boys could only marry Christian girls. Around the same time, Helen Nevius, Maria Brown Davis, and Mary Porter Gamewell each helped their natural-footed girl students to marry boys in neighboring Christian schools to encourage other girls to unbind their feet.[26]

In the twentieth century, missionaries had less need to help find husbands for girls with large feet, since among educated Chinese families the custom was increasingly repugnant, and girls with unbound feet were less of an oddity. In the new century, one change indicative of the erosion of parental authority was the increasingly commonplace practice of young men seeking their own brides rather than following tradition and waiting for their parents to arrange a match. For mission school boys and men, the natural hunting ground was the mission girls' school.[27]

Strangely enough, although missionaries rarely hesitated to break up an engagement between a Christian and non-Christian, they were more diffident about acting as go-betweens for their students. When a young man asked Matilda Thurston to help him choose a wife among Ginling College students in 1918, Thurston commented, "I do not care to go into the match-making business altho [sic] I have much sympathy for a nice young man who wants an educated Christian wife, instead of the stupid heathen girl his relatives would pick out for him." Mildred Test Young likewise "hesitated to be a matchmaker." When students asked for her help, she recalled, "I would usually give them a list of several girls whom I thought would be suitable."[28]

The twentieth-century trend toward men choosing their own brides, although it was an important departure from traditional Chinese ways, brought nothing like Western-style courtship. American missionaries, accustomed to long courtships, were startled by the rapidity of Chinese wooing. They were also disappointed when they tried to interest Chinese couples in getting to know each other before consenting to become engaged. "When a young man goes wife-hunting on Thursday, and is engaged to her the following Monday," Episcopalian missionary Venetia Cox wrote her family in 1920, "I call that going rapidly." Since the girl was a student in Cox's school, she brought the couple together and encouraged them, contrary to Chinese custom, to see and speak to each other. Both young people were discomfited by this innovation. "They evidently did not choose to speak," Cox lamented, "and I doubt that they really saw each other, they hung their heads so low."[29]

Elevating the esteem in which Chinese women were held by their society was another missionary goal. In preaching against female infanticide, foot-binding, and polygamy, missionaries stressed the worth of every individual, male and female, in the eyes of God. At a 1906 Women's Christian Conference, after an emotional session led by women missionaries and Chinese Christian preachers, a group of Chinese women unanimously resolved to "show no more partiality" in their treatment of their sons and daughters.[30] But here, too, mission schools were crucial to missionary efforts to improve the position of Chinese girls and women. In the early years of Christian education in China, some Chinese ridiculed attempts to teach girls, and the girls themselves were hampered by their low self-esteem.[31] Because education was highly respected in China, however, once girls began to prove their intellectual capabilities, mockery from outsiders diminished, and the girls increasingly took pride in their accomplishments.[32]

Missionaries rarely discussed among themselves how they might deal with the problem of low self-esteem among their girl students, although they often mentioned it as one of the features of Chinese life that they wished to alter. Yet it is clear that education emboldened Chinese girls to think of themselves in new ways. Evidence of this may be seen in some of the topics girls addressed in graduation speeches at the Methodist Girls' High School in Beijing in 1905: "The Relationship Between China and the Anti-Footbinding Society," "Do Not Look Down on Women," and "The Miserable Condition of Chinese Women."[33]

Christian college magazines written by students often included essays indicating that the position of women was a question of some importance to them. By the 1920s, the "emancipation" of Chinese women was a burning issue among students and young radicals, many of whom attacked the Chinese family system as intemperately as the early missionaries. However, by this time missionaries were considerably more conservative than many students in their approach to gender issues. Some students in mission schools adopted the conservative missionary viewpoint, which put them at odds with their radical peers in government schools. For example, Wu Ming-ying, a student at Ginling Women's College, attributed recent changes in women's status in China to the coming of Christianity. "Jesus came to emancipate women," she wrote in 1924, "and this saved China....[M]en began to realize more and more that women are the equals of men."[34]

Women missionaries often took advantage of opportunities to teach their own vision of gender to their students. Elsie Clark led a discussion of women's suffrage in her second-year English class at Ginling in 1916. A suffragist herself, Clark was elated with the girls' response:

> [I]t was amazing to hear these young young [*sic*] things, quite out of their own heads, saying that women should help their country as much as men did, that their wisdom, though different from men's, would also be valuable, that they

should take an interest in things outside their home, that they should have greater opportunity to develop all their different sorts of power, that they should lead a larger life, and most of all, again and again, that they should help their country.[35]

It is hardly astonishing that Clark was pleased, for in their discussion, the Ginling students reiterated a number of missionary beliefs about gender roles: the distinctness but equality of the sexes, a role for women that was not strictly limited to the domestic sphere, and an emphasis on service and reform.

In addition to encouraging students to think, write, and speak about the position of Chinese women, missionaries also set before their students examples of great women from the Western world. At the Hangchow Union Girls' School, for instance, two male Chinese teachers spent Friday afternoons translating the lives of "famous women in America." In a similar vein, at the fiftieth anniversary celebration of the Methodist Mary Porter Gamewell School in 1922, guest speaker Sherwood Eddy praised women who had pioneered in various areas, including Susan B. Anthony, Frances Willard, Elizabeth Fry, and Florence Nightingale. The Gamewell School, Eddy concluded, "was preparing such women today and...the nation looked to this and sister schools to raise up the pioneers in social uplift for China."[36]

Just as missionaries tried to impart their vision of Christian womanhood to girls in their schools, so those who taught in boys' schools sought to teach Chinese boys what it meant to be a Christian man. In addition to trying to build up their students physically and develop the manly virtues of competitiveness and sportsmanship, American missionaries wanted male students to learn the gentler ways of Christian manhood. Boys in the Gotch Memorial College, for instance, were reminded that Christian teachers and preachers "must not strive, but be gentle unto all men, apt to teach, patient, in meekness instructing those that oppose themselves."[37]

Boys in mission schools were also expected to display a "Christian attitude" toward women and girls. In the nineteenth century, missionaries exhorted Chinese boys and men that the primary responsibility for ending the practice of foot-binding rested with them, for the custom would continue as long as they continued to marry women with bound feet. Missionaries likewise taught the boys that plural marriage degraded women, expecting them to abstain from this practice themselves and condemn it in others.[38] Missionaries further believed that witnessing the interaction between foreign men and women would set a good example for their schoolboys. As one missionary noted in 1893, "No Chinese boy can see the daily behavior of his teacher toward foreign or Chinese ladies without receiving an object lesson." Baptist missionary Adam Groesbeck wrote in 1927 that first encounters with a missionary's wife startled non-Christian students because of the courtesies she received from men.[39]

Not only did missionaries give students a living demonstration of Western chivalry, but they also insisted that their boys follow the same code. Some schools even had formal rules telling boys how to conduct themselves in the presence of women. Nanking University authorities listed these: "Ladies should always be treated with the utmost respect and given preference on every occasion. When you meet a lady whom you know, raise your hat (or, if wearing a Chinese hat, simply bow). In a crowded room, offer your seat. When a lady enters the room stand up. Be of service in every way possible."[40]

By the 1920s, when these rules appeared in Nanking University's Student Handbook, presumably most urban Chinese had at least a passing familiarity with Western ways, either from movies or witnessing the behavior of foreigners in China. In the nineteenth century, however, relations between male and female missionaries had often shocked the Chinese deeply. The spectacle of men and women walking publicly arm in arm or of a man shaking a woman's hand in greeting violated the Chinese sense of propriety, for open displays of affection, even between husband and wife, were regarded as being in extremely poor taste. For a man to touch a woman who was not his wife was a serious breach of morality.[41]

American displays of deference toward women did not necessarily imply equality. Since Chinese tradition required women to defer to men, however, missionaries' public courtesies to women challenged this tradition.[42] Missionaries also made pointed efforts to demonstrate to the Chinese that girls were as worthy of attention as boys. One missionary woman wrote to her family that she had deliberately and ostentatiously lavished praise on the girls in a village she visited while all but ignoring the boys.[43] The Methodist mission decided in 1915 that from that time on, all students in the Theology Department of Peking University must permit their wives to attend school. Any man who prevented his wife from receiving an education was not to be allowed to continue his own studies.[44] Women missionaries who taught in boys' schools found themselves in a strategic position to influence the boys' ideas about women. Methodist Clara Collier, for example, wrote that she sought to teach her boys that "Christianity is not for them alone, but that womankind is worth saving."[45]

Although missionaries objected to the strict sexual segregation in traditional Chinese society, when they first opened schools in China, they accommodated the different mores of the Chinese. It is curious that in this one realm the missionaries should display sensitivity to Chinese beliefs while attempting to alter so much of the rest of the Chinese gender system. Perhaps American missionaries felt no particular urgency about this reform and were content to promote it gradually. Coeducation, after all, was slow to develop in their own country, particularly in high school and college. It might equally be the case that missionaries were willing to compromise with Chinese beliefs in order to attract students into their schools, as they had done with the teaching of the Chinese classics. Whatever the reason, before the turn of the century, all mission schools were single-sex, with rare exceptions on the primary school level. Furthermore, as we have seen, girls had to be chaperoned when taught by a man, and all girls' schools were encircled by walls to shield the girls from the improper gaze of passersby. When girls from one mission school took part in famine relief efforts, they were not permitted to go into the courtyard of the relief center when there were men present.[46]

After 1900, however, American missionaries began attempting to break down some of this segregation. Missionaries did not record instances of Chinese opposition to mixing among younger students. For instance, in 1911, when boys and girls from two local mission elementary schools gave a joint public concert, "[n]ot a word of disapproval greet[ed] this innovation," according to missionary Mary Swail Taft. Mission colleges had to be more conservative. At the public opening of Ginling Women's College in 1916, male and female guests sat on opposite sides of the chapel during the program. Segregation was still the rule at the first graduation exercises three years later. By the 1920s, however, most missionaries agreed that Christian schools offered "a safe place in which to experiment cautiously."[47]

Experimentation with sexual integration in mission schools took several forms. Joint concerts and programs involving boys' and girls' schools were common; so too were joint commencement exercises. There was also interaction between schools. One boys' school, delighted at having been invited to attend a program at a girls' school, immediately returned the favor, hosting the girls at a play at their school the following evening.[48] The first attempts in the mission schools to teach Chinese students how to socialize in the Western style were not always successful, as the students often regarded one another with embarrassed indifference.[49]

The purpose of breaking down the walls of rigid propriety that divided men and women in traditional China was, the missionaries claimed, to facilitate the adoption of Christian gender relations. In order to shift from Confucian hierarchical gender relations to Christian complementarity, Chinese men and women had to get to know one another in a new social context. "We are trying to build up a new society in which people of both sexes are expected to co-operate and to work together on a basis of equality," asserted an official at Fukien Christian College in 1930.[50] However, coeducation, a logical extension of this philosophy, proved problematic for some women missionaries, revealing the limits of Christian gender ideology in terms of the equality of the sexes.

Coeducation and Woman's Work

There had been little coeducation in mission schools before 1919. In areas where there was no Christian elementary school for girls, they were sometimes allowed to study for a few years in the local mission boys' school. The opposite was also true. On at least one occasion, a Chinese girl disguised herself as a boy and attended a mission boys' school for some time before her masquerade was discovered. The missionaries then sent her away to a Christian girls' school, paying the travel costs the girl's family could not afford.[51]

When the Chinese government in 1912 began permitting coeducation in its lower schools, missionary educators began to debate coeducation as a formal policy. Few missionaries objected to coeducation in elementary schools, although it is not clear how many schools actually became coeducational. Most American missionaries agreed with Chinese officials that coeducation was not a good idea for middle schools.[52]

The controversy over coeducation in Christian colleges was the most heated. Many missionaries believed that coeducation on the college level was desirable. The Commission for Christian Education, for instance, argued in 1922 that students "should be given ample opportunity for natural social relationships together." This could help ease the maladroitness of Chinese students at mixed social functions.[53] It would further the cause of gender reform, because as one man put it, "There is no place where boys can be so efficiently taught the intellectual equality of women as in the classroom."[54] Some missionaries further argued that coeducation would develop strength in girls and courtesy in boys. Others thought that coeducation would enhance moral behavior and militate against early marriages by promoting "wholesome disillusion with regard to the relation of the sexes." It would also permit pooling of the resources of male and female mission boards and make Christian education more efficient. Finally, Chinese patrons of the schools often wanted coeducation. The adoption of coeducation by the government schools posed a challenge to the single-sex mission schools, which some Chinese now criticized for being "out of touch with the currents of modern life, and producers of an unsocial type of graduate."[55]

The first Christian college to admit women was Canton Christian College (later Lingnan University), which opened its preparatory department to a handful of girls in 1906. The regular college department did not become coeducational until 1919, the same year that coeducation began in the government university in Beijing. Other Christian colleges followed more slowly: Shantung Christian Medical College in 1921; West China Union University in 1924; Shantung Christian College (also known as Cheeloo University) and Huachung College in 1926; Soochow University in 1928; and Hangchow University in 1929.[56]

There seems to have been little friction between men and women missionaries in men's colleges that opened their doors to women. Women who worked in these newly coeducational institutions were supportive of the policy. "After two years of co-educational work," Alice Brethorst of the West China Union University wrote in 1926, "we think that we made a step in the right direction."[57] At the three existing independent women's Christian colleges, however, attempts to initiate coeducation led to conflict between male and female missionaries.

The general boards in the United States and male missionaries in the field wanted to merge the women's colleges with near-by men's colleges: the North China Union Women's College with Yenching University; Hwa Nan College for Women with Fukien Christian College; and Ginling Women's College with Nanking University. Interest in merging women's colleges with men's began in 1914 when the North China Union University (the men's college later took the name "Yenching") voted to combine all of the North China Union institutions into one federated university. They agreed, however, that the women's college and the medical college would not be compelled to move their campuses "for the purpose of centralization unless they so desire."[58]

But by 1920, the women's college president, Luella Miner, was "alarmed" when she thought about the extent to which coeducation had been "forced" on the women's college. The Women's College was physically moved onto Yenching's campus in 1920, although it retained its administrative autonomy. The men soon began pressing the women for a complete merger of the two institutions. The women were able to resist this demand, and the Women's College was still a separate administrative unit in 1930. The long skirmishing had, however, exacted a price; Luella Miner was ousted as dean of women after the Women's College was moved, and her successor, Alice Frame, had a nervous breakdown as a result of continual conflict with Yenching's president, John Leighton Stuart, who failed to comply with the conditions the women had laid down for the partial merger.[59]

Efforts at merger were less successful at the other two women's colleges. In the late 1920s, Fukien Christian College urged Hwa Nan College for Women to move its campus closer to the men's college to facilitate the sharing of classes and joint use of libraries and laboratories. Correspondence between the two colleges makes it clear that the missionaries at Hwa Nan feared that moving their campus was the first step toward the ultimate surrender and the absorption of the women's college.[60] Although Hwa Nan women couched their resistance in the politest terms, among themselves they were more candid. Lucy Wang, the first Chinese president of Hwa Nan, wrote bluntly in 1929, "We who are working on the field know very well that they want to swallow us." Hwa Nan was not swallowed, but only because the women missionaries were able to stand fast against "subtle and strenuous pressure...over a long period of years."[61]

The relationship between Ginling Women's College and its neighbor, Nanking University, was similar. Ginling's president, Matilda Thurston, wrote that no one opposed genuine cooperation between the two colleges but that it had to be "on the basis of recognized equality." Because of the constant stream of pressure, threats, and criticism from Nanking University, Thurston understandably concluded that "there is a most unbrotherly spirit in the [Nanking] group." Like Hwa Nan, Ginling did not merge with the men's college.[62]

Four matters surfaced in the proposed merging of men's and women's colleges. One was money. The men naturally favored a common treasury as part of the integrative plan, arguing that it would be more efficient to have a single budget. Women missionaries, however, suspected that the men simply wanted to get their hands into the women's till. "They want our money into their general pool because their overhead is so high," explained Methodist Elsie Reik. "We who keep our overhead low as only thrifty women can have no wish to pay overhead for them, of course."[63]

A second issue was the women's belief that men and women had different educational needs and that coeducational institutions would not be able to accommodate women's special needs. When a renewed attack was made on the autonomy of the women's colleges in 1930 in the guise of a "Correlated Program" to enhance the efficiency of the Christian colleges, women at Ginling highlighted the differences between the needs of students at Ginling and Nanking University. "In chemistry, for instance," they declared, "Nanking University would be inclined to stress industrial chemistry and agricultural chemistry, while Ginling would be more apt to find the interest in the direction of household chemistry and physiological chemistry."[64] Ironically, these women used the gender distinctions inherent in "domesticizing" the sciences to defend their educational autonomy, while men, who had not always supported women's desire to teach the hard sciences to girls, now criticized the lack of laboratories and advanced science courses in the women's colleges.[65]

The key issue in the conflict over merging the colleges concerned power and the preservation of "woman's work." Women wanted to ensure that they would be granted adequate representation in the administration of any merged college. Among the conditions laid down by women of the North China Union Women's College for merging with Yenching was that the Women's College have control over its faculty appointments and its own money.[66]

Here is an example of what Estelle Freedman calls "separatism as strategy." Freedman argues that the establishment of "female institutions" paralleling those organized and run by men gave women a chance to play the executive roles from which they were barred, by virtue of their sex, in male organizations.[67] This was the case in China. In the protected areas known as "woman's work," American women were permitted to establish and administer their own schools and colleges, whereas there is no evidence that boys' middle schools or colleges ever had female principals or presidents. Women who taught in coeducational Christian schools tended to cluster in "feminine" subjects such as English, music, and art. It is instructive to note that none of the coeducational Christian colleges had women presidents or even vice-presidents; the highest administrative position open to women in these institutions was dean of women.[68] Thus, the commitment to "female equality" that ostensibly underlay the drive for coeducation in mission schools threatened to deprive women of executive roles and force them back into a much more limited range of activities.

Women missionaries not only worried about their own representation in coeducational colleges but also feared that their female students would suffer the same disadvantages because they were greatly outnumbered by men students. This was a fourth obstacle to merging the colleges. Many women missionaries agreed with Matilda Thurston that women's colleges provided a unique opportunity for Chinese women to consider their existing status and future plans "unhampered by the domination of masculine authority and point of view."[69] Chinese male students, like their missionary mentors, wanted coeducation on the college level. But Thurston believed that beneath male students' call for cooperation there was "a desire to have women fall in line with *their* program, attend *their* movies, take part in *their* social entertainment and entertain *their* dull lives." According to women missionaries, Chinese Christian college women were more conservative than men, both socially and politically, and were not greatly interested in coeducation. There was, in fact, a good deal of friction between male and female college students in the Christian schools over political and social issues.[70]

The conflict over coeducation is one of the rare instances of documented gender conflict among missionaries in the field. American missionaries usually concealed disputes among themselves in order to present a united front to American supporters at home and the Chinese. The fact that they were willing to reveal their differences over coeducation to their home boards shows how deep those differences were.[71] The controversy over coeducation also illuminated the profoundly ambiguous social space that "woman's work" occupied. Because women missionaries undertook the same tasks as men, their work could be categorized as part of the public sphere. Because women missionaries worked only with women and children, however, they claimed that their work belonged to the private sphere. When male missionaries promoted coeducation, they were implicitly proposing to raid women's private sphere and force women more fully into the public sphere where, women missionaries feared, both Chinese and missionary women would be subject to the rules of subordination that dictated women's position outside of their own privileged sphere.

Thus the paradox of Christian gender ideology was that only by separating their work from that of men could women missionaries maintain the illusion of equality between the sexes. The coeducation battle exposed the equivocal nature of women's status and demonstrated to missionary women what other American women were discovering at home: entry into the public world might result in women's being forced into positions that were not as satisfactory as those that women had held in a separate women's sphere.[72] In other words, the mere passage of women into the male world might not yield true equality; in fact, it might be the case that women were better off maintaining their distance from men's work. Rather than give up the status they had held in their own sphere and join the male world on a less-than-equal basis, most missionary women preferred to remain in the half-way house of "woman's work" that straddled the gap between public and private and allowed women to believe that their work was "separate but equal." These women continued to defend women's work in the traditional language of separate spheres. However, changes in twentieth-century China, as well as in the United States, constantly challenged missionaries' beliefs about gender.[73]

An Awakened China

Following the Boxer Uprising at the turn of the century, American missionaries often stated that China was "awakening" for it was quite evident to them that urban China, in particular, was in the midst of fundamental social change. Urban women and youth were most strikingly touched by the changes that were taking place. Marital customs were undergoing a slow metamorphosis. Chinese women acquired greater standing in society as increasing numbers of them were educated and moved into a widening public sphere. Chinese young men, displaying a new attitude toward women and their abilities, welcomed women into student and protest activities. Because a number of these changes had been goals of missionary gender reform, the missionaries liked to credit themselves for having had a beneficial effect on Chinese society.[74]

But the pleasure missionaries felt as they observed these social changes, particularly those involving gender, was mixed with anxiety, guilt, and hostility: anxiety because many of the new developments shocked the missionaries; guilt because they assumed that they and their culture were the source of many of these changes; and hostility because the new climate of China did not seem hospitable to missionaries or their Christian beliefs. Two changes in missionary thinking followed. First, missionaries softened their earlier critique of traditional China and argued instead that some of the older ways should not be abandoned. Second, as the Chinese increasingly adopted certain external manifestations of Western culture, the missionaries, contrary to their prior practice, began to exhort the Chinese to distinguish between Christian and secular Western features and to keep the former but resist the encroachment of the latter. In the missionary-Chinese *pas de deux*, the roles were now reversed: it was American missionaries who played the part of cultural conservatives while young radical Chinese urged their compatriots toward deeper change.

It took time, however, for American missionaries to perceive and then articulate the dangers of rapid social change in China. They were dazzled at first by what seemed to them to be the tremendous new opportunities of the twentieth century. For example, although the missionaries had not specifically called for the overthrow of the Qing dynasty, the proclamation of the Republic in 1911 delighted them. With the old dynasty gone and a new spirit of change in the air, missionaries concluded hopefully that the time was ripe for Christianity; China would have to become Christian in order to become powerful.[75] Missionaries were encouraged when the new government proclaimed the principle of religious liberty. They were astonished and pleased when the government asked all Christians to pray for China on April 13, 1913. There was an upsurge of interest in Christianity and Western culture, notably among younger urban Chinese and the number of Chinese Protestant communicants soared to 366,524 by 1920, nearly four times the number at the turn of the century.[76] Educational missionaries were particularly exultant because, with the coming of the Republic, many Chinese believed that modern (as opposed to Confucian) education was more important than ever before. In chapter five, we will look more closely at changes in China's educational system and the impact this had on teaching missionaries.

There were also a number of specific changes relating to Chinese women, their roles in society, and their interactions with men that gratified American missionaries. Education had grown more popular for urban Chinese girls and women, and teaching missionaries observed that this helped to raise the status of women within their homes, both because of their potential earning power and their attractiveness as wives. One Chinese woman who had no sons, for example, took in sewing in order to finance the education of her granddaughter. The woman planned for her granddaughter to train as a teacher, doctor, or Bible woman so that she could support her grandmother in old age. The fact that the girl was a potential source of income made it possible for her to take the place of a son in the Chinese scheme of filiality. Similarly, the mother-in-law of one of Mary Margaret Moninger's pupils had sent the girl to school to be trained as a teacher, since she was not strong enough to work in the fields. Without education the girl would have been a burden on her marital family but as a teacher she could contribute to its well-being.[77]

Education, in fact, replaced footbinding as a desirable feature for a marriageable girl. Mildred Test Young recalled that mission school graduates "proudly displayed their school diplomas along with their trousseaus," making this concept of "education-as-dowry" explicit.[78] Not only were Chinese women proud of their schooling, but young educated men began to demand it of women who were to become their wives. Speaking of one young man who had become engaged to a student at Ginling Women's College in 1922, Matilda Thurston wrote, "The lad is in no haste to be married....He wants to graduate from the University and he wants her to go on in college. The world moves, you see." American college degrees were more highly prized on the marriage market than domestic ones, but the demand for educated wives affected both the missionary and government educational systems in China.[79]

The preference of educated men for educated brides reflects two aspects of cultural change in China in the early twentieth century. First, the Chinese elite was now being drawn from the ranks of those who had received a modern education in either government or mission schools. Students were well aware that many older Chinese regarded them as China's only hope, and therefore the students took seriously their role as the modernizers of their country.[80] The second cultural change was a new conception of marriage. This new view, to be sure, did not reach Western extremes of individualism since the young couple still usually obtained the consent of their families before entering into an engagement. Now, however, the initiative often rested with sons, not their parents, and there was an increasing sense that rather than the wife's marrying into the husband's lineage, the young couple married each other. Margaret Burton noted in 1911 that men wanted their wives to be "congenial companions"— a shift away from viewing marriage as primarily for procreation and the continuity of the male lineage.[81]

Due to the impact of these new ideas, it became increasingly common for an educated boy to refuse to wed an uneducated girl unless some provision was made for her education. Irene McCain, a Presbyterian missionary, wrote to her home church in 1920 that a number of local boys brought their wives-to-be to her George C. Smith Girls' School in Suzhou for schooling. Sometimes the girls' parents were willing to pay the school fees; in other instances the young men themselves or their families accepted the responsibility. On at least one occasion the roles were reversed, when an educated young woman paid for the education of the "ignorant country boy" to whom her family had betrothed her in infancy.[82] This development reveals the degree to which young Chinese were struggling to adjust to the rapid social changes taking place in their country in the first decades of the twentieth century. That young men—and occasionally women—now dared to defy their parents or to attach conditions to their obedience suggests the withering of absolute parental authority over their children and the tentative emergence of a new relationship in which parents and children might negotiate some issues.[83]

American missionaries had encouraged a certain amount of independence in their students when it came to choosing their spouses and thus undoubtedly contributed to the undermining of traditional patriarchal authority. The rising status of urban Chinese youth and the overturning of customary patterns of deference, however, are not attributable to the missionaries in any direct way. The advent of the modern educational system, particularly after the abolition of the classical examinations, was more significant in undoing the old relationship between educated children and their parents since it created a wide gap in knowledge, experience, and expectations. The succession of crises that battered China in this era and the widespread belief that students in the modern schools were the key to China's future further widened the gulf, for each crisis seemed like an indictment of the old society and increased the students' conviction that the older generation was incapable of dealing with China's problems. This belief fueled the development of a student movement, which, as we shall see in the next chapter, posed problems for teaching missionaries.

It is worth noting, however, that when it came to marriage arrangements, young men did not simply break long-standing engagements to find an educated partner. In this time of transition between the old world of tradition and a new social world with dizzying freedoms, even young Chinese were reluctant to break an engagement. It was, in fact, the seriousness of breaking a betrothal that gave the rebellious young men the leverage necessary to win their parents' acquiescence to the education of their fiancees. It was preferable for all concerned to pay for a girl's education and delay a marriage rather than to sunder an engagement.

American missionaries, as previously noted, thought little of breaking a betrothal. They were shocked, however, when some Chinese men simply abandoned their uneducated wives and wed women who were more to their taste, often women whom they had met while in school. In traditional Chinese culture it was acceptable to have more than one wife, but the missionaries regarded this as a sin. They found the position of the cast-off wife tragic.[84] They were also sympathetic toward young women who were suddenly thrust into school at the insistence of their future husbands. Irene McCain pitied one twenty-four-year-old woman who was enrolled in the mission school's first grade in 1920; she was not only the oldest student in her class but had never been away from home and did not even know how to put up her own hair. Another girl ran away from the Methodist Keen School after her parents enrolled her there against her will.[85]

Although some Chinese women were forced to go to school, many others eagerly sought education. Novelist Xie Bingying resolved as a girl to starve herself to death if her conservative mother would not permit her to go to school. The mother capitulated after Xie took to her bed and did not eat for three days. Even women who were already married clamored to go to school: eighteen of the seventy-eight pupils at the Kachek Daughters' School in 1923 were married.[86]

It was not only Chinese young men who acted more independently in choosing their mates; Chinese women were also voicing their preferences. In 1925, the *Missionary Review of the World* claimed that Chinese women had new, higher standards for husbands and were often attracted to Christian men because they believed their chances for a happy married life were better if they were "the wives of clean purposeful men." In a striking example of a woman's exercising control over her marital options, one Miss Chang, reputedly "a girl of strong character," told missionaries at Yenching University that she had chosen her mate with the understanding that he would not impede her work as headmistress of a girls' school in Shanxi.[87]

The Chinese government began to play a role in the marriage patterns of China beginning in 1909, when the Qing dynasty announced that students under the age of twenty would not be allowed to marry. Missionaries were pleased with the decree but it is not clear whether this stricture applied to both sexes or how rigorously, if at all, it was enforced.[88] Some years later, the GMD also turned its attention to legislating marriage reform. In 1924, it proposed to uphold adult, monogamous marriage, freedom in marriage and divorce, equal treatment of widows who remarried, and the "overthrow of traditional rites enslaving the female sex." Some of these recommendations became part of the 1930 Family Code. Again, however, this ideal was honored more on paper than in practice.[89]

Yet another significant change was that some Chinese women now preferred not to marry at all. In traditional society, apart from a handful of "filial daughters" who stayed home to care for aged parents, Buddhist nuns (and, in the nineteenth century, Chinese Catholic nuns), and a few other quite anomalous groups, the vast majority of Chinese women were married. "Not one girl in a thousand can escape marriage," commented Presbyterian missionary Louise Johnson in 1902.[90] In the late nineteenth and early twentieth centuries, however, the growing availability of paid labor and careers for women made spinsterhood an option for a few women at the same time that the birth of nationalism encouraged some women to devote their lives to the service of their country. Some Chinese women were reluctant to wed if it meant relinquishing a career. Indeed, some argued that it was unfilial to do so and throw away the opportunities that parents had sacrificed to provide. The implication that marriage itself was a private pleasure rather than a filial duty demonstrates the dramatic degree to which the traditional conception of marriage was being transformed. Likewise, the arguments of some young Chinese that the claims of country were higher than those of clan evidence both the power of nationalism and the decline of the family as the primary focus of Chinese loyalty.[91]

Some missionaries, like Methodist Elsie Reik, claimed that Christianity had been responsible for creating "old maids" in China. Insofar as missionaries encouraged education for women and promulgated an ideal of service, Reik's statement is not altogether inaccurate. The Chinese government, however, was also promoting women's education, and the emergence of Chinese nationalism made service to the country and to the Chinese people a patriotic duty. It is impossible to separate the various factors that motivated mission-educated Chinese women to avoid marriage in favor of a service career; the fact that women educated in government schools acted in the same way as those educated by missionaries should caution against the hasty conclusion that exposure to Christian ideals was the decisive factor.[92]

It is not clear what Reik or other missionaries thought of Chinese women who did not marry. Although a large number of missionary women were single, they constantly reiterated that the highest role to which a woman could aspire was wife and mother. At the 1907 China Centenary Conference, a consensus emerged among the missionary women that they would not encourage their girl students to remain single, not even to become sorely-needed teachers in mission schools. The ideal, instead, was to be Christian marriage and motherhood. Luella Miner urged her fellow missionaries to consider careers for Chinese women as the exception, not the rule.[93]

By far the most popular career for Chinese women in the early twentieth century was teaching. Although in the past the overwhelming majority of teachers in formal settings had always been men, in the twentieth century, the Chinese gradually came to accept and even prefer women as teachers, at least in the lower levels of education. As in the United States, this acceptance was based on the association of teaching with women's maternal role. Tellingly, the only higher-level education for girls that the government supported before 1912 was normal training.[94]

American teaching missionaries had long believed that women have a special aptitude for teaching and had worked to reform Chinese prejudices against women teachers. A 1904 report from the Presbyterian Pui-kei Boys' School noted a change in the attitude of local Chinese regarding women teachers: "We are surprised and pleased that they are willing to place their sons under the supervision of women, which is so contrary to the Chinese custom, but it has been an object lesson to them, enabling them to understand that educated consecrated Christian women are eminently fitted to instruct and lead boys through their tender and impressionable years." From the inception of Christian education in China, missionary women had taught in both boys' and girls' schools.[95]

After 1911, American missionaries urged the Chinese government to provide normal training for young women since the Christian schools alone were unable to assure an adequate supply of Chinese teachers. Missionaries believed that it was preferable for young children to be taught by women. "Women teachers for the elementary schools in China are needed by the tens of thousands," Congregationalist missionary Henry Graybill stressed in 1916. "Women teachers are now so few that practically all primary schools have men teachers."[96] Chinese officials in the government schools agreed with the missionaries. "It is universally recognized that women are more fit to be teachers, especially to younger students, than men," was the judgment of the Chinese National Association for the Advancement of Education in 1923. Thus Republican China emphasized the establishment of girls' schools, particularly normal schools. As had been the case in the United States, two ideas were woven together in the promotion of Chinese women as teachers: one was the notion that unless children were trained from the cradle in how to be good citizens, the republic could not succeed; and the second was that this training fell within women's special sphere, because women were believed to be naturally better teachers for young children.[97]

Although American missionaries were happy to see Chinese women take up teaching, it disturbed them that many of these women continued to teach after they married. This departed from the career pattern of women teachers in the United States, who were often forced to resign after they wed.[98] It is not clear just how many Chinese women teachers were also married, but some continued working even after they had borne children. Missionaries found this most unsettling. Methodist missionary Elsie Reik wrote to her family in 1925 that the casual observer might not recognize that these Chinese women with their babies on their backs in the classroom were actually teachers. "I do not mind their having the baby strapped on their backs," she stated in a later letter, "but when they nurse it right before the children, I am rather nervous."[99]

Although nursing babies in public struck the missionaries as immodest, they worried more about married women working because they assumed that this created a conflict between domestic and professional duties. The question of whether or not the domestic duties of married women precluded their working in a professional capacity was a burning issue in the United States throughout the 1920s. It is not clear where missionaries stood in this debate since their views regarding domesticity were complex and sometimes conflicting. Matilda Thurston, who was uncommonly outspoken on gender issues, wrote critically in 1928: "Men seem to have cleared the way more completely so that career has the right of way but, married or unmarried, women seem to be expected to put family into a place of higher claim." Some missionaries insisted, contrary to the implications of Thurston's comments, that nothing was more important than a woman's work in the home. Others highlighted the domestic duties that conflicted with careers. "We hope that in a few years we will have enough teachers so that we need only employ the unmarried ones," reported Eva Sprunger in 1922. "Many of the preachers are asking for unmarried teachers. They say that the married ones who have babies spend and must spend so much time with the babies that they have no time for outside work."[100] A conflicting consideration for missionaries was that given the constant shortage of teachers in both mission and government schools, they often had no choice but to accept the fact that some Chinese women would have to combine domestic and public life. Some women's schools praised the ability of their alumnae to juggle these dual roles[101]

Changes in family and marital life, the increasing availability of education, and entrance into the public world of work and politics were the major factors transforming the lives of Chinese women in the early decades of the twentieth century. Discussing the social changes that she had witnessed in China since her arrival in 1923, missionary Emily Case Mills told an International Recreational Congress in Los Angeles in 1932 that changes in family life had resulted in smaller family size, improved standards of living, greater freedom for women, and less sexual segregation. "Democracy," she noted, "with its emphasis on individual self-expression, social reform, and equal rights for women has caught the popular imagination." Perhaps the most significant development, as Mills saw it, was the new attitude among young Chinese women. "Educational institutions may strive to stem the rising tide of emancipation," she warned, "but the Chinese girl has tasted a new freedom...her mind is shedding its conventional restrictions and she is beginning to demand liberty of expression and an opportunity for development equal with men."[102] Although American Protestant missionaries had claimed to support the "emancipation" of Chinese women since their arrival in China, by the early twentieth century many missionaries were disturbed to realize that this emancipation might run counter to their own conceptions of Christian womanhood.

Liberty and License

American missionaries had not been the first to attack the Chinese gender system, but their teachings and Western contact itself added a new dimension to indigenous critiques since they provided Chinese critics with a visible alternative to the Confucian pattern and a political context that made reform a pressing concern. In the late 1880s, male reformers such as Wang Tao and Zhang Guanying, comparing the relative positions of women in China and the West, agreed that Confucian social relations oppressed women.[103] It was not until China had suffered repeated humiliations at the hands of the Western powers and Japan, however, that the issue of reforming the Chinese gender system assumed a prominent position in the national program for reform. Chinese reformers generally did not go so far as to argue that women were equal to men or that they ought to be granted rights on the basis of their personhood. Instead, the reformers urged an end to customs such as footbinding on the grounds that these practices sapped national strength and made China a laughingstock among the powerful nations of the world. The issues of Chinese women's status and nationalism were thus entwined for Chinese reformers and radicals alike.[104]

By the turn of the century, Chinese women began to speak and organize on their own behalf. Historian Charlotte Beahan describes three different types of women's organizations that were founded in the first years of the twentieth century: women's rights groups, philanthropic organizations, and nationalistic societies. Some of the women who launched these organizations had ties to mission schools in China, while others had been politicized while studying in Japan. The organization of public women's groups was a new phenomenon.[105] The transformation of women's roles quickened after the 1911 revolution as their private and subordinate roles were undermined by the beginnings of industrial development in China. New cotton mills and tobacco factories in Shanghai and other large cities drew increasing numbers of girls and young women into the world of wage labor. A handful of admittedly exceptional women became doctors, lawyers, dentists, and government officials. Other women took jobs as waitresses, barbers, shop assistants, radio announcers, journalists, and policewomen. The increased availability of education for Chinese women and new attitudes toward their capabilities opened new jobs for them.[106]

Although American missionaries regarded favorably some of the social changes that were reshaping gender relations in twentieth-century China, they had mixed emotions about others. Their ambivalence stemmed from the lack of fit between the new social conditions in China and their own gender beliefs.[107] Missionaries were amazed and pleased, for example, when the traditional seclusion of women and older girls of the wealthier classes began declining around the turn of the century. But this loosening of past restraints on Chinese women often went further than missionaries were willing to countenance and they feared that Chinese women had transgressed their proper sphere. An uneasy counterpoint accompanied missionaries' rhapsodizing about the ways in which Chinese women were becoming liberated from the Confucian past.[108]

Just before the turn of the century, a few missionaries began to question the wisdom of destroying the traditional culture, even for the sake of reforming its gender practices. At the Second Triennial of the EAC in 1896, one woman asserted that "the secluded lives which women and girls live is their safety, and to desire their emancipation from it before China has been leavened with Christian thought and principle is to risk too much." Three years later, at the Third Triennial, the principal of the Methodist McTyeire Girls' School, Laura Haygood, said that she was "so conservative as to shudder with a nameless fear" at the idea of Chinese women riding bicycles. She advised against "liberating" Chinese women from the constraints of traditional culture until there was "a Christian community into which they may be set free."[109]

The need to protect Chinese women from the wrong sort of social change was reiterated with still greater urgency by missionary women at the educational session of the 1907 China Centenary Conference. They noted with disapproval that in the Chinese newspapers "woman's claim to 'freedom' and 'power' is strongly asserted, in notes not unworthy of Susan B. Anthony in her most strenuous, self-assertive days."[110] American missionary women clearly believed it was their responsibility and within their power to set the limits of social change. After a critical discussion of recent developments in China, the missionaries resolved to enlist their schools in opposing "masculine dress and manners" for Chinese schoolgirls, to promote marriage and motherhood even though new career opportunities were unfolding and "to take a conservative attitude as to the position, rights, and privileges of women."[111]

Unlike the "nameless fears" of the late nineteenth century, missionaries in the twentieth century were increasingly explicit about their dread of the changes taking place in China. One alarming development was political radicalism. An astonishing aspect of the 1911 revolution was the (very limited) participation of radical Chinese women as soldiers. Warfare is one of the most clearly demarcated sexual boundaries and one whose transgression the missionaries would be expected to condemn. Yet oddly, although American missionaries were aware of the female "Dare-to-Die" corps, the written record has preserved very few missionary comments on this phenomenon. Their reticence is peculiar, particularly since they did not hesitate to lambast other offenses against their gender beliefs. Perhaps the anti-feminist backlash that followed the Chinese Revolution convinced missionaries that the Dare-to-Die units had been a momentary aberration that could be safely ignored.[112]

There was, however, a visible missionary critique of Chinese women who attempted to gain the vote in 1912. The Chinese women's suffrage movement was quite small; these women demanded the vote as a right based on revolutionary egalitarianism. After the Chinese legislators ignored their calls for enfranchisement, two groups of Chinese women, following the example set by British suffragists, stormed the Nanjing Assembly in early 1912 and the Beijing Assembly later in the year. In the conservative political atmosphere of 1912, the National Assembly denied women's suffrage, effectively barring women from citizenship in the new republic and making a mockery of the feminist rhetoric that some of the makers of the revolution had previously espoused.[113]

There is no evidence that American missionaries lent their support to the movement for Chinese women's suffrage. Although by 1912 a number of liberal missionary women favored suffrage themselves, the majority probably would have identified themselves as "moderate non-militant suffragist[s]," as did Methodist missionary Laura Marsden White. The violence of the Chinese suffrage movement shocked the missionaries, who argued that the reason the movement had failed was that "the wrong element gained control" and therefore "it was not helping the legitimate feminist movement in China."[114]

For American missionaries, determining which public activities were and were not permissible for women depended on the underlying motive for the activity. They sanctioned public work if the purpose was service, a Christian and a feminine virtue safely within the bounds of women's sphere. Suffrage was acceptable, but only if those who sought it were concerned with "the life and rights of others," as one missionary put it, rather than selfishly demanding their own due. This was a leading justification for seeking votes for women among non-radical suffragists in the United States as well. It was also an ideal that missionary women constantly reiterated to their female students in Christian schools in China. "We should always try to keep before them," one missionary stated in 1907, "that they should long for knowledge, not to improve their own position but to benefit others."[115]

Missionary misgivings about Chinese feminism were related to their concern that missionary gender ideology was either being ignored or misinterpreted. "In this new education," one missionary said, "there seems to be a confounding of the idea of equality of sex with that of identity, that is, the girls are in dress and manners aping boys." To what degree this was actually occurring and to what degree it was an exaggeration reflecting missionary gender anxiety is not clear. Although Christian gender ideology permitted some blurring of gender lines, missionaries had never envisioned a world peopled by ungendered human beings. "Masculine" and "feminine" were still significant and largely opposing categories for them.[116]

American missionaries also feared something that they vaguely referred to as "Westernization." "Our object," missionaries stated in 1907, "should be to Christianize and educate the Chinese women, not to Anglicize them." There is a good deal of irony here. In their schools, missionaries taught "Western subjects," introduced Western pedagogical methods, required Western standards of cleanliness and politeness, attempted to teach a variety of Western concepts ranging from "the value of labor" to "the emancipation of women," and they increasingly taught in English. It is hard to imagine a more thorough program to "Anglicize" the students, intentionally or not.[117]

Missionaries now began to alter their stance regarding Westernization. Whereas they had previously connected Christianity with Western culture, in the early twentieth century they began to draw distinctions between the two, arguing that although the Chinese needed the former, the latter was irrelevant, if not downright harmful. "Let us remember that nothing Western is essential but the gospel of Jesus Christ," said one missionary in 1912. Similarly, Helen Daringer, who applied to teach at Ginling Women's College around 1922, wrote on her application that "unless the education given to Chinese children is crystallised [sic] on a Christian foundation, it will do more harm than good."[118]

Worries over political radicalism, gender ideology, and Westernization continued to haunt missionaries after the 1911 revolution. Their apprehension regarding the first fear—radicalism—grew markedly, most noticeably when Chinese girls and women were involved. Some missionaries were stunned to discover, after the fact, that some of their schoolgirls had abetted the revolutionaries by smuggling bombs and weapons under their school uniforms. Even before the revolution, some Chinese women had taken part in patriotic protest movements such as the anti-American boycott in 1905 and the railroad and mining rights recovery movements in 1908–1911. Missionaries wondered how the political awakening among Chinese women might be diverted into innocuous channels.[119]

Along with a new interest in politics among students came the dissolution of strict sexual segregation. Although missionaries believed this to be desirable, and had in fact promoted it in their schools, the new informality in relations between some Chinese men and women disturbed the missionaries. The relaxation of previous taboos led, inevitably, to sexual experimentation and what one Chinese woman termed "matrimonial anarchy" in reference to the flurry of divorces, fraudulent marriages, and bigamous unions caused by the sudden fluidity in the social practices surrounding marriage. Lida Ashmore wrote her daughter in 1913 that the Baptist Girls' School in Shantou had to be "shut up for awhile" after one of the students became pregnant by a young man in the nearby Theological School. "Too much liberty has been given the girls," Ashmore opined, "but they took more than was given them."[120]

Obliteration of traditional sexual segregation did not occur all at once; throughout the 1920s missionaries in some schools were still attempting to throw bashful boys and girls together. Missionaries in other schools, however, regarded the new laxity in relations between the sexes as a moral danger and moved swiftly to control and regulate such contact. One measure to control the social behavior of students in the Christian girls' schools was to refuse to grant them a diploma or even to expel them for what missionaries deemed improper behavior. Luella Tappan disclosed in 1922 that one graduate of the Pitkin Memorial School on the island of Hainan was not to receive her diploma because she was "a flirt," "not to be trusted with men," and, most damningly, "not a good one to represent Pitkin." Female students complained to the missionaries at Presbyterian Harriet Stroh's school about a classmate's "improper communication with boys" because they did not want any shame reflected on their school. Although the girl's mother kowtowed to Stroh and begged her to save the daughter's face by letting her finish the term, Stroh expelled the girl at once since she was concerned about the "face" of her school.[121]

In addition to wanting to prevent pregnancies, runaway marriages, and other evils, the solicitude missionaries exhibited for the reputation of a Christian school also led them to clamp down on unsupervised socializing between the sexes. Mission schools for both girls and boys were known and praised by the Chinese for their strict discipline.[122] This was of special importance in the mission girls' schools, since after the establishment of government schools for girls, missionaries claimed that those non-Christian

Chinese parents who continued to send their daughters to the Christian schools tended to be of a conservative bent.[123] Any hint of impropriety in the behavior of staff or students in a mission school tainted its reputation and could make it the target of community censure.[124]

By the second decade of the twentieth century, there was a consensus among missionaries that many Chinese students, especially girls and young women, were confusing "liberty" with "license." Missionary Lois Young commented that for Chinese youths in general the early twentieth century was a time of difficult adjustment because the old social controls had been cast aside and the Chinese did not know with what to replace them. Discouraged by the numerous disciplinary problems in her school, she remarked, "It is so hard to know how far to let them go. You can't cramp everything, things are changing everywhere and must here too, but there are going to be many tragedies in the change."[125]

As they revealed concern about the behavior of their students, missionaries simultaneously criticized some Western practices and amusements that were creeping into China, especially in the treaty ports. Monona Cheney was incensed to learn in 1918 that a California brewery planned to begin operations in China. "I get so wrathy [sic] every time I go down the street...," she wrote, "and remember the slogan of the American Tobacco Co., 'a cigarette in the mouth of every man, woman, and child in China' — we will all be a heap *wrathier* if the liquor business is transported bodily." Cheney also denounced American movies that played in China as "sickeningly suggestive." Episcopalian missionary Venetia Cox agreed, stating bluntly, "Moving pictures do more to corrupt morals out here than anything else I know."[126]

Missionaries rallied quickly to defeat these fresh menaces to Chinese morality. Mission school students were not permitted to drink or smoke, but from time to time a school had problems with students who wanted to experiment with alcohol or tobacco.[127] An emphasis on community service and self-government organizations in Christian schools, which we will examine in greater detail in the next chapter, was likewise expected to occupy students in healthy activities and keep them out of mischief. The Chinese YMCA, first introduced into China in 1885, by the early twentieth century defined its mission in part, as providing wholesome forms of recreation for urban youths, many of whom lacked parental supervision.[128] Missionaries also organized a "Committee on Film Censoring for China" in

1915 that published a guide to films that the committee deemed morally repugnant. By 1917, the committee had viewed approximately six hundred films, but it only rejected thirty of them.[129]

American Protestant missionaries had always defined their duty to include reforming vice. Prior to the First World War, however, they had been engaged primarily in attacking what they considered to be native Chinese vices, notably prostitution, opium smoking, gambling, and theater performances.[130] Now, to their chagrin, they found themselves in the position of having to oppose practices that originated in their own culture. World War I was a turning point in terms of missionaries' disposition toward the West, for they were profoundly embarrassed by the spectacle of the allegedly "Christian" nations using their superior technology to slaughter one another.[131] Following the war, some of the manifestations of American youth culture of the 1920s—cigarettes (especially for women), alcohol, bobbed hair, dancing, and cabarets—appeared in China. Although historians deny that the changes in American cultural life in the 1920s were particularly dramatic, the Hollywood stereotype of a free-wheeling, gangster-ridden, anti-Victorian American society horrified the missionaries, since they feared that movie images and the antics of Western adventurers in Chinese treaty ports might be interpreted by the Chinese as accurately reflecting the values of Western society.[132]

Missionary concern about the importation of Western vices into China, in tandem with the social changes that had already begun in China, led to a radical reorientation of missionary attitudes toward both their own culture and Chinese traditional culture. In the nineteenth century, although missionaries could and did point to specific deplorable Chinese customs and beliefs (such as footbinding and plural marriage, to name but two), they were rather vague about the Christian-Western amalgam they wanted to introduce into China. Missionaries generally wrapped the Christian and the Western aspects of their culture into a single bundle and presented it to the Chinese with the implication that Westernizing meant Christianizing and vice versa. Among themselves, missionaries agreed that even seemingly extraneous material goods from the West could help to "break down Chinese exclusiveness" and enhance Chinese receptivity to the Christian message.[133]

The certainty of American missionaries about the superiority of their culture and the indivisibility of Western and Christian characteristics was in decline by the late nineteenth and early twentieth centuries. Discussing their work in China, they often reminded each other ominously of what had happened in Japan; Japan had Westernized and become a world power without adopting Christianity. Some missionaries believed that this had occurred because educational missionaries in Japan had failed to gain control of the modern national school system, established in Japan in 1886. Others, like Southern Baptist T. F. McCrea, argued that the mission schools were more directly responsible for Japan's secularism. "The mission schools in Japan," McCrea wrote in 1912, "have been guilty of inoculating the church of Japan with Western materialism, a Godless evolutionism, higher criticism of a destructive kind, and other isms that run in our Western colleges and universities." This statement represents an early salvo in a battle between conservative and liberal Christians over education in China; in ten years these same charges would be leveled at educational missionaries in China.[134]

It was obvious to missionaries of this era that China would, if possible, follow the Japanese path of modernization and self-strengthening while rejecting Christianity. Because of this threat, missionaries retreated from their earlier assertion that "Western" and "Christian" were synonymous. They argued instead that Western culture was good only insofar as it was Christian. "[L]et us think of the dangers of Western civilization without Christianity," warned Luella Miner at the China Centenary Conference in 1907. "They are appalling and impossible to enumerate in the short time at my disposal." Miner's cryptic criticism and her assumption that she did not have to elaborate on it indicate that American missionaries were coming to share a common view of the shortcomings of Western civilization.[135]

American missionary attitudes toward the West became harsher in the aftermath of the war. Increasing numbers of missionaries took a dim view of the moral atmosphere in the United States and doubted that the West was a fit role model for China. Missionary Maynard Owen Williams concluded glumly as early as 1914 that the United States was going to the dogs. "The sanctity of the home and marriage tie is being lost in the land of the chorus girl and the sensational press," he wrote. James Webster, writing about Christian education in 1923, asked his readers how one could differentiate between Chinese polygamy and "the continuous polygamy through divorce and remarriage in the United States?" The West, it seemed, was not really very Christian after all.[136]

At the beginning of the century, missionaries remained confident that Christianity could protect the Chinese from the temptations of a rapidly evolving society. According to Luella Miner, Christian women, in particular, were "surrounded by that invisible shield which Christianity throws about womanhood."[137] By the early 1920s, however, some missionaries argued that Christian education had not proven an adequate replacement for traditional conventions and that it was ineffective as moral armor. After investigating the status of Christian education in China, James Webster pointed out that in attacking Confucian traditions, American missionaries "are destroying religious sanctions that have been essential to social control in China." He wondered: "What equally powerful religious sanctions, what definite institutions that provide adequate school and home training, and what constructive social customs is Christian education offering?"[138]

While few Americans matched Webster's pessimism or readiness to pose prickly questions, it became increasingly common for missionaries to hark back to the days of traditional China with a kind of nostalgic fondness that belied their former hostility. Speaking at the fifty-year anniversary celebration of the Beijing Mary Porter Gamewell School in 1922, Methodist Bishop Birney said: "Modern education must preserve the noble traditions of Chinese womanhood. There is danger that in breaking away from restrictions, the new woman will also break away from the glorious things of the past. This must not be."[139] Similarly, without defending women's traditional lack of education or the custom of footbinding, missionaries recognized that Confucian teachings had enforced a moral rectitude that was now being lost.[140] Some missionaries argued that Christianity should complete Confucianism by supplying what it lacked rather than supplanting it altogether. What Confucianism lacked, they argued, was the moral strength to live up to the standards it set. Although they still believed that Christianity was an exclusive religion, by defining Confucianism not as a religion but as a "noble ethical system," they cleared the way for an implicit acceptance, among missionaries, of some of its tenets. Ironically, although the Chinese agreed that Confucianism was not and never had been a religion *per se*, some Chinese intellectuals launched in

1919 their own attack on Confucianism even as missionaries were discovering its value.[141]

Alarming as missionaries found the state of affairs in China with the outbreak of World War I, the scene grew bleaker yet after the war ended. By 1920, missionaries had to contend with both the continuing corrosive social effects of prolonged political disorder in China and the rise of a vociferous student movement. The latter not only attacked Confucian tradition but also assailed the missionaries, their schools, Christianity, and religion itself. Under these circumstances, it is not to be wondered that Confucianism and traditional society appeared increasingly benign to the beleaguered missionaries. Expressions of nationalism among Chinese women in the Christian schools, however, provided missionaries with some solace.

ENDNOTES

1 Olga Lang, *Chinese Family and Society* (New Haven: Yale University Press, 1946; reprinted New York: Archon Books, 1968), p. 43.

2 Samuel Colcord Bartlett, *Sketches of the Missions of the American Board* (New York: American Board of Commissioners for Foreign Missions, 1872), pp. 123, 130.

3 George Barbour to family, Nov. 18, 1911, George and Dorothy Barbour Papers, RG 8, Box 13, Folder 1911, YDSL; and *China Centenary Missionary Conference* (Shanghai: Centenary Conference Committee, 1907), p. 586.

4 Elizabeth Perkins to family, Oct. 21, 1907, Elizabeth Perkins Papers, RG 8, Box 154, YDSL; Lois Young to family, April 26, 1918, Lois Young Papers, H85. 128491, BWM; Elsie Clark to family, May 10, 1914, Elsie Clark [Krug] Papers, RG 8, Box 42, YDSL; Lois Young, diary, p. 11, uncatalogued, YDSL.

5 *Woman's Work for Woman* 25 (March 1893): 81–82.

6 Ruth Chester to Elizabeth Bender, Nov. 23, 1924, Ginling College, Correspondence, UBCHEA, RG 11, Box 135, Folder 2721, YDSL.

7 *Centenary Conference*, 1907, p. 158; Fung Hin Liu, "About our School," in "Canton Christian College Girl Students," pamphlet, 1915, RG 31, Box 273, Folder 1944, YDSL; *Missionary Review of the World* (January 1927): 73.

8 Jane Hunter, *The Gospel of Gentility: American Women Missionaries in Turn-of-the-Century China* (New Haven: Yale University Press, 1984), p. 182; Elsie Clark to family, May 22, 1915, Elsie Clark [Krug] Papers, RG 8, Box 43, YDSL; Gladys Bundy to family, May 11, 1924, Robert and Gladys Bundy Papers, RG 8, Box 240, YDSL; Bertha St. Clair to family, March 30, 1924, Bertha St. Clair Papers, RG 8, Box 174, YDSL.

9 Jeanie Graham McClure to family, November 11, 1917, Robert and Jeanie Graham McClure Papers, RG 8, Box 120, YDSL; Ida Belle Lewis to family, on removing Chinese children from their families and substituting the Christian school for the home, January 16, 1921, October 17, 1921, and November 27, 1921, Ida Belle Lewis [Main] Papers, RG Ax 216, Box 1, UOSC. In the early twentieth century, some Chinese agreed with the missionary assessment of the average Chinese home, stating that it was necessary for the

government to establish kindergartens, in part, to counteract "the bad influences that have been associated with our family life." *Republican Advocate* 1: 14 (July 6, 1912): 545. See also Helen Barrett Montgomery, *Western Women in Eastern Lands: An Outline Study of Fifty Years of Woman's Work in Foreign Missions* (New York: MacMillan Co., 1910), p. 87.

10 Lang, *Chinese Family and Society*, pp. 198–199; Michael Grossberg, *Governing the Hearth: Law and the Family in Nineteenth-Century America* (Chapel Hill: University of North Carolina Press, 1985).

11 Elsie Reik to family, April 27, 1925, Elsie Reik Papers, UOSC.

12 Caroline Lee to her home church, Nov. 5, 1921, Microfilm #107, BFM. It should be noted that only men who were well-to-do could afford more than one wife or a concubine, which meant that these practices were considerably less common than missionaries implied in their writings.

13 Margaret Burton, *Women Workers of the Orient* (West Medford, Mass.: Central Committee of the United Study of Foreign Missions, 1918), pp. 123–124.

14 Joan Jacobs Brumberg, "Zenanas and Girlless Villages: The Ethnology of American Evangelical Women, 1870–1910," *Journal of American History* 69 (September 1982): 347–371; Clifton Jackson Phillips, *Protestant America and the Pagan World: The First Half-Century of the ABCFM, 1810–1860* (Cambridge: East Asian Research Center, Harvard University Press, 1969), ch. 9; and Montgomery, *Western Women in Eastern Lands*, p. 48.

15 Some of these adoptions were legal, but most missionaries who "adopted" Chinese children did so informally and limited their responsibilities toward the children to paying for their education. If the children did not perform satisfactorily, the missionaries reserved the right to cease all support. Not all of these children were orphans; some simply came from families too poor to pay for education. Lucerne H. Knowlton, "One Hundred Years of Methodism in China," p. 5, Lucerne H. Knowlton Papers, Box 1, HIA; Gladys Bundy to family, May 4, 1924, Bob and Gladys Bundy Papers, RG 8, Box 240, Folder 4, YDSL; Martha Wiley, essay, n. d., about Donald and Catherine Hsueh, Martha Wiley Papers, RG 8, Box 218, YDSL; Ida Belle Lewis to family, March 14, 1912, Ida Belle Lewis [Main] Papers, RG Ax 216, Box 1, UOSC. Venetia Cox ultimately stopped supporting her "adopted" Chinese daughter after the girl disobeyed Cox and left school without permission. Venetia Cox to family, October 15, 1922, Venetia Cox Papers, RG 236, Box 1d, ECMC.

16 Anna and Oswald Brown, *Life and Letters of Laura Askew Haygood* (Nashville: Publishing House of the Methodist Episcopal Church, 1904), p. 287.

17 Myrtle Smith to family, Aug. 7, 1922, Myrtle Smith Papers, RG A 164, Box 1, UOSC.

18 Montague Bell and H. G. W. Woodhead, eds., *China Yearbook* (London: George Koutledge and Sons, Ltd., 1913), pp. 440–441; *Centenary Conference*, 1907, p. 177.

19 Shanghai Conference report, 1890, p. 53; Lida Ashmore to daughter, Oct. 9, 1898, William and Lida Ashmore Papers, RG Ax 564, Box 1, UOSC.

20 Report of the Foochow Mission of the American Board, 1895–1896.

21 Knowing that this might be misunderstood by Americans at home, Cheney hastened to caution her parents not to mention the story to anyone else. Monona Cheney to family, Sept. 10, 1922, Monona Cheney Papers, RG Ax 275, Box 1, UOSC.

22 Elizabeth Perkins to family, March 28, 1908, Elizabeth Perkins Papers, RG 8, Box 154, Folder 7, YDSL.

23 Mary Margaret Moninger to family, Feb. 24, 1918, Mary Margaret Moninger Papers, RG 240, Box 1, Folder 10, PC (USA).

24 Chester Fuson to family, April 18, 1920, Chester Fuson Papers, RG 8, Box 71, YDSL. The missionaries then undertook to train the woman as a Bible woman so that she could earn a living. Clearly, Chinese women with ties to the Protestant community had options that other women lacked, making divorce economically feasible.

25 Matilda Thurston, Typed Excerpts from Letters, March 17, 1922, Ginling College, Correspondence, UBCHEA, RG 11, Box 144, Folder 2856, YDSL.

26 Clarence Burton Day, *Hangchow University, A Brief History* (New York: United Board for Christian Colleges in China, 1955), p. 7.

27 Lang, *Chinese Family and Society*, pp. 122–123.

28 Matilda Thurston, May 5, 1918, Ginling College, Correspondence, UBCHEA, RG 11, Box 143, Folder 2855, YDSL; Mildred Test Young interview, p. 45, MCOHP, 1978, ELCA.

29 Venetia Cox to family, March 7, 1920, Venetia Cox Papers, RG 236, Box 1b, ECMC. Missionaries also tried to get Chinese brides to wear virginal white instead of Chinese red—symbolizing happiness—at their weddings. Schools played a limited role in this effort, although teachers sometimes attempted to clarify the symbolism of the Western bridal color. See, for example, Elsie Clark to family, April 18, 1915, Elsie Clark [Krug] Papers, RG 8, Box 43, YDSL.

30 "Yenching College, Peking, China," possibly written by Luella Miner, p. 4, 1921, Yenching University, Publicity, UBCHEA, RG 11, Box 376, Folder 5719, YDSL; Mary J. Bergen, Women's Christian Conference, May 12, 1906, Shantung Christian College, UBCHEA, RG 11, Box 267, Folder 4269, YDSL.

31 Montgomery, *Western Women in Eastern Lands*, p. 91; Foochow Girls' School, Seventieth Anniversary pamphlet, p. 8, 79-16: 1459-4-2: 11, GBGM.

32 Lida Ashmore, "My Life Story," p. 53, William and Lida Ashmore Papers, RG Ax 564, Box 1, UOSC.

33 *"Tian Zu Hui Yu Chongguo zhi Guanxi," "Bu Ke Qingshi Nuzi,"* and *"Chongguo Nuzi zhi Kukuang."* History of the Peking Station of the North China Mission of the Woman's Foreign Missionary Society of the Methodist Episcopal Church (WFMS), RG 8, Box 73, YDSL.

34 *Ginling College Magazine*, 1924, Ginling College, UBCHEA, RG 11, Box 151, Folder 2947, YDSL. The degree to which mission and government school students, especially female students, were in conflict on social issues will be discussed in chapter 4.

35 Elsie Clark to family, Oct. 15, 1916, Elsie Clark [Krug] Papers, RG 8, Box 44, YDSL.

36 Hangchow Union Girls' High School minutes, Board of Directors meeting, April 1915, RG 31, Box 276, Folder 1963, YDSL; Mary Porter Gamewell School, 1922 report, 79-16: 1459-4-3: 50, GBGM.

37 Gotch Memorial College, 1906, Cheeloo University, Publicity and Brochures, UBCHEA, RG 11, Box 267, Folder 4269, YDSL; Reverend O. G. Reuman, "Some Suggestions toward a Progressive Program of Projects for Young Adolescent Boys in China," n. d., Reuman Family Papers, RG 8, Box 164, YDSL.

38 *Records of the Second Triennial Meeting of the Educational Association of China* (Shanghai: American Presbyterian Mission Press, 1896), p. 287; *University of Nanking Magazine* (March 1912): 6, Nanking University, UBCHEA, RG 11, Box 235, Folder 3919, YDSL.

39 *Records of the First Triennial Meeting of the Educational Association of China* (Shanghai: American Presbyterian Mission Press, 1893), p. 36; Adam Groesbeck, "How the Chinese Boy Finds Christ, or stated psychologically and less intelligently; the Conversion Experience among Adolescent Chinese," n. d., Adam and Clara Groesbeck Papers, RG Ax 818, Box 1, UOSC.

40 *Nanking University Student Handbook*, 1924–1925, p. 69, Nanking University, UBCHEA, RG 11, Box 236, Folder 3920, YDSL.

41 Matilda Thurston, Typed Excerpts from Letters, December 17, 1916, Ginling College, Correspondence, UBCHEA, RG 11, Box 143, Folder 2855, YDSL; mimeographed sheet "Contacts with non-Christian Cultures," n. d., Bob and Gladys Bundy Papers, RG 8, Box 240, Folder 3, YDSL; Harlan Beach, *Dawn on the Hills of T'ang or Missions in China* (New York: Student Volunteer Movement for Foreign Missions, 1898), p. 13.

42 Arthur J. Brown, *New Forces in Old China: An Unwelcome but Inevitable Awakening* (New York: Fleming H. Revell, 1904), p. 88.
43 Elsie Reik to family, April 27, 1925, Elsie Reik Papers, UOSC.
44 *Woman's Missionary Friend* 47 (January 1915): 45.
45 *Woman's Missionary Friend* 53 (March 1921): 97.
46 Harriet Stroh to family, October 12, 1919, Harriet Stroh Papers, RG 187, Box 1, Folder 3, PC (USA); Grace Boynton, "The Famine Refuge," n. d., around 1922, Yenching University Correspondence, UBCHEA, RG 11, Box 321, Folder 4904, YDSL. It must also be kept in mind that coeducation was not widespread in the United States until the late nineteenth century. See Lynn D. Gordon, "Coeducation on Two Campuses: Berkeley and Chicago, 1890–1912," pp. 171–193, in Mary Kelley ed., *Woman's Being, Woman's Place: Female Identity and Vocation in American History* (Boston: G. K. Hall and Co., 1979).
47 *Woman's Missionary Friend* 43 (February 1911): 47; Matilda Thurston, Typed Letters, May 7, 1916, Ginling College, Correspondence, UBCHEA, RG 11, Box 143, Folder 2855, YDSL; Elsie Clark to family, Feb. 4, 1918, Elsie Clark [Krug] Papers, RG 8, Box 44, YDSL; Matilda Thurston, Typed Letters, June 4, 1922, Ginling College, Correspondence, UBCHEA, RG 11, Box 144, Folder 2856, YDSL.
48 Wan L. Hsu to John Edwards, July 27, 1929, 73-43: 1043-3-2: 03, GBGM; Monona Cheney to family, July 5, 1920, Monona Cheney Papers, RG Ax 275, Box 1, UOSC; Bertha Magness to family, October 9, 1920, Bertha Magness Papers, RG Ax 846, Box 1, UOSC; Harriet Stroh to family, December 16, 1923, Harriet Stroh Papers, RG 187, Box 1, Folder 6, PC (USA).
49 Jeanie McClure to family, June 1, 1918, Robert and Jeanie Graham McClure Papers, RG 8, Box 120, YDSL.
50 Administrative Committee on Co-Education, April 1930, Fukien Christian College, UBCHEA, RG 11, Box 108, Folder 2391, YDSL.
51 Hinghua Woman's Conference Report, 1909, Missionary Miscellany, RG 846, UOSC; Mildred Test Young interview, p. 13, MCOHP, 1978, ELCA; Arthur Braden Coole, *A Trouble Shooter for God in China* (Kansas: Intercollegiate Press, 1976), pp. 136–138, Arthur and Ella Coole Papers, Ax 793, Box 1, UOSC.
52 Hwa Nan faculty to the Trustees, August 31, 1928, Hwa Nan College, UBCHEA, RG 11, Box 114, Folder 2476, YDSL.
53 *Christian Education in China: A Study Made by an Educational Commission Representing the Mission Boards and Societies Conducting Work in China* (New York: Committee of Reference and Counsel of the Foreign Missions Conference of North America, 1922), p. 271; Fukien College Committee on Coeducation, April, 1930, Fukien Christian College, UBCHEA, RG 11, Box 108, Folder 2391, YDSL.
54 F. S. White, "Co-Education in China," *Chinese Recorder* 50 (Oct. 1919): 666–673, see p. 669.
55 *Ibid.*; Administrative Committee, April 1930, Fukien Christian College, Fukien Christian College, UBCHEA, RG 11, Box 108, Folder 2391, YDSL; George T. Scott, "Higher Education by Missions in the Far East—Observations and Suggestions," Hangchow Christian College, Publicity, UBCHEA, RG 11, Box 162, Folder 3046, YDSL; Grace Boynton, "A Coeducational Celebration in China," March 15, 1920, pamphlet, Yenching University, Correspondence, UBCHEA, RG 11, Box 321, Folder 4904, YDSL.
56 Chester Fuson to family, April 28, 1906, Chester Fuson Papers, RG 8, Box 71, YDSL; Charles Hodge Corbett, *Lingnan University* (New York: Board of Trustees for Lingnan University, 1963), pp. 44, 71; Charles Hodge Corbett, *Shantung Christian University (Cheeloo)* (New York: United Board for Christian Colleges in China, 1955), pp. 124–125; Shantung Christian College, Report of the Woman's Unit, 1926, Shantung Christian College, UBCHEA, RG 11, Box 244, Folder 3993, YDSL; *West China Union University Bulletin*, 1927–1928, p. 2, West China Union University, UBCHEA, RG 11, Box 227, Folder 4387, YDSL; John L. Coe, *Huachung University* (New York: United

Board for Christian Higher Education in Asia, 1962), p. 48; W. B. Nance, *Soochow University* (New York: United Board for Christian Colleges in China, 1965), p. 20; and Clarence Burton Day, *Hangchow University, A Brief History* (New York: United Board for Christian Colleges in China, 1955), p. 70.

57 Alice Brethorst to Frank D. Gamewell, Aug. 19, 1926, 73-43: 1113-1-1: 04, GBGM.

58 Luella Miner to Miss Lee, n. d.; Miner to Lee, August 6, 1917, Yenching University, Correspondence, UBCHEA, RG 11, Box 344, Folder 5280, YDSL.

59 Luella Miner to Miss Lee, Oct. 3, 1920, Yenching University, Correspondence, UBCHEA, RG 11, Box 344, Folder 5280, YDSL; "Guide to Yenching University," pamphlet, 1930, p. 13, 79-16: 1459-5-1: 07, GBGM; Philip West, *Yenching University and Sino-Western Relations, 1916–1952* (Cambridge: Harvard University Press, 1976), p. 130.

60 "Correspondence Between Fukien Christian University and Hwa Nan," Hwa Nan College, UBCHEA, RG 11, Box 114, Folder 2476, YDSL.

61 Lucy Wang to Mrs. Wallace, Sept. 25, 1929, Hwa Nan College, UBCHEA, RG 11, Box 114, Folder 2476, YDSL; Mrs. Thomas Nicholson to Dr. John Edwards, Feb. 9, 1931, Hwa Nan College, UBCHEA, RG 11, Box 114, Folder 2476, YDSL.

62 Matilda Thurston to Miss Hodge, Sept. 6, 1928, Ginling College, Correspondence, UBCHEA, RG 11, Box 143, Folder 2845, YDSL.

63 Elsie Reik to Mrs. Nicholson, n. d., 1935, "Correspondence between Fukien Christian University and Hwa Nan," Hwa Nan College, UBCHEA, RG 11, Box 114, Folder 2477, YDSL.

64 "Notes on the Correlated Program," 1930, Ginling College, UBCHEA, RG 11, Box 143, Folder 2485, YDSL.

65 Matilda Thurston to Miss Hodge, Sept. 6, 1928, Ginling College, Correspondence, UBCHEA, RG 11, Box 143, Folder 2845, YDSL; Hwa Nan's Board of Managers to Fukien University, June 28, 1928, "Correspondence Between Fukien Christian University and Hwa Nan," Hwa Nan College, UBCHEA, RG 11, Box 114, Folder 2476, YDSL. Just as men in the field were trying to push women missionaries into "cooperation," the male general mission boards were attempting to persuade the women's boards to merge with them, in the interests of efficiency. See R. Pierce Beaver, *American Protestant Women in World Mission: The History of the First Feminist Movement* (Grand Rapids, Mich.: William B. Eerdmans Publishing Co., 1968), pp. 184–205; Montgomery, *Western Women in Eastern Lands*, chapter six; and Robert G. Torbet, *Venture of Faith: The Story of the American Baptist Foreign Mission Society and the Woman's American Baptist Foreign Mission Society, 1814–1954* (Philadelphia: Judson Press, 1955), pp. 201–205.

66 Administrative Committee minutes, Oct. 20, 1928, Yenching University, College for Women, UBCHEA, RG 11, Box 302, Folder 4687, YDSL; Luella Miner to Miss Lee, April 17, 1921, Yenching University, Correspondence, UBCHEA, RG 11, Box 344, Folder 5280, YDSL.

67 Estelle Freedman, "Separatism as Strategy: Female Institution Building and American Feminism, 1870–1930," *Feminist Studies* 5 (1979): 512–529.

68 At Ginling Women's College, for example, in 1922 all of the eighteen instructors were women, three of them Chinese; by the academic year 1927–1928, there were nine foreign women, eight Chinese women and seven Chinese men. Although one foreign woman taught chemistry and two women, one foreign and one Chinese, taught biology, the men had otherwise taken over the teaching of Chinese, biology, physics, mathematics and chemistry. Previously, all of these subjects had been taught by women. *Ginling College Bulletin*, 1922, Ginling College, UBCHEA, RG 11, Box 128, Folder 2633, YDSL; *Ginling College Bulletin*, 1926–1927, Ginling College, UBCHEA, RG 11, Box 143, Folder 2844, YDSL.

69 Matilda Thurston to Miss Hodge, Sept. 6, 1928, Ginling College, UBCHEA, RG 11, Box 143, Folder 2845, YDSL. Women made up only 14 per cent of the students in the Christian colleges and only 2.54 per cent of the students in government colleges. Djung

Lu-dzai, *A History of Democratic Education in Modern China* (1934; reprint, Taipei: Ch'eng Wen Publishing Co., 1974), pp. 155–156.

70 Matilda Thurston to Miss Hodge, Sept. 6, 1928, Ginling College, Correspondence, UBCHEA, RG 11, Box 143, Folder 2845, YDSL, emphasis in original; Randolph Sailer interview, pp. 20–21, MCOHP, 1980, ELCA.

71 For example, Alice Reed wrote to her parents in 1919: "I don't know that I ought to write such things to you but you ought to understand that keeping things running smoothly and avoiding friction is one of the most trying parts of living here." December 14, 1919, Excerpts from Letters, p. 51, Alice Reed Papers, RG 8, Box 163, YDSL. Similarly, after hinting strongly that there was conflict between missionaries and local Chinese Christians, Frank Gamewell cautioned Frank Cartwright, "Please take this as confidential, for you know my interest in the work and can read between the lines as far as necessary." Gamewell to Cartwright, April 16, 1929, 73-43: 1041-1-3: 22, GBGM.

72 Paula Baker, "The Domestication of Politics: Women and American Political Society, 1789–1920," *American Historical Review* 89:3 (June 1984):620–647.

73 Irwin T. Hyatt, Jr., *Our Ordered Lives Confess: Three Nineteenth-Century Missionaries in East Shantung* (Cambridge: Harvard University Press, 1976), p. 86. Jane Hunter disagrees with Hyatt. Hunter, *Gospel of Gentility*, pp. 84–85.

74 Elsie Clark to family, May 26, 1913, Elsie Clark [Krug] Papers, RG 8, Box 41, YDSL; Reverend Edward A. Smith, "Beautiful Foochow," pamphlet, n. d., pp. 8–9, 18, Reuman Family Papers, RG 8, Box 164, YDSL.

75 C. Spurgeon Medhurst to the *Republican Advocate* 1: 11 (June 15, 1912): 431.

76 *Republican Advocate* 1: 4 (April 27, 1912): 141; *Republican Advocate* 2: 4 (April 26, 19123): 133–134; Elsie Clark to family, April 30, 1913, Elsie Clark [Krug] Papers, RG 8, Box 41, YDSL; Paul Varg, *Missionaries, Chinese and Diplomats: The American Protestant Missionary Movement in China, 1890–1950* (Princeton: Princeton University Press, 1958), pp. 88–89.

77 Alice Reed to family, Nov. 30, 1919, Excerpts from Letters, p. 51, Alice Reed Papers, RG 8, Box 163, YDSL; Report from the Kachek Daughters' School, 1923–1924, Mary Margaret Moninger Papers, RG 230, Box 1, Folder 25, PC (USA).

78 Mildred Test Young interview, p. 89, MCOHP, 1978, ELCA.

79 Matilda Thurston, Typed Excerpts from Letters, March 17, 1922, Ginling College, Correspondence, UBCHEA, RG 11, Box 144, Folder 2856, YDSL; Djung, *Democratic Education*, p. 140.

80 Joseph Esherick, quoting historian Chang P'eng-yuan, noted that in the early Republican National Assembly, only 20 per cent of the legislators had received their education completely in traditional schools, whereas 80 per cent had obtained some combination of modern and traditional schooling. Joseph Esherick, "1911: A Review," Symposium on the 1911 Revolution, *Modern China* 12: 2 (April 1976):139–226, see p.186; Olga Lang, *Chinese Family and Society*, pp. 93, 98; C. K. Yang, *The Chinese Family in the Communist Revolution* (Cambridge: Massachusetts Institute of Technology Press, 1959), p. 9.

81 Margaret Burton, *The Education of Women in China* (New York: Fleming H. Revell Co., 1911), p. 153; Sophia Chen, "The Chinese Woman and Four Other Essays," Yenching University, UBCHEA, RG 11, Box 459, Folder 6107, YDSL; *Woman's Missionary Friend* 59 (November 1927): 399.

82 Irene McCain to home church, March, 1920, Microfilm #108, BWM; Ida Belle Lewis Main, "Memoirs," p. 15, the Dorothy Walters Collection of Ida Belle Lewis [Main] Papers, RG 29, Box 1, UOSC; Eliza Anne Hughes Davis to family, Jan. 5, 1907, Eliza Anne Hughes Davis Papers, RG Ax 285, UOSC.

83 Lang, *Chinese Family and Society*, pp. 122–123.

84 George Barbour, "The Position of a Student in a Christian University in China Today," 1926, George and Dorothy Barbour Papers, RG 8, Box 13, Folder 1926, YDSL. It was likewise shocking for the educated Chinese women to discover that her "modern" husband already had a wife secreted in his home village. See Celia Huaguen Chao, "The Story of

Mali, an Ideal Biography of My Mother," p. 84, unpublished manuscript, Harlan Hatcher Graduate Library, University of Michigan, Ann Arbor, Michigan; Yang, *The Chinese Family*, p. 60.

85 Irene McCain to home church, March, 1920, Microfilm #108, BWM; Main, "Memoirs," p. 15, Dorothy Walters Collection of Ida Belle Lewis [Main] Papers, RG 29, Box 1, UOSC.

86 Hsieh Ping Ying, trans. Adet and Anor Lin,*The Girl Rebel: The Autobiography of Hsieh Ping Ying* (New York: The John Day Co., 1940), pp. 30–32; Report of the Kachek Daughters' School, 1923–1924, Mary Margaret Moninger Papers, RG 230, Box 1, Folder 25, PC (USA); Fung Hin Liu, "Some Educational Problems in China," 1916, p. 9, Pamphlet Collection, RG 31, Box 273, Folder 1945, YDSL.

87 *Missionary Review of the World* (January 1925): 72; George Barbour, "The Position of a Student in a Christian University in China Today," George and Dorothy Barbour Papers, RG 8, Box 13, Folder 1926, YDSL.

88 *Woman's Missionary Friend* 41 (November 1909): 401.

89 Djung, *Democratic Education*, pp. 156–157; Marc van der Valk, *An Outline of Modern Chinese Family Law* (Peking: Henry Vetch, 1939), p. 49; Lang, *Chinese Family and Society*, pp. 115–118, 226; and Yang, *The Chinese Family*, pp. 12 and 17; Kiang Kang-hu, *On Chinese Studies* (Shanghai: Commercial Press Ltd., 1934), p. 194.

90 Marion Levy, Jr., *The Family Revolution in Modern China* (Cambridge: Harvard University Press in cooperation with the Pacific Institute, 1949), p. 94; Kenneth S. Latourette, *A History of Christian Missions in China* (New York: The MacMillan Co., 1929), p. 234; Marjorie Topley, "Marriage Resistance in Rural Kwangtung," pp. 67–88, in Wolf and Witke, eds. *Women in Chinese Society*; Sara Collins, "Presbyterian Schools in China," 1902, NT6.3 C69p, PC (USA).

91 Chao, "The Story of Mali," p. 36. The author's mother and aunt both vowed when young not to marry and to spend their lives helping China and contributing to women's emancipation by becoming doctors. Both of them ultimately did marry. See also Mary Ninde Gamewell, *New Life Currents in China* (New York: Missionary Education Movement in the U. S. and Canada, the Methodist Book Concern, 1919), p. 69; Topley, "Marriage Resistance."

92 Elsie Reik to family, June 15, 1925, Elsie Reik Papers, UOSC; Chao, "The Story of Mali"; and Hsieh, *Girl Rebel*, p. xiv.

93 Gamewell, *New Life Currents*, p. 182; *Centenary Conference*, 1907, p. 176.

94 Carl F. Kaestle, *Pillars of the Republic: Common Schools and American Society, 1780–1860* (New York: Hill and Wang, 1983), p. 123.

95 Electa Butler, "Historical Sketch of the Pui-kei Boys' School," 1904, NT6.3 B976hp, PC (USA); Hyatt, *Our Ordered Lives Confess*, p. 171.

96 Henry Graybill, "Developing a Woman's College," April, 1916, p. 31, Pamphlet Collection, RG 31, Box 273, Folder 1944, YDSL. The fact that fewer girls than boys went to school meant that there was always a shortage of Chinese women to serve as teachers. The *Chinese Recorder* was disappointed to note in 1922 that only 28 per cent of the Chinese teachers in the mission school system were women. *Chinese Recorder* 53 (April 1922): 268.

97 Chindon Yiu Tang, "Women's Education in China," *Bulletins on Chinese Education* 9 (1923): 32; Djung, *Democratic Education in Modern China*, p. 159; *Chinese Recorder* 50 (October 1919): 663.

98 Nancy Cott, *The Grounding of Modern Feminism* (New Haven: Yale University Press, 1987), p. 183; *Christian Education in China*, p. 266.

99 Elsie Reik to family, Feb. 28, 1925, and April 14, 1925, Elsie Reik Papers, UOSC.

100 Cott, *Grounding of Modern Feminism*, chapter six; Matilda Thurston, Typed Excerpts from Letters, June 3, 1928, Ginling College, Correspondence, UBCHEA, RG 11, Box 144, Folder 2859, YDSL; Eva Sprunger, Kutien Report, July 28, 1922, Myrtle Smith Papers, RG A 164, UOSC.

101 See, for example, W. Henry Grant, "Educational Requisites of the Church in China," 1924, p. 22, Lingnan University, Publicity, UBCHEA, RG 11, Box 187, Folder 3308, YDSL; "Yenching Alumnae," pamphlet, n. d., Yenching University Correspondence, Grace Boynton, UBCHEA, RG 11, Box 321, Folder 4904, YDSL.

102 Paper given at the First International Recreational Congress, Los Angeles, July 29, 1932, Emily Case Mills Papers, RG 8, Box 141, YDSL.

103 Lin Yutang, "Feminist Thought in Ancient China," *T'ien Hsia Monthly* 2 (September 1935): 127–150. Joanna Handlin points out that the writings of the eighteenth-century feminists were also rooted in past writings. See Handlin, "Lu Kun's New Audience: The Influence of Women's Literacy on Sixteenth Century Thought," pp. 13–38, see p. 16, in Margery Wolf and Roxane Witke, eds., *Women in Chinese Society* (Stanford: Stanford University Press, 1975).

104 Charlotte Beahan, "The Women's Movement and Nationalism in Late Ch'ing China" (Ph.D. diss., Columbia University, 1976), chapter one; Mary Backus Rankin, "The Emergence of Women at the End of the Ch'ing: The Case of Ch'iu Chin," pp. 39–66 in Wolf and Witke, *Women in Chinese Society.*

105 Charlotte Beahan, "In the Public Eye: Women in Early Twentieth-Century China" in Richard Guisso and Stanley Johannesen, eds., *Women in China: Current Directions in Historical Scholarship* (Youngstown, N.Y.: Philo Press, 1981), pp. 215–238. Women had long been members of secret societies and religious sects, which were auxiliary to similar male organizations. Susan Naquin, *Millenarian Rebellion in China: The Eight Trigrams Uprising of 1813* (New Haven: Yale University Press, 1976), pp. 14, 38, 41–42, 47; S. Y. Teng, *The Taiping Rebellion and the Western Powers—A Comprehensive Survey,* (Oxford: Clarendon Press, 1971), p. 115.

106 Beahan, "In the Public Eye," pp. 236–238; Lang, *Chinese Family and Society,* pp. 81–87, 102–107; Bobby Siu, *Imperialism and Women's Resistance, 1900–1949* (London: Zed Press, 1982), pp. 83–89; "Careers for Chinese Women," *Missionary Review of the World* (December 1926): 988.

107 Luella Miner, "A Pioneer College for Women in the East," n. d. Yenching University, Correspondence, UBCHEA, RG, 11, Box 313, Folder 4798, YDSL.

108 *Chinese Recorder* 42 (July 1911): 389.

109 *Second Triennial of the EAC,* 1896, p. 231; *Records of the Third Triennial Meeting of the Educational Association of China* (Shanghai: American Presbyterian Mission Press, 1899), p. 167.

110 *Centenary Conference,* p. 179.

111 *Centenary Conference,* pp. 587–588.

112 The *Chinese Recorder* did refer to women's martial role in the revolution as a "perversion" and recommended that women be trained as kindergarten teachers, not soldiers. *Chinese Recorder* 43 (October 1912): 622. Chinese men criticized the women soldiers; see the *Republican Advocate* 1: 33 (November 16, 1912): 1319 and 1:24 (September 14, 1912): 946–948.

113 Beahan, "In the Public Eye," pp. 236–238.

114 *Woman's Missionary Friend* 45 (February 1913): 60; *Woman's Missionary Friend* 46 (July 1914): 245; Nancy Cott, *Grounding of Modern Feminism,* p. 7.

115 *Woman's Missionary Friend* 47 (January 1915): 9; *Centenary Conference,* p. 574.

116 *Centenary Conference,* 1907, p. 178.

117 *Centenary Conference,* 1907, p. 180.

118 *Chinese Recorder* 43 (May 1912): 259; missionary application of Helen F. Daringer, probably around 1922, 73-43: 1109-1-1: 36, GBGM.

119 Ida Belle Lewis Main, "Memoirs," p. 11, Dorothy Walters Collection of the Ida Belle Lewis [Main] Papers, RG 29, Box 1, UOSC; Luella Miner, "Evolution of a Woman's College in China," 1912, Yenching University, Yenching College for Women, Publicity, UBCHEA, RG 11, Box 376, Folder 5719, YDSL.

120 Chao, "The Story of Mali," p. 107; Lida Ashmore to daughter, Sept. 21, 1913, William and Lida Ashmore Papers, RG 564, Box 1, UOSC.

121 Luella Tappan to family, May 20, 1922, David and Luella Tappan Papers, RG Ax 103, Box 1, UOSC; Harriet Stroh to family, May 20, 1923, Harriet Stroh Papers, RG 187, Box 1, Folder 6, PC (USA). I assume that boys could be expelled from mission schools for misbehaving with girls, although I have seen no reference to any such instances. Instead, missionary correspondence about boys being disciplined has to do with political protests.

122 *Republican Advocate* 2: 11 (June 14, 1913): 420; "Jefferson Academy at Tungchow and its Significance for Christian Education in China," pamphlet, n. d., Pamphlet Collection, RG 31, Box 297, Folder 1967, YDSL.

123 Buwei Yang Chao, trans. Chao Yuenren, *The Autobiography of a Chinese Woman* (Westport, CT: Greenwood Press, 1947), p. 75; Alice Brethorst to family, June 11, 1927, 73-43: 1113-1-1: 04, GBGM.

124 Having a "good character" was often a condition of matriculation in a mission school; Mada McCutcheon wrote to her home church that no students with a hint of the unsavory about themselves or their families were admitted to her school. Mada McCutcheon to home church, July 18, 1923, Microfilm #108, BWM. See also a description the trouble caused by the improper behavior of a missionary teacher at Ginling, Matilda Thurston, Excerpts from Letters, Dec. 17, 1916, Ginling College, Correspondence, UBCHEA, RG 11, Box 143, Folder 2855, YDSL.

125 Both James Webster and Mary Ninde Gamewell use the expressions "liberty" and "license," as do a large number of missionaries. See James Webster, *Christian Education and the National Consciousness in China* (New York: E. P. Dutton & Co., 1923) pp. 236–237, and Gamewell, *New Life Currents,* p. 177; Lois Young to family, date uncertain, probably 1925, Lois Young Papers, H85. 128491, BWM.

126 Monona Cheney to family, Dec. 22, 1918 (emphasis in original) and Feb. 11, 1922, Monona Cheney Papers, RG Ax 275, Box 1, UOSC; Venetia Cox, Diary, Oct. 29, 1917, Venetia Cox Papers, RG 263, Box 2c, ECMC.

127 Reverend O. G. Reuman, "Some Suggestions toward a Program of Progressive Projects for Young Adolescent boys in China," 1923, Reuman Family Papers, RG 8, Box 164, YDSL; Ida Belle Lewis to family, n. d., Ida Belle Lewis [Main] Papers, RG Ax 216, Box 1, UOSC.

128 *Republican Advocate* 1: 13 (June 29, 1912): 518–520.

129 *Chinese Recorder* 47 (February 1916): 131–132; and 48 (March 1917): 206.

130 *Chinese Recorder* 45 (April 1914): 229.

131 *Chinese Recorder* 45 (October 1914): 596–597.

132 Roderick Nash, *The Nervous Generation: American Thought, 1917–1930* (Chicago: Rand McNally Publishing Co., 1970). Venetia Cox wrote in her diary: "Because America is a Christian country [the Chinese] think anything they copy from us cannot be harmful and many times the very worst is copied quite innocent of the wrong." Venetia Cox, Diary, October 29, 1917, Venetia Cox Papers, RG 263, Box 2c, ECMC.

133 *Woman's Work for Woman* 26 (February 1894): 32.

134 Jon Livingston, Joe Moore, and Felicia Oldfather, eds., *Imperial Japan, 1800–1945* (New York: Pantheon Books, 1973), p. 149; *Chinese Recorder* (September 1912): 546.

135 *Centenary Conference*, 1907, p. 574.

136 Maynard Owen Williams to "Muvver," November 1, 1914, Maynard Owen Williams Papers, RG 8, Box 218, YDSL; Webster, *Christian Education*, p. 240.

137 *Centenary Conference*, p. 573; *World Missionary Conference, 1910, Report of Commission III, Education in Relation to the Christianization of National Life* (New York: Fleming H. Revell, Co., 1910), p. 98.

138 Webster, *Christian Education*, p. 242.

139 Mary Porter Gamewell School, Report, 1922, 79-16: 1459-4-3: 50, GBGM.

140 Mary Raleigh Anderson, *A Cycle in the Celestial Kingdom or Protestant Mission Schools for Girls in South China (from 1827 to the Japanese Invasion)* (Mobile, Ala.: Heiter-Starke Printing Co., 1943), p. 16; *Chinese Recorder* 43 (November 1912): 636.

141 Chow Tse-tsung, *The May Fourth Movement: Intellectual Revolution in China* (Cambridge: Harvard University Press, 1960), pp. 300–313; *Chinese Recorder* 47 (December 1916): 812. For the missing ingredient in Confucianism, see an article in the *Kansas City Journal-Post*, Oct. 21, 1928, by missionary Mabel Ruth Nowlin, Mabel Ruth Nowlin Papers, RG 8, Box 147, YDSL.

Chapter 4:
"A Spirit of Nationhood:" Chinese Student Nationalism and the Mission Schools

The rising social status of Chinese women and the swift unraveling of certain Confucian traditions were not the only changes that missionaries found noteworthy in the early twentieth century. They simultaneously became aware of a growing spirit of nationalism among the Chinese. Students, in particular, exhibited a new national consciousness and began to claim the right to speak and act on behalf of their country and its sovereignty. Missionaries initially welcomed this as a positive development, since they believed that China's political and military weakness reflected not only the physical flabbiness of the elite but also the country's lack of popular patriotism. Although a few voices cautioned that the emergence of Chinese nationalism might not work to the benefit of Christianity or Christian education, in the period before 1919 most missionaries regarded the manifestations of patriotism among their students with benevolent and proprietary pride. Some missionaries even claimed credit for arousing this nationalistic spirit by asserting, without further explication, that Christianity was the root of all patriotism.[1]

Just as the delight missionaries originally felt about developments in the lives and status of Chinese women was ultimately superseded by the gloomy certainty that the liberation of Chinese women had gone in undesirable directions, so too their pleasure concerning student nationalism reversed sharply in the mid-1920s. Sympathetic when students protested the exclusionary immigration policies of the United States, the depredations of Japan, or corruption in the Chinese government, American Protestant missionaries were antagonized when students attacked missionary activities or the Western presence in China. Even when student protests were not specifically aimed at missionaries or their schools, their boycotts, strikes, and demonstrations led to a serious disruption of educational work. By 1925 teaching missionaries had grown tired of student activism and believed that it had gotten out of hand.

Chinese students began to mobilize for patriotic activities out of a new consciousness of themselves as political actors. This developed first among radical students in China and overseas in Japan. The establishment of the national system of education in 1903 furthered the perception that China's future depended upon students with modern education and heightened the sense of responsibility that students felt for China's fate. Although missionaries had long hoped that educated Christian students would be able to wield great influence in China, they also believed that these former students would continue to rely upon missionary guidance. Missionaries thus hoped that the ascension of their students into positions of power would ultimately enhance the power of the missionaries in China.

Students in the mission schools, however, were at an immediate disadvantage in participating in the student patriotic movement. Because Chinese nationalism grew out of hostility toward foreign encroachment on China's sovereignty, students in foreign schools, which were protected by extraterritoriality, were often accused of complicity in foreign imperialism. Students from government schools taunted mission school students with the epithets "running dog of the foreigner" and "foreign slave." To prove that they were every bit as patriotic as students in government schools, mission school students sometimes joined in attacks on foreigners and their institutions in China. The anti-foreignism of the student movement partly explains why American missionaries eventually soured on it.

American teaching missionaries first attempted to deal with patriotic protests within their schools by linking patriotism to social service. Service to others was a characteristic feature of Christian belief; missionaries argued that a key purpose of Christian education was to awaken a sense of service within their students. The theology of the Social Gospel, which emphasized social rather than individual salvation, became increasingly prevalent among China missionaries in the early twentieth century and added impetus to the focus on community service in the mission schools. As the student movement gathered momentum, missionaries argued that if the students really wanted to help their country, they should engage in service activities rather than wasting their energy on ineffective types of protest, such as striking or parading.

It was in the mission girls' schools, curiously, that the students conformed most closely to the missionaries' beliefs about service and patriotism. On numerous occasions, mission school girls refused to participate in protest activities, even if boys from a neighboring mission school were involved, preferring to lend their support to missionary-sanctioned works of community service. In harmony with the missionaries, the girls and young women claimed that these works were equally patriotic and much more practical than the protests of the mission school boys. Although missionaries interpreted the differing responses of their male and female students as evidence of inherent gender differences, Chinese girls and young women themselves asserted that the fundamental issue was the right of women to determine independently how they would fulfill their duties as patriotic citizens.

Because the missionaries were unable to defuse the student movement within their schools by channeling student energy into social service, they came to view the movement as a disciplinary rather than a political problem. This allowed them to downplay the degree to which their own presence had served as a catalyst to the development of Chinese nationalism among students. The primary means by which missionaries dealt with outbreaks of protest activities in their schools, then, were punitive. In some schools, the student movement caused missionaries to re-open a debate about the role of the Christian school and the admission of non-Christian students. The greatest effect of the student movement on the missionary educational endeavor, however, was to increase missionary pessimism regarding the direction in which China had been moving since the turn of the century.

The New Role of Chinese Students

The genesis of Chinese student nationalism cannot be pinpointed exactly, but it seems reasonable to argue, as does Roger Hackett, that the experience of study in Japan was pivotal for a generation of Chinese youths. According to Hackett, although the Chinese had long regarded China as "the Middle Kingdom," the center of all civilization, they did not begin to develop a modern conception of nationhood until the late nineteenth century. For overseas students, the impact of life in newly modernized and powerful Japan was critical to their understanding of China as one nation among many.[2]

Revolutionary Chinese student societies, organized in Japan prior to the fall of the Qing, were the first political organizations to emerge among

Chinese students in non-Confucian schools.[3] Chinese students in Japan not only began to develop nationalistic ideas but also to regard themselves as the future leaders of China. It was not the first time that Chinese students had taken an interest in politics, but whereas Confucian students had validated earlier protests on the grounds of tradition, students now argued that their exposure to modern education qualified them to speak.[4]

The initiation of non-Confucian education on the Chinese mainland further changed the roles and expectations of students. When the Qing abolished the imperial examinations in 1905, an entire status group was eliminated. Elite status was no longer predicated on conversance with the Chinese classics but rather on knowledge of Western subjects. This upset the traditional hierarchies of the elder over the younger and the teacher over the student, as was painfully evident when the Qing attempted to use modern-educated youths to retrain traditional degree-holders for employment in the new government schools. Putting young modern-trained Chinese in positions of authority over older teachers was an "inversion of customary relationships" that was distressing for both parties.[5]

Even before the establishment of government schools, mission schools had already begun to undermine traditional Chinese hierarchies. But their influence was limited to the tiny population they served and did not constitute a major threat to the social order. Missionary intervention in the parent-child relationship through their strictures on footbinding, betrothal and marriage were important aspects of the disruption of tradition. Chinese parents had also inadvertently contributed to the weakening of traditional relations between student and teacher when they advised their children to obey the missionaries but to ignore their religious proselytization. Distinguishing the authority of the teacher from the authority of the teaching was an innovation that enhanced the status of the student, as judge of what teachings should be heeded, at the expense of the missionary teacher.[6]

In the atmosphere of national crisis in the early twentieth century, Chinese educators pinned their hopes for the development of Chinese wealth and power on the modern educational system. Students were repeatedly told by their elders that China's future was in their hands.[7] Students in mission schools believed that they, no less than students in government schools, would play a large role in saving China. Cha Tsuen Kwei, a student in Nanking University in 1911, wrote that "young energetic students...are the only ones who are able to make wise plans for national progress in all spheres; they are the ones who will become the efficient and competent leaders in the coming reformation; they are the ones who will be able to restore China to a position of power and significance...." American teaching missionaries encouraged this belief among their students.[8]

In the early twentieth century, students in both mission and government schools expressed increasing intolerance of inefficiency in the schools, inadequately prepared teachers, and old-fashioned customs of deference. "There has been a complete reaction against the old recognized relationship between teacher and pupil," stated an astonished 1908 editorial in the *Chinese Recorder*.[9] Interest in the internal management of the schools was a constant issue in both mission and government schools. When the first student strike occurred at Shantung Christian College in 1906, for example, the majority of the student demands were related not to national political matters but rather to internal rules governing student behavior and the curriculum. The students wanted the missionaries to abolish kneeling during the classics tutorial, as their Confucian teacher required, and to permit students to go freely into the city on Sundays. They also demanded the elimination of two unspecified subjects and the introduction of a course in English. Only their demand for military drill might be construed as quasi-political since it stemmed from the students' belief that if China was to survive, its people had to be physically stronger and prepared to defend themselves.[10] In the government schools as well, many of the earliest student strikes centered on the corruption of school officials or the political appointment of specific teachers and administrators rather than foreign aggression.[11]

Before 1911, when students in either Chinese government or mission schools addressed themselves to larger political issues, such as the recovery of Chinese railway rights, they usually adhered to the older pattern of social relations, following the lead of their teachers rather than their own initiative. These teachers, to be sure, were not traditional Confucianists but younger men and women who had studied in Japan and were already beginning to reject older modes of behavior.[12] In the years following the Republican Revolution, however, Chinese teachers exhorted students not to neglect their studies and to maintain order. Students no longer listened to the admonitions of their teachers and were, in fact, somewhat bitter when their teachers refused to provide them with leadership. From one student's perspective, it was outrageous that "at times of national crisis, they [teachers] fail to have the courage to step forward, thus making it necessary for us students to protest again and again."[13]

Students in Christian schools presumably did not expect missionaries to lead them in protesting imperialism, although they may have expected, since missionaries had been vocal critics of Confucianism and ardent reformers, that their teachers would understand why students felt it was incumbent on them to solve China's internal problems. The reluctance of their elders to protest against foreign imperialism, warlordism, and corruption in the Chinese government convinced many students that China's salvation was truly in their hands. Chen Duxiu's famous "Call to Youth" in 1916 perfectly matched student sentiments. Chen argued that Chinese veneration for the past and respect for elders had led to China's contemporary weakness and national humiliations. He urged students to "discard resolutely the old and rotten" and not waste time looking to the older generation for answers.[14] With patriotism and modern education as their credentials, Chinese students arose repeatedly in the early twentieth century to protest both the feebleness and corruption of the Chinese government and the predatory actions of the foreign powers.

Mission Schools and the Emergence of Patriotic Protests

The first modern Chinese student protest involved the Russian refusal to remove troops from Manchuria in 1903, but mission school students did not engage in patriotic protest activities until the anti-American boycott two years later. The boycotters—led by merchants, students, and patriotic groups—were angered by the refusal of the United States government to rescind its discriminatory Chinese immigration policies. Although American law permitted Chinese teachers, merchants, students and tourists to enter the United States, in practice, immigration authorities defined the exempt categories increasingly narrowly. The Chinese also resented the harassment of Chinese in the United States, and the 1892 Geary Act, which stipulated that to enter the United States, Chinese citizens had to prove that they were exempt from exclusion and forced all resident Chinese in the United States to be registered.[15]

Although their own country was the target, American missionaries generally supported the boycott and its aims. Before the boycott began, a dozen members of the missionary Educational Association of China (EAC) wrote to President Roosevelt urging him to promote better treatment of Chinese students in America. They feared that otherwise Chinese hostility toward the United States might hinder their own educational work in China. Other missionaries attended protest meetings with their students and helped draft letters to William Rockhill, the American Minister in Beijing.[16] This sympathetic stance blunted Chinese animosity toward American missionaries and so although a few students withdrew from American mission schools in protest, total enrollment in American mission schools in China was not much diminished.[17]

Some Chinese women participated in the 1905 boycott, but there is no direct indication that girls and young women from mission schools had been involved. This changed during the next significant protest activity, the Railway Rights Recovery Movement. Beginning after the American boycott and continuing until the eve of the 1911 revolution, students and other patriotic Chinese formed associations to raise money in order to buy back railway concessions that had been granted to various foreign powers by the Qing government.[18] For the first time, girls from mission schools played an active role. In Fuzhou, for example, girls in the Methodist Boarding School hosted a women's meeting to protest the British railway loan. The participation of Chinese women and girls in public protests dramatized both the degree to which a new spirit was arising among the Chinese and the changing role of Chinese women.[19]

Although American missionaries had often derided Chinese lack of patriotism, they responded ambivalently to the first stirrings of nationalism in their schools. Sensitive to Chinese accusations that foreign schools denationalized students and believing that patriotism was a virtue, the missionaries did not, initially, denounce the new movement. As Methodist missionary Ella Shaw wrote in 1908, "We surely wanted our students to learn lessons of patriotism and to be loyal to their country." At the same time, however, missionaries were uneasy about the tone of Chinese nationalism. Editors of the *Chinese Recorder*, noting that the new spirit was an "astonishing contrast to the apathy of former years," added that it was disturbing that "much of the lauded patriotism of the day is fed by anti-foreignism rather than pro-China enthusiasm."[20]

Since the Chinese had developed their sense of nationalism in response to the aggressive nationalism of the foreign powers and since they felt humiliated by the inability of their country to protect itself against the imperialists, it is not surprising that they expressed little "pro-China enthusiasm" while vociferously criticizing the foreigners. Although the missionaries regarded this attitude as unreasonable and continued to criticize the anti-foreign element in Chinese nationalism, they seemed to sense that this was a potentially explosive issue and attempted to avoid offending the Chinese as much as possible. During the Railway Rights Recovery Movement, for example, although American missionaries found themselves more in sympathy with the British than with the Chinese point of view, the *Chinese Recorder* advised against open avowals of pro-British sentiment for fear of raising "a new and unnecessary barrier" between American missionaries and the Chinese.[21]

Torn between their conviction that Chinese patriotism was a positive development and their distrust of its anti-foreign undertones, American missionaries hesitated to quell the first manifestations of nationalism within their schools. Some students took advantage of this. Chao Yang Buwei humorously recounted how students at the Shanghai McTyeire School maneuvered the missionaries into granting them a holiday to mourn the death of the Empress Dowager in 1908:

The principal, Miss Richardson, said that McTyeire was a missionary institution, and had nothing to do with Chinese national affairs. We replied that we were Chinese people; that a missionary school was to teach us to embrace religion, not to renounce our country. We had not been particularly loyal subjects of the Ch'ing [Qing] dynasty, and I had been proud of having come from a revolutionary-minded family. But now national honor was at stake, and when it took the form of a one-week vacation, the movement was irresistible....[22]

Although missionaries sometimes compromised with student demands (McTyeire students were given a three-day holiday instead of the week for which they had asked), as time went on they asserted their authority over their students more strongly. Many suspected that their students, like Chao, used patriotism as a pretext to put off school work and examinations. Other missionaries simply believed that students had no right to disrupt school activities and that, moreover, students should not attempt to intervene in national and international affairs. This led to serious clashes between students and mission school administrators as the student movement progressed.[23]

Before 1919, however, there was no consensus among American teaching missionaries that the student movement ought to be curbed. Between the years 1911 and 1919, student protests, although widespread, were primarily directed against internal Chinese events. After 1914, some protests focused on Japanese encroachment on Chinese territory and sovereignty. Since none of these protests was particularly threatening to missionaries or to the status of their work in China, the missionaries continued to give qualified support to their students. Moreover, the student role in these protests paled in comparison to that of merchants and older intellectuals.[24]

In the government schools in this era, the Republican educational establishment made deliberate attempts to foster nationalistic ideals in students through a new textbook series, the *National Readers*. These books were extravagant in their praise of Western culture, particularly Western science and technology, while harshly criticizing the Chinese social system. Educators hoped that by stirring shame in the students for the weakness and backwardness of their country, they would develop strong nationalist sentiments and devote their lives to the regeneration of China. Both mission and government schools used these textbooks until 1922.[25]

The May Fourth Movement of 1919, aimed at both Japan and the Chinese government, is generally acknowledged to be the beginning of a genuinely national student movement in China. In 1915, Japan issued the infamous Twenty-one Demands, which aimed to bring China under virtual Japanese control. President Yuan Shikai was able to put off one set of demands for later consideration but was compelled to accede to the others. Japan also got the Allies to agree that German concession in Shandong, which Japan had seized in 1914, should be turned over to Japan after WWI. When all of these secret agreements were revealed at Versailles, a storm of protest swept China. In Beijing, some three thousand students met at Tiananmen Square and, after a mass meeting, burned the home of Cao Rulin, a pro-Japanese cabinet member whom the students condemned as a traitor. Students also tracked down and beat another prominent pro-Japanese official, Zhang Zongxiang. After police arrested thirty-two students, new demonstrations erupted to demand their release. This led to a spiraling increase in demonstrations as students who had not originally been involved came out into the streets to protest both the Versailles Treaty and the government arrests of student protesters. Student Unions sprang up all over China in the months following May 4, and helped to coordinate student protest activities in the years that followed.[26]

The May Fourth demonstrations had a great impact on educational institutions in China. Government and mission schools in over two hundred cities were closed by striking students. Although students in mission schools had not taken a leading role in this movement, they were not far behind the government school students in voicing their outrage at the Versailles "sell-out" and subsequent government action against protesters. One student from Yenching University was among the first to be arrested in Beijing. Mission schools that did not initially participate in the movement found it difficult to remain uninvolved. In Fuzhou, for example, although the mission boys' schools in the city had closed immediately, the Foochow Girls' College continued to hold classes. "But when our girls learned that a neighboring girls' school had closed," wrote missionary Elizabeth Perkins, "they were fearful of being called unpatriotic by the already free students." The missionaries obligingly canceled the final examinations and sent the girls home.[27]

The sudden and tempestuous emergence of a national student movement startled the missionaries after the relative quiescence and pessimism of students during the war years. The permanent organizational base formed to structure and guide future student protests was another surprising element of the May Fourth Movement. The missionary response to the new movement varied considerably. Some missionaries applauded the students. "To some of us foreigners in China this recent demonstration of national consciousness on the part of the students is a most encouraging sign," wrote Robert McClure. "We have often felt shame for the Chinese for the way they have sat by and watched their country being gambled away by corrupt officials, and imposed upon by selfish neighbors." On the other end of the spectrum, a few missionaries were determined not to have their schools upset by the patriotic movement. Lois Young, writing shortly after the movement began, threatened to "wave her big stick" if the girls in her Suzhou school joined other students in the city in demonstrations.[28]

For the majority of missionaries, the issue of whether or not to support the student movement was not clear cut. Alice Reed found the spectacle of mission school boys, on strike along with students from government schools, going about the countryside giving patriotic speeches "strange but fine." Abbie Sanderson, a Baptist missionary, thought the student movement was both gratifying and dangerous; she approved of the spirit of patriotism but hoped it would not get out of hand. Even Lois Young, who initially did not want her students involved, unbent slightly by August. "[T]here are promising signs in the Student Association [of Suzhou]," she wrote. "If it can only be led and guided right, it may be able to do great things for China."[29]

These ambivalent statements were characteristic of the missionary response to the May Fourth Movement. It was clearly an advance for the student movement in terms of organizational unity and enhanced communication, but the fact that the students were once again focusing on anti-imperialism undoubtedly contributed to missionary ambivalence toward the movement. There is also evidence to suggest that the collective nature of Chinese student nationalism was repellent to the missionaries. One missionary disparaged the Chinese by saying that they were "the original strikers," incapable of individual action. Episcopalian missionary Venetia Cox agreed, adding, "It disgusts you lots of times."[30]

The real turning point, however, in the missionary attitude toward nationalism among Chinese students was the May Thirtieth Incident of 1925, when the twin issues of anti-foreignism and anti-imperialism surged to the forefront. The death of a Chinese worker at the hands of a Japanese foreman in a Japanese-owned cotton mill in Shanghai touched off student protests when police from the International Settlement, an enclave of foreign privilege and sovereignty on Chinese soil, dispersed Chinese who were attempting to hold a memorial service. A group of students took to the streets to rouse public opinion against both the police of the International Settlement and the Japanese. When a number of the students were arrested, an angry mob gathered in front of the precinct where the students were being held and demanded their release. The police, under orders from a British officer, fired on the crowd. Eleven Chinese were killed on the spot; others died later from their injuries. The consequent uproar reverberated throughout China with local, national and international implications. On the local level, the Chinese demanded drastic revisions in the governance of the Shanghai International Settlement. Nationally and internationally, the Chinese reopened the explosive question of abolishing extraterritoriality.[31]

Since the majority of foreigners in China were protected by extraterritoriality, American missionaries found themselves targets, although not the primary ones, of the protests that followed the May Thirtieth Incident. A few Chinese students claimed that the protests were not anti-foreign, but the experiences of most missionaries led them to the opposite conclusion. Even Abbie Sanderson, who was not given to exaggerating events, noted apprehensively that the atmosphere in the Baptist Boys' Academy in Shantou was "far from cordial to foreigners."[32]

Unlike the 1905 boycott, in which American missionaries successfully disassociated themselves from the immigration policies of their government and presented themselves as friends of the Chinese, the May Thirtieth Incident allowed no such escape. American missionaries, along with foreigners of other nationalities, were implicated in the imposition of extraterritoriality on China and were among its direct beneficiaries. It was at this time that American missionaries began to debate the wisdom of maintaining their extraterritorial privileges. Although some missionaries took the position that these privileges were necessary until the Chinese government had proven itself capable of protecting foreigners within its boundaries, other groups began to campaign for the immediate renunciation of extraterritoriality and the revision of the entire nineteenth-century treaty system.[33]

The fact that some American missionaries were ready to relinquish extraterritoriality or at least to consider doing so did not greatly impress the Chinese. Again, as during the May Fourth Movement, the mission schools felt the impact of an aroused Chinese public as, led by local and national Student Unions, students all over China refused to go to classes, took to the streets in mass parades, and boycotted British and Japanese goods. The mission higher primary and middle schools were particularly affected, although different schools had different experiences. Mary Margaret Moninger in Quongzhou and Lois Young in Suzhou were both relieved that their schools had already closed for the term when the disturbances broke out. The two independent women's Christian colleges weathered the storm fairly well: Ginling suspended classes for a few weeks but managed to finish the term's work, while Hwa Nan simply closed two weeks early. Students at Yenching University, bolstered by the faculty's supportive "Yenching Manifesto," contented themselves with a boycott of British goods. Faculty at Soochow University also issued a sympathetic manifesto and their students did not strike.[34]

Other mission schools were less fortunate. Abbie Sanderson reported that although the girls from the Shantou Baptist School had been sent home to avoid trouble, the boys had refused to leave. "The teachers have practically lost power over them," Sanderson wrote worriedly. "They are pretty nearly a mob most of the time." Lida Ashmore, who also taught at this school, told her daughter that the boys had hissed at the missionary leading the chapel exercises and shuffled their feet until he was forced to dismiss them.[35]

One of the most damaging incidents occurred in Shanghai, at St. John's University, an Episcopalian institution with roots reaching well back into the nineteenth century. In the weeks after the May Thirtieth Incident, students demanded that the school flags be lowered to half-mast as a sign of mourning for those killed by the police in the International Settlement. The missionaries refused to permit the American flag to be lowered because they feared that this would "indicate that Americans were in sympathy with the rioters." According to Gladys Bundy, a teacher at a nearby Episcopalian high school, the students then "struck en masse, left the school in a body and signed a paper that not one of them would ever enter the place again." Quite possibly none of them did, for with the help of local sympathizers and returned students, the striking students established their own university, Guang Hua [Kwang Hwa] University. The new university opened within a year, with an enrollment of one thousand students.[36]

Although St. John's was the only mission school to suffer so severe a blow, missionaries were aware that, in the wake of the May Thirtieth Incident, Chinese government schools often made appeals to the patriotism of Christian school students, trying to persuade them to withdraw from foreign-run schools. In Nanjing, local patriots established the May 30th School and offered special inducements to mission school students if they would enroll in what Presbyterian Caroline Lee called "that school of hate."[37] The fortunes of Christian education in China had not yet reached their nadir. In the two years preceding the Nanjing Incident of 1927, however, mission and government schools alike were in an almost constant state of uproar.

By this time, the unease missionaries had initially expressed about Chinese nationalism hardened into solid antipathy. One missionary went so far as to liken Chinese nationalism to idolatry.[38] Until the May Thirtieth Incident, most educational missionaries had harbored the hope that the patriotic energies of their students could be put to use in Christian service. Although the emphasis on social service in the mission schools was not a direct response to the student movement, missionaries did attempt to link the two in an effort to control the activities of students in mission schools. Ultimately the missionaries did not believe that they had succeeded in redirecting student activism into Christian channels, but they had some successes, especially with female students.

The Student Movement and the Missionary Service Ideal

Service to others, along with sacrifice of self, were two fundamental hallmarks of a Christian, according to American missionaries. Although they recognized that the Chinese also lauded service to others, missionaries criticized the Chinese for limiting this spirit of helpfulness to members of their own family and clan. One missionary argued that until the Chinese realized the necessity of extending service beyond the ties of kinship, there could be no true patriotism in China.[39] Service, then, was touted by missionaries as both a Christian and a patriotic virtue.

An emphasis on service had long existed in Christian schools in China, many of which claimed to embody an ideal of service. Yenching University, for example, adopted the motto, "Freedom through Truth for Service" (*I Zhen-li De Ziyou Er Fuwu*). Ginling Women's College proclaimed that its purpose was to educate "Christian women for Christian service." Hangchow Christian College similarly wanted to train men "for leadership in service to church, state, and society." Missionaries did not reserve service for one sex alone, and they promoted it as both Christian and patriotic.[40] Before the turn of the century, however, most mission schools urged service to the Christian church rather than to the Chinese people or nation. Although missionaries never gave up hoping that their students would give service to the Christian church, either as preachers, teachers, or evangelists, in the twentieth century Christian service also meant social service, and the missionaries began to require that their students put in time doing a variety of work in the local community.

There were three main reasons for this shift in emphasis from narrow church-related service to a broader commitment to serving the community and nation. The evolution of the Social Gospel among liberal Protestants in the United States was one significant factor. The Social Gospel focused less on individual salvation and the afterlife than on the regeneration of human society and the realization of the Kingdom of God on earth. In China, this meant that missionaries, while still striving for individual conversions, worked also to ameliorate the numerous social problems they observed in the country. As we will see, the service activities into which the missionaries directed their students had both Christian and social applications.[41]

It was not until the early twentieth century that missionaries influenced by the theology of the Social Gospel arrived in China. Only in 1914 did the *Chinese Recorder* begin publishing a substantial number of articles concerning the Social Gospel and how it affected missionary work.[42] It is difficult to gauge how many missionaries considered themselves part of the Social Gospel movement. Even within the theologically conservative denominations it is likely that missionaries involved in medical or educational work, which naturally had a social orientation, believed in the efficacy and value of social service work. One missionary argued that the majority of American missionaries in the twentieth century supported the Social Gospel, although it is unclear how he arrived at this conclusion.[43]

The other two factors behind the emphasis on social service in the mission schools were grounded not in theological developments in the United States but rather in conditions in China itself. One of these was the desire to promote a sense of solidarity or "school spirit" in their students; the other was the need to respond to the emergence of the Chinese student patriotic movement. The issue of encouraging a group spirit among students was particularly urgent in higher level mission schools, because these schools recruited beyond the immediate neighborhood and it was not uncommon for their students to speak different dialects. This was a distinct obstacle to the formation of school unity. "A thing that has puzzled and worried us," wrote George Barbour, a teacher at Yenching University, in 1924, "has been the curious difficulty we have had in trying to fuse the student group and produce anything resembling a college loyalty or esprit de corps of any kind, beyond rather pathetic cliques of a definitely provincial character...."[44] The Chinese Ministry of Education mandated that Mandarin (*Guoyu*) be taught in the elementary schools beginning in 1920 and in the upper-level schools in 1922, but it took time before the effect of the uniform language policy was felt on the high school and college level.[45]

Some schools adopted school uniforms as a means of drawing students into a kind of visible community. Social service, however, was a more substantial effort to bring students together outside the classroom and help break down provincial clannishness. Students engaging in community service worked in groups and were clearly identified to the local Chinese community as students from the neighborhood mission school, which enhanced the cohesiveness of the group. One missionary mentioned that when boys from his school went out to teach hygiene and preach Christianity in the surrounding villages, they marched under the banners of their school.[46] The mixture of social and Christian service is clearly evident here.

The third factor, the emergence of the Chinese student movement, was probably the most significant in the focus on social service in the mission schools, and yet the relationship between the two is by no means simple. Although the missionaries often linked patriotism and service, as previously noted, it is not clear that social service within the mission schools was necessarily a response to the student movement. It seems more likely that the two movements evolved separately, although the missionaries hoped that the enthusiasm of the student movement could be harnessed for Christian purposes. Noting with approval the patriotic fervor of boys in the Caroline Johnson Memorial School in Fuxing in 1911, the principal commented, "If such students as these, full of patriotism, can be used as preachers, our church will surely become a very strong and prosperous church in China."[47]

Although American missionaries hoped to use the student movement to further the Christian cause, they did not really strive to control it until after 1919, and particularly after the May Thirtieth Incident in 1925. It therefore cannot be argued that the missionaries required social service of their students solely to restrain the student movement. Moreover, as we shall see, the primary means of controlling student activism within the mission schools was to punish students who insisted on flouting the rules of the school. There was, nevertheless, a link between social service and the student movement in the mission schools. Missionaries were not only apprehensive about activism that lacked a Christian focus, particularly if it was anti-foreign, but they also argued that running charity schools, helping victims of natural disasters, and spreading scientific and hygienic knowledge were all positive and constructive things that students could do to help their country while they prepared themselves for more substantial leadership roles in adulthood. These actions also contrasted with striking and demonstrating, which American teaching missionaries regarded as destructive. They frequently told their students that they ought to attend to their studies rather than shouting slogans on the streets.[48] Recognizing and generally sympathizing with the restlessness and dissatisfaction of Chinese students in the early twentieth century, missionaries offered Christian service as a legitimate outlet.[49]

Thus students in mission schools, especially in middle or higher level schools, were expected to undertake social service in their communities. In one early report on social service in a mission school, Chester Fuson wrote that since 1910, students in Canton Christian College had engaged in a variety of community volunteer work; they ran a village school for poor children, did open-air speaking on Sunday afternoons, and ran a night school where the college's workmen studied Chinese, arithmetic, the Bible, history, geography, English, and singing. By 1916, the students were in charge of two schools for poor boys and one for poor girls. Students also established and taught Sunday Schools, distributed pamphlets as part of a science lecture band, and went with preaching groups into the countryside to speak on Christianity, agriculture, and hygiene. The Student Christian Association further operated a Farming and Industrial School for poor village children.[50]

This list of service activities for students in Christian schools was fairly typical. In addition to charity schools, Sunday Schools, night schools, and lecture or preaching bands, students also established famine refuges, where refugees were not only provided with the necessities of life but were also offered a wide range of courses. Women students often ran mothers' meetings, where they could air their knowledge of childcare, psychology, health and hygiene. "Well baby" clinics were common, as were exhibitions demonstrating the proper way to care for a child. Some students worked with medical missionaries, giving vaccines and founding clinics in poor villages.[51]

By the early 1920s, social service was already an integral part of student life in most mission schools, with the possible exception of lower primary schools. A report of the education committee of the American Presbyterian mission recommended that social service begin on a voluntary basis in the second year of middle school and form part of the regular school curriculum in the third year. The report listed a number of social problems for students to investigate: industrial conditions, sanitation and public health, crime and delinquency, "defectives," boat people, education, amusements, family life, and religion. The influence of the Social Gospel is clearly evident in this program, which also reflects missionary awareness of the considerable changes, like industrial development, that had occurred in Chinese social life since the late nineteenth century. Moreover, the emphasis on investigating crime, delinquency, and amusements was almost certainly indicative of the missionaries' critique of the Westernization of Chinese social life in the urban areas.[52]

This report also made clear gender distinctions in the types of work recommended for boys and girls. For boys, the report suggested work in YMCA night schools, health exhibits, Boy Scouts, prison visitation, training schools for "boat boys," preaching and running vacation Bible schools. The list for girls contained certain significant additions and omissions: hospital visitation replaced prison visitation for girls; they were to work with "boat girls" and organize playgrounds for girls; there was no mention of preaching; and cooking, sewing, and teaching mothers' courses, along with assistant nursing were added to the list.[53]

It is impossible to know to what degree this gender specificity mirrored missionary gender beliefs and to what extent Chinese gender beliefs were a factor, but student social service followed the gender patterns of the American missionaries. Although the work itself was quite similar, "boys' work" focused on Chinese men and boys, while "girls' work" was confined to efforts to aid Chinese women and girls. Boys did not hold mothers' (or fathers') meetings, and girls did not establish or teach in farming schools, but some girls were permitted to preach to audiences of Chinese women. In all likelihood, these distinct sexual spheres for voluntary activity stemmed from both missionary beliefs about "woman's work" and Chinese beliefs about sexual segregation, because even though the latter was rapidly being undermined by more open relations between the sexes in the urban areas, the villages where much of this work was carried out were slower than the cities to adopt the new ways.

American teaching missionaries regarded social service as a tangible, meaningful way of expressing both patriotism and Christianity. Had the student movement never emerged in China, mission schools would still have committed themselves to serving the local communities in which they existed. Because the student movement did develop, however, and particularly because the missionaries believed that the volatile students had to be "guided right," as Lois Young put it, missionaries attempted to push their students into service work as a substitute for forms of patriotic protest that the missionaries abhorred. Interestingly, this tactic was more successful with mission school girls than with the boys.

Gender in the Christian Student Movement

A quite striking pattern of gender differentiation, unremarked by historians, appeared in the student movement in the Christian schools.[54] When girls participated, they initially did so separately, reflecting Chinese beliefs about sexual segregation. By 1919, these traditional ideas had declined drastically among students so in the May Fourth protests the sexes worked together for the first time, rather than maintaining separate meetings or marches.[55] The old taboos had not entirely lost their potency, however, for when the seven hundred members of the Kiungchow [Quongzhou] Student Association on the island of Hainan decided to invite girls from the local mission and government schools to attend a three-day meeting in 1920, they did so with some trepidation. According to missionary Mary Margaret Moninger, the boys feared "the rowdy element" among the Student Association might behave inappropriately toward the girls, causing the entire Association to lose face.[56]

In spite of the developing trend for cooperation between the sexes in the student movement, it soon became obvious to missionaries that Chinese women and girls in the Christian schools had a fundamentally different approach than male students to nationalistic protests. Missionaries regarded Chinese women as playing a unique role within the student movement as the practical, level-headed members who reined in the excessive zeal of their male comrades. Luella Miner described a student meeting at Yenching University at which two women students exercised their calming influence over the men:

> The young men are excited, and in a moment of passionate disagreement the meeting seems about to break up, when one of these young women rises and in a few earnest words pleads that the great cause may not be forgotten. The storm calms, the presiding officer thanks the speaker, and after several hours, when darkness begins to fall and the two young women withdraw, all rise to show their respect.

Miner was thrilled by the men's respect, but even more so by the role the women had played. Having feared that some educated Chinese women might become, in Miner's words, "Amazons or frenzied suffragettes," she was relieved to observe Christian young women behaving in a manner consistent with Christian gender ideology.[57]

It is tempting to speculate that Miner and others were simply projecting their own gender beliefs onto the student movement in the Christian schools since their approach to women's political action favored reconciliation over confrontation and was enmeshed in beliefs about the higher moral tone that women would bring to politics. There may indeed have been an element of missionaries' seeing what they wanted to see in the participation of Chinese girls in the student movement. There is, however, also clear evidence that Chinese girls and young women, at least in the mission schools, were active in different ways than boys and young men.

In some instances, mission school girls stood aloof from patriotic protests. Following an anti-Japanese boycott and the destruction of Japanese goods in the local shops by boy students in Changsha in 1920, all of the schools in the city, with the exception of the I-Chang Girls' Collegiate School (and one other unspecified school), were temporarily shut down by striking students. The I-Chang students did not take part in the protests, nor was their school closed, which led outside students to revile them as unpatriotic. Similarly, when mission and government school boys in Nanjing decided that a parade was the only appropriate way to commemorate "National Humiliation Day" (the day on which Yuan Shikai had agreed to most of the Japanese Twenty-one Demands), women from

Hwa Nan College for Women declined to join them. According to Methodist missionary Elsie Reik, the women "sympathized absolutely in the spirit of responsibility felt by the students, but they were convinced that for them as Christian Chinese young women, they had found a more effective expression of their loyalty to China." Rather than marching, the young women went into the surrounding villages to do patriotic work, explaining to villagers the meaning of the Chinese flag and some of the current events in the country.[58]

When young women joined men in student activities, they may well have enjoyed the courtesy and deference that Luella Miner described. When they did not participate or refused to follow the lead of male students, however, the women and girls had to endure a good deal of verbal and, on one or two occasions, physical abuse. George Barbour, a missionary teacher at Yenching University in Beijing, noted that Yenching men resented the unanimity of the women students, who would not vote for a student sympathy strike in 1925 for a protester killed by the police. When they denounced the women as cowards, the men precipitated a quarrel with the women that disrupted school work for over a week because the women refused to attend classes on the men's campus until they had received a suitably abject apology.[59]

Female students often found their own ways of expressing their love of China, even when this meant going against the current of the larger student movement or against the actions of local mission school boys. Doing patriotic propaganda work among village children and adults (particularly mothers) was a favorite form of activism by mission school girls. Sometimes, the girls performed patriotic plays and gave "entertainments" within the school to which the public was invited. Girls at the Methodist Keen School in Tianjin incorporated prayers into their patriotic meetings and refused to attend city Student Union meetings held on Sundays.[60]

This gender-linked pattern of behavior was consistent throughout the student movement of the 1920s, although the pressure the young women had to withstand increased as the temper of the students grew more heated. This was especially true when student protests began to target foreign missionaries and their schools. Although they grew progressively more distressed by the unruliness of their boy students, missionaries believed that they had every reason to be proud of the girls in their schools. "The girls are just as responsive [to nationalistic appeals as the boys], but they have a more balanced and truly practical and constructive reaction," Matilda Thurston wrote in 1928. "This is 'conservative' in the good sense of the word," she noted, "the correct opposite is destructive [*sic*]."[61]

Thus when girls in Christian schools responded to the call of Chinese nationalism in the 1920s, they most often did so in ways that paralleled the social service activities to which they were already accustomed. It was the boys who diverged from missionary ideals of appropriate student activism when they turned to striking, demonstrating, and boycotting. Missionaries often attributed this gender-linked nationalism to inherent gender differences, arguing that "girls have much more sense of service than boys" or, more bluntly, that "girls are more civilized than boys."[62]

Since their gender beliefs predisposed American missionaries to identify women as inherently inclined to an ideal of service, missionaries were not surprised that female students were more tractable than the boys. Yet the missionaries also believed that Christianity had the power to mold male behavior. Missionary men, having devoted their lives to the service of Christ, were also advocates of the service ideal. For this reason, missionaries were often deeply disappointed in their boy students, which contributed to the deepening sense of discouragement among American missionary educators in China in the twentieth century.

Gender was not the only component of differing responses to the student movement in the mission schools. Age, or the level of schooling, was also important. Although mission girls' schools of all grades were generally less disrupted by the student movement than the boys' schools, young women in the Christian colleges were by far the most conservative among the students. According to the missionaries, the most active students were in high school.[63] Abbie Sanderson reported ruefully in 1921 that thirty-four of her middle school students had decided that they could not in good conscience promise to obey the rules of the school, for "in matters of patriotism they would decide for themselves and would in no wise hearken to the voice of teachers, matron, principal, or anyone!" Similarly, Elsie Reik described her high school students as "naughty...little rascals" in comparison with her college students, who gave her no trouble.[64]

It is not clear why there should have been this visible difference between high school girls and college women or, indeed, why the male and female response to the student movement should have been so distinct in the mission schools. Discussing the role of the mission school students in protests of the 1930s, sociologist Olga Lang has argued that mission school students were generally more conservative than those in government schools because they frequently came from wealthy families and because they had been imbued with Christian precepts, both of which made them less open to radical ideas than government school students. But before 1950, very few Chinese youths were educated and the majority of them came from elite backgrounds, particularly in high school and college. It is not clear, moreover, that there is anything innately conservative about Christianity, particularly in the Chinese context. Nor does Lang's argument explain the remarkable gender differences within the Christian schools.[65]

Lang asserts that women in the Christian schools were less active than men because they believed that their own position could best be improved through liberal political reform. However well this argument applies to the Nanjing Decade (1927–1937), it cannot be said to fit the earlier phases of the student movement. If political reform was in fact their goal, it is curious that women from the mission schools eschewed the political-pressure tactics of the male students in favor of educating village women or undertaking charitable works. From the actions engaged in by women and girls from the Christian schools, moreover, it is far from obvious that they were seeking only to improve their own lot. In addition to offering lessons in childcare and hygiene to their less-educated sisters, female students from mission schools tried to spread patriotic ideas among the villagers and to promote the manufacture and use of Chinese goods in order to reduce dependency upon foreign imports.[66]

The fact that Chinese women in the Christian schools were motivated by patriotism no less than young men means that there must be some other explanation for their different responses to the student movement. In addition to citing inherent gender differences, missionaries offered their own explanations for this phenomenon. Some missionaries agreed that "the girls realize that if they do not get their education here and now they will not get any." This is reasonable, for although by the late 1920s most of the government and mission colleges were open to women and there were increasing numbers of lower level girls' schools, education for women was still a rare privilege. College women in China were particularly conscious of their elite, pioneer status and did not take it lightly; missionaries observed with awe how hard all of their female students worked at their lessons. Chinese women did not like to miss classes in order to attend mass meetings or demonstrations. Even when they did go to meetings of the Student Union, some girls' schools sent representatives rather than attending *en masse*, a practice that displeased some male students, who wondered sardonically if one could show one's patriotism by proxy.[67]

Chinese women students were also aware that many people regarded women's education as experimental and that it therefore behooved the women to be particularly circumspect in their behavior. When middle school students from a government girls' normal school became embroiled in a quarrel with boys from a nearby mission school and posted insulting placards on the streets, it was the girls, not the boys, who were criticized. Another indication of the girl students' perceived need for caution in their social behavior was that they shared with the missionaries a deep concern for the reputation of the schools they attended.[68]

On certain occasions, however, girls did strike or demonstrate just as the boys did. To the missionaries the explanation was simple: the girls who demonstrated were either too easily swayed by male students or had been browbeaten into compliance. "If our girls were left alone," Elsie Reik insisted, "they would be reasonable and we would have no trouble, but boy agitators get after them and tell them they are unpatriotic and under the domination of foreigners, who are alienating them from their own people." Abbie Sanderson's opinion was similar to Reik's. She explained that girls were often influenced by boy students because they were tied to the boys through kinship or marriage.[69]

Assertions that the girls and women were unpatriotic if they would not join in the larger student movement were exactly the charges that were leveled at mission school boys and men by students from the government schools. Both male and female students in the mission schools were caught between the conflicting demands of the student nationalist movement and Christian education. For the older female students, a desire to play an independent role in the student movement prompted them to reject male leadership. Because of their thirst for education, their consciousness of their unique status in China, and the changing roles of women in the society at large, college women were both disinclined to jeopardize their status and determined to choose their own paths in politics, careers, and marriage.

This is best illustrated by examining a complex battle between male and female Christian college students, ostensibly over patriotism, that was waged in May 1928. The quarrel erupted after male students from Nanking University discovered that women from neighboring Ginling had danced with British sailors on the cruiser *Cumberland*. A group of university men posted a placard on the back wall of Ginling that read, "You who danced with the foreign soldiers are not worthy to step on the ground of the university." One man wrote sarcastically to a Shanghai newspaper that "Ginling girls have opened a new chapter in the history of women in China." Missionary administrators at Ginling were barraged with letters that equated the women students with prostitutes and charged them with being "slaves to the foreigners" and not understanding the meaning of patriotism. Ginling women responded indignantly, calling the university men "rude and crazy."[70]

The issue, however, involved more than the patriotism of the women students; it was linked to long-standing disagreements between the men and women over issues such as coeducation, closer social contacts between the two schools, and marriage. Changing mores concerning the relations between the sexes and the end of traditional sexual segregation led the men eagerly to seek friendship with the women. Men students at Nanking wanted the women's college to merge with their own to create a coeducational college. They also wanted to socialize with the women. The point of all of this activity was the search for a mate. Now that Chinese young men were permitted to choose their own brides, they tended to look upon the neighboring Christian women's college as a source of potential wives. The primary reason the Nanking University men were so outraged to learn of the women's behavior on shipboard was that women had steadfastly refused to have anything to do, socially, with the male students. The fact that the men in question were British sailors on a gunboat protecting foreign privileges simply compounded the insult.[71]

Women from Ginling did not regard any of these issues—coeducation, social contacts, and marriage—in the same way that the men did. We have seen, in the previous chapter, their negative reaction to the suggestion that their school merge with Nanking University. In terms of increased contacts between the sexes, including their participation in the student movement, the women argued that although the men paid lip service to the ideal of "cooperation," what they really meant was that women ought to follow the lead of the men. The women refused to play a subordinate role, saying that they would work with the men only on the basis of equality. "The unwillingness of University students to have sufficient regard for the woman's point of view," wrote Matilda Thurston, caused Ginling students to be highly suspicious of male pleas for "cooperation."[72]

Marriage was similarly a contentious issue, because many of the women hoped to defer marriage in favor of a career. From their perspective, this was a patriotic thing to do. "I believe in homes," wrote Lucy Wang, the first Chinese president of Hwa Nan College for Women in Fujian, "but China is in the time of building and some of us young women must turn our backs [on] such blessing and comfort [if] China is to be saved." Linking the elite status of educated women with both nationalist and service ideals, Wang added, "Trained women are so few that everyone who has any education ought to work for our people and society."[73]

The fundamental issue underlying these various conflicts was the right of Chinese women to determine their own lives independently. Although younger students were perhaps more easily swayed by appeals to their patriotism, college women preferred to define patriotism in their own way, rather than allowing the men to dictate to them the forms their patriotism should take. To American teaching missionaries, upset by the direction women's emancipation and the student nationalist movement had taken in China, it was a relief to find that the patriotism of the college women, at least, was service-oriented, Christian and womanly.

Missionary Disenchantment with the Student Movement

With the exception of college women, it was clear to American missionaries by the late 1920s that Christian social service would not in itself absorb the energies of their students. Seeking to quell the unrest in their schools, teaching missionaries generally treated student protests as infractions of discipline rather than taking seriously their political content. Initially, missionaries blamed the Student Unions for fomenting trouble. American missionaries had been ambivalent about these organizations since their inception and soon came to believe that the Unions were inimical to the interests of democratic, Christian-oriented patriotism. They were convinced, for example, that the Unions were not democratically run. Missionaries claimed that the majority of Christian school students were not radical or interested in protests, but a handful of hot-headed students overrode the objections of the majority and forced the entire Student Union to follow their lead. Missionaries often expressed disgust that their male students were not manly enough to stand up to the more radical students. "'[B]ut they [government school students] *scowl* at me,'" Gladys Bundy wrote, mocking a mission school student's explanation of why he had gone along with a protest against his better judgment. "I can just imagine a bunch of American boys acting that way!"[74]

Missionaries also believed that the Student Unions were not, in fact, controlled by students. On the contrary, "outside elements" manipulated students for their own political ends. It was these outsiders, whom the missionaries usually identified as communists, who were behind anti-imperialist agitation. The students were simply pawns.[75] While recent studies of the student movement of the 1920s make clear that both the Guomindang and Chinese Communist Party attempted to use the Student Unions to spread their propaganda and recruit new members, this does not mean that the students were completely manipulated by either group. Weaned on the *National Readers* that emphasized China's humiliations by foreigners and schooled, for the most part, in large cities, where current events were widely discussed and the foreign presence was visible, high school and college students in China did not require outside manipulation to kindle their patriotism.[76]

American missionaries may have blamed outsiders for the disturbances among their students as a way of explaining to mission supporters in the United States the seeming ingratitude of mission school students. In their letters home, missionaries often stressed that although other schools had suffered from the student movement, their own students had remained loyal. Gladys Bundy, for example, wrote: "The more we hear of what was done in some of our other schools, the prouder we feel of our Boone students." Presbyterian William Cummings was forced to tell his home church that twenty-six boys had left his school after a friend of theirs had been expelled. Cummings hastened to add, however, that given the spirit of the times, the incident was not really very serious. When their own schools were forced to close, missionaries noted that, in comparison with the government schools, they had not experienced much turmoil. American missionaries feared that anti-foreign student protests might be one cause of declining donations to missions in the 1920s.[77]

In addition to their fears that the student movement might adversely affect their financial support, missionaries worried that their own counsel counted for less and less among their students. For years, missionaries had claimed to be training the future leaders of China and thus to have an indirect but genuine influence over the course of China's development. The Student Unions contradicted missionary claims to authority and influence over their students. This, as much as anything else, was responsible for missionary hostility toward the Student Unions. At the Mary Porter Gamewell School in Beijing, for example, missionaries were outraged when their female students "ignored the authority of the mission" and contacted representatives of a Student Union. The girls won their battle to join the Union when Gamewell alumnae threatened the missionaries with some unspecified retribution.[78]

Mission school students were in the middle of this tug-of-war. Because they attended foreign-run schools, these students were eager, as missionary Alice Margaret Huggins wrote in 1925, "to prove that they weren't under the thumb of the foreign missionaries." But when students in one mission school joined the local Student Union against the advice of the missionaries, the Student Union turned on them and, by pressure and threats, forced the most prominent Christian students to drop out of school.[79] The problem was that while the government school students encouraged the participation of mission school students in the nationalist movement, they often regarded these students with suspicion or hostility. When the Student Unions linked the Christian schools to foreign imperialism, students in the mission schools became legitimate targets of abuse. Government school students often taunted the mission school students as "foreign slaves" or "Chinese in face but not in action." During demonstrations, government school students sometimes marched to local mission schools and shouted under the classroom windows for the students to come out and join them. If they refused, the government school students would continue to shout in order to disrupt classes. Minnie Vautrin noted in her diary in 1927 that some mission schools received anonymous letters warning that if the students did not follow the lead of the Student Unions, their school would be attacked and forced to close. Methodist Elsie Reik reported in the same year that one school had discovered carbolic acid in its rice, apparently an attempt by outsiders to intimidate the students and compel the closing of the school.[80]

In some instances, however, mission school students were able to call upon the Student Unions to aid them in their private battles with the missionaries over issues of authority and discipline. Pressure from outsiders could sometimes compel missionaries to permit their students to take part in patriotic activities, as happened at the Gamewell School when the alumnae took a hand. If students were expelled from a Christian school due to their protest activities, the Student Unions helped to pull strings to get the students enrolled in government institutions.[81]

Although a handful of Christian schools, notably St. John's University and Yale-in-China, had bitter experiences with student uprisings in their schools, the majority were able to continue their work, at least until the upheavals of 1927. It was a trying time, however, for mission school students, who were often torn between their desire to show their love for their country and their appreciation for the Christian school they attended and the missionaries who taught them. It was one thing to talk about foreign imperialism in the abstract; it was another to give imperialism the familiar face of a teacher or principal. Educational missionaries understood and, to some degree, sympathized with their students who struggled with competing allegiances, but they felt they had to curb the student movement in order to carry on their work. When Christian social service failed to contain and channel student activism, missionaries adopted disciplinary measures to maintain a modicum of order.

Missionaries summarily expelled the ringleaders of strikes and boycotts in their schools when they were able to identify these students. Expelled for his role in establishing a society for "Discussion of Foreign Relations," a student at the Presbyterian Han Mei Boys' School wrote one of the missionaries in charge, asking, "In the Bible wasn't it Peter who was told to forgive his enemies seventy times seven? Well, how would it be to forgive me just once?" His appeal to the religious sensibilities of the missionary failed; although she was inclined to be lenient, she was not convinced that the student's repentance was genuine.[82]

Once the instigators were removed, the missionaries were more forgiving of students whom they judged to have been mere followers. Those students were nevertheless often required to submit written apologies and sign pledges promising to obey the rules of the school in the future. As Mary Margaret Moninger commented, "Our schools are way past the place where we have to beg pupils to come to them," indicating that missionaries did not fear that taking a strict stance toward student discipline would diminish the enrollment in their schools. Students who refused to apologize or pledge good behavior were expelled. Some schools suspended students for a year or readmitted them with nearly a full slate of demerits so that one more misdemeanor would result in their expulsion.[83]

A more serious step was simply to close the school for the rest of the term and send the students home.[84] Mission schools also began, often for the first time, to exercise caution in enrolling students. Because since the late nineteenth century large numbers of youths had been clamoring to register, many mission schools used entrance examinations to determine who could enroll. Some had also insisted that students come with character references, either from their home church or, if they were not Christians, from some prominent, respectable person in their community. Prior to the emergence of the student movement, however, this practice had been primarily an expedient means of allowing the missionaries to select students from a large pool of applicants.[85] Now, many mission schools began to pick their pupils with considerably greater care. Even at Ginling Women's College, where missionaries were proud of the loyalty of their students, missionaries admitted in 1927 that they were not going to risk having unknown new students upset the calm of the school; only thirty new students were to be admitted and they were to be chosen based on how well they seemed likely to conform to Ginling's atmosphere. Henry Lacy, a Methodist missionary, wrote that in order to eliminate troublemakers, all students in his school would henceforth have to provide the names of three men who would guarantee their good behavior.[86]

At the same time a renewed debate broke out over whether Christian schools should limit themselves to educating children with some connection to the Chinese Christian community or whether they should continue to receive all students who cared to register, requiring letters from guarantors and pledges of obedience from the students. As a result of student unrest in the 1920s, a number of mission schools concluded that it would be prudent to retreat from the open policies of previous years and attempt to fill their schools primarily with Christians. These missionaries argued that it was the non-Christian students who were responsible for disturbances in the mission schools, and that it was a mistake to take in too many students who were not religious. Lida Ashmore wrote her daughter in 1926 that she had "never believed in taking in such hordes of boys not in any way connected with our [Christian] families" since it meant lowering the Christian atmosphere of the school. Similarly, when the American Lutherans planned their new college in China in 1919, they decided that no more than 25 per cent of the students could be unbaptized and none would be accepted who were hostile to Christianity.[87]

Following the May 30th Incident in 1925, the optimism that had characterized nineteenth-century educational missionaries all but disappeared. Upset when they observed social changes in China that diverged from Christian ideals, missionaries were likewise disillusioned with the student nationalism that had seemed so promising a quarter of a century earlier. Some missionaries regarded the tempestuous mass movements of the 1920s not as the sign of a revitalized China but as the work of the devil.[88] Other missionaries despaired of the future of missionary work in China. Frank Gamewell, a survivor of the Boxer siege in 1900, wrote to Reverend John R. Edwards less than a month after the May 30th Incident that the atmosphere in China reminded him of those days. Another Methodist missionary, A. J. Bowen, wrote to Gamewell in deep discouragement, saying that he had advised his children against making the China mission their life's work. It seemed to him that the situation in China could only get worse, in which case he believed all missionaries should be sent home indefinitely. "At any rate," he concluded, "only the strongly optimistic should stay, and I fear that I and the family are rapidly getting out of that class, as are a good many others."[89]

As disenchanted as educational missionaries were with the state of affairs in China in 1925, they were still in control of their schools. Within two years, this was to change. It was not only nationalistic students but also the Chinese Christian community and educational officials who pushed for fundamental changes in the status of the foreign educational system. In their assessment of the student movement, missionaries focused primarily on the negative aspects of Chinese nationalism, reacting bitterly to the voices that called "Foreigners out!" But Chinese nationalism also demanded the empowerment of the Chinese within the Christian church. The cry "Chinese in!" was reiterated by the GMD as, following its ascension to power, it sought to assert its sovereignty by curtailing the independence of mission schools in China. Under these various pressures, missionaries were forced to restructure the staffing policies and curriculum of their schools, as the next chapter will explain.

ENDNOTES

1 Chapter title quotation comes from the Katherine Ward interview, p. 17, MCOHP, 1977, ELCA. See also Georgiana Baucus, "Jack, the Giant-Killer," *Heathen Woman's Friend* 27 (May 1895): 304; *World Missionary Conference* (New York: Fleming H. Revell, Co., 1910), p. 84; Irene McCain to home church, Aug. 14, 1919, Microfilm #108, BWM.

2 Roger Hackett, "Chinese Students in Japan, 1900–1910" *Papers on China*, Vol. 3 (Cambridge: Harvard University Press, 1949), pp. 134–169; Y. C. Wang, *Chinese Intellectuals and the West, 1872–1949* (Chapel Hill: University of North Carolina Press, 1966), p. 26; Gilbert Rozman, ed. *The Modernization of China* (New York: The Free Press, 1981), p. 23.

3 Joseph Esherick, "1911: A Review," Symposium on the 1911 Revolution, *Modern China* 2: 2 (April 1976): 139–226.

4 Another major difference was that in the twentieth century, the students were younger, lived together in crowded dormitories, and were mostly concentrated in large cities and provincial capitals, which were both seats of government and areas with the greatest foreign presence and activity. John Israel, *Student Nationalism in China, 1927–1937* (Stanford: Stanford University Press, 1966), p. 1; Chow Tse-tsung, *The May Fourth Movement: Intellectual Revolution in Modern China* (Cambridge: Harvard University, 1960), pp. 11–12.

5 C. K. Yang, *The Chinese Family in the Communist Revolution* (Cambridge: Massachusetts Institute of Technology Press, 1959), p. 6; Sally Borthwick, *Education and Social Change in China: The Beginnings of the Modern Era* (Stanford: Hoover Institution Press, 1983), p. 119.

6 When Francis C. M. Wei first entered a mission elementary school, his father warned him not to heed the Christian teachings. This advice did not have the desired effect, since Wei not only became a Christian but later the president of the Christian Huachung University. It seems logical that other children did resolutely close their minds to Christianity. See Howard Boorman, ed., *Biographical Dictionary of Republican China*, Vol. 3 (New York: Columbia University Press, 1967), p. 403.

7 Matilda Thurston, Typed Excerpts from Letters, October, 1918, Ginling College, Correspondence, UBCHEA, RG 11, Box 143, Folder 2855, YDSL; William Overholt Interview, p. 102, MCOHP, 1980, ELCA.

8 Cha Twuen Kwei, "The Responsibility of Chinese Students Today," *Nanking University Magazine* (May 1911): 9, Nanking University, UBCHEA, RG 11, Box 235, Folder 3913, YDSL.

9 *Chinese Recorder* 39 (January 1908): 14.

10 Charles Hodge Corbett, *Shantung Christian College* (New York: United Board for Christian Colleges in China, 1955), pp. 75–79. Shantung Christian College students' demand for English might be read as political, assuming it were based on the belief that knowledge of this language would contribute to self-strengthening in China, but it might also be related to students' hopes for employment after graduation.

11 *Republican Advocate* 1: 17 (June 27, 1912): 649–650, 1:31 (November 2, 1912): 1219, and 2: 11 (June 14, 1912): 424, 428.

12 Chow, *The May Fourth Movement*, p. 3; Charlotte Beahan, "The Women's Movement in Late Ch'ing China" (Ph.D. diss., Columbia University, 1976), p. 227; Liao Kuang-

sheng, *Anti-Foreignism and Modernization in China, 1860–1980: Linkage Between Domestic Policies and Foreign Policy* (Hong Kong: The Chinese University Press, 1984), p. 76.

13 Quoted in Tsang Chih Sam, *Nationalism in School Education Since the Opening of the Twentieth Century* (Hong Kong: South China Morning Post, Ltd., 1933), p. 158.

14 Wang, *Chinese Intellectuals and the West*, p. 308; see Teng Ssu-yu and John K. Fairbank, eds., *China's Response to the West: A Documentary Survey, 1839–1923* (Cambridge: Harvard University Press, 1961), pp. 241–245, for a translation of Chen's essay.

15 Charlotte Furth, "May Fourth in History," pp. 59–68, see p. 60, in Benjamin I. Schwartz, ed., *Reflections on the May Fourth Movement : A Symposium* (Cambridge: East Asian Research Center, Harvard University Press, 1972); Delber L. McKee, *Chinese Exclusion vs. the Open Door Policy, 1900–1906: Clashes over China Policy in the Roosevelt Era* (Detroit: Wayne University Press, 1977), chapters one and two; Margaret Field, "The Chinese Boycott of 1905," *Papers on China* Vol. 11 (Cambridge: Harvard University Press, 1957): 63–98.

16 McKee, *Chinese Exclusion*, p. 212; letter from three Corresponding Secretaries of the Methodist Board of Foreign Missions to the U. S. Senate, March 31, 1890, 73-44: 1261-6-1: 05, GBGM.

17 McKee, *Chinese Exclusion*, p. 212.

18 Joseph Esherick, *Reform and Revolution: The 1911 Revolution in Hunan and Hubei* (Berkeley: University of California Press, 1976), pp. 78–80.

19 Margaret C. Burton, *The Education of Women in China* (New York: Fleming H. Revell Co., 1911), p. 177; Charlotte Beahan, "In the Public Eye: Women in Early Twentieth-Century China," pp. 215–238, see p. 226, in Richard Guisso and Stanley Johannesen, eds., *Women in China: Current Directions in Historical Scholarship* (Youngstown, N.Y.: Philo Press, 1981); Chester Fuson to family, Jan. 10, 1908, Chester Fuson Papers, RG 8, Box 71, YDSL.

20 Ella C. Shaw, "A Patriotic Holiday in Nanking," *Woman's Missionary Friend* 40 (July 1908): 238; *Chinese Recorder* 39 (January 1908): 22.

21 *Chinese Recorder* 39 (January 1908): 26.

22 Chao Yang Buwei, trans. Chao Yuenren, *The Autobiography of a Chinese Woman* (Westport, Conn.: Greenwood Press, 1947), p. 78.

23 Randolph Sailer interview, pp. 20–21, MCOHP, 1980, ELCA.

24 Elsie Clark to family, Nov. 12, 1915, Elsie Clark [Krug] Papers, RG 8, Box 43, YDSL; Chow, *The May Fourth Movement*, pp. 23–25; and the *Chinese Recorder* 50 (July 1919): 434.

25 Tsang, *Nationalism in School Education,* chapter four.

26 Chow, *The May Fourth Movement*, pp. 21, 123, 129.

27 John K. Fairbank and Edwin O. Reischauer, *China, Tradition and Transformation* (Boston: George Allen and Unwin, 1979), p. 435; "Report of the Foochow Girls' College," Feb. 1919–Jan. 1920, Elizabeth Perkins Papers, RG 8, Box 159, Folder 50, YDSL.

28 Robert McClure to family, Sept. 1, 1919, Robert and Jeanie Graham McClure Papers, RG 8, Box 121, YDSL; Lois Young to cousin, May 25, 1919, Lois Young Papers, H85.128491, BWM.

29 Alice Reed to family, June 8, 1919, p. 46, Excerpts from Letters, Alice Reed Papers, RG 8, Box 163, YDSL; Abbie Sanderson to family, Aug. 4, 1919, Abbie Sanderson Papers, RG 8, Box 183, YDSL; Lois Young to family, Aug. 16, 1919, Lois Young Papers, H85. 128491, BWM.

30 Alice Reed to family, Jan. 25, 1925, and June 14, 1925, Excerpts from Letters, pp. 52, 81, Alice Reed Papers, RG 8, Box 163, YDSL; Venetia Cox to family, May 17, 1920, Venetia Cox Papers, RG 263, Box 1b, ECMC.

31 Nicholas Clifford, *Shanghai, 1925: Urban Nationalism and the Defense of Foreign Privilege*, Michigan Papers on Chinese Studies, #37 (Ann Arbor: Center for Chinese Studies, 1979), pp. 22, 71.

32 The students of Shanghai College, "Our Point of View," n. d., and Abbie Sanderson to family, June 10, 1925, both in the Abbie Sanderson Papers, RG 8, Box 179, YDSL; Paul Chih Meng, "A Chinese View of the Situation in China," *Missionary Review of the World* (May 1927): 331–336.

33 However, even missionaries who called for the immediate abrogation of the unequal treaties continued to insist that Christian missionaries and their institutions in China ought to have special consideration from the Chinese government. According to Reverend Beach, this caused some "caustic comment" from Chinese in the Shanghai newspapers. Reverend Beach to Frank M. North, December 10, 1925, and Beach to Reverend John Edwards, February 3, 1926, 73-43: 1041-1-1: 18 and 1: 19, GBGM.

34 Mary Margaret Moninger to family, June 20, 1925, Mary Margaret Moninger Papers, RG 230, Box 1, Folder 28, PC (USA); Lois Young to family, July 9, 1925, Lois Young Papers, H85.128491, BWM; W. B. Nance, *Soochow University* (New York: United Board for Christian Colleges in China, 1956), pp. 43–44; Matilda Thurston and Ruth M. Chester, *Ginling College* (New York: United Board for Christian Colleges in China, 1955), pp. 50–51;

35 Abbie Sanderson to family, June 31, 1925, Abbie Sanderson Papers, RG 8, Box 188, YDSL; Lida Ashmore to daughter, June 13, 1925, William and Lida Ashmore Papers, RG Ax 564, Box 2, UOSC.

36 Mary Lamberton, *St. John's University* (New York: United Board for Christian Colleges in China, 1955), pp. 101–102; Gladys Bundy to family, June 21, 1925, Bob and Gladys Bundy Papers, RG 8, Box 240, Folder 9, YDSL; Tsang, *Nationalism in School Education*, pp. 203–209.

37 Caroline V. Lee to home church, Nov. 9, 1926, Microfilm #107, BWM.

38 Matilda Thurston from Japan, possibly to Miss Hodge, August 20, 1927, Ginling College, Correspondence, UBCHEA, RG 11, Box 143, Box 2844, YDSL.

39 W. H. Jeffreys, *James Addison Ingle (Yin Teh-sen): The First Bishop of the Missionary District of Hankow, China* (1913; reprint, Taipei: Ch'eng-Wen Publishing Co., 1971), p. 167.

40 Dwight Edwards, *Yenching University* (New York: United Board for Christian Higher Education in Asia, 1959), p. 131; Ginling College, 1915, Publicity, UBCHEA, RG 11, Box 155, Folder 2965, YDSL; Hangchow Christian College, Yearbook, "The Tide," 1924, Hangchow Christian College, UBCHEA, RG 11, Box 161, Folder 3040, YDSL.

41 Ronald C. White and C. Howard Hopkins, *The Social Gospel: Religion and Reform in Changing America* (Philadelphia: Temple University Press, 1976).

42 John Stewart Burgess, "Peking as a Field for Social Service," *Chinese Recorder* 45 (April 1914): 226–230. Beginning in September 1915, the *Chinese Recorder* regularly featured articles about the Social Gospel, including letters and articles from conservative Christians who opposed the social emphasis.

43 Paul Hutchinson, "The Conservative Reaction in China," *Journal of Religion* 2: 4 (July 1922): 337–361, see p. 350, in the Paul Hayes Papers, ELCA.

44 George Barbour to Nina Kidder, Sept. 30, 1924, George and Dorothy Barbour Papers, RG 8, Box 13, Folder 1924, YDSL.

45 Marianne Bastid, trans. Paul Bailey, *Educational Reform in Early Twentieth-Century China* (Ann Arbor: Center for Chinese Studies, 1988), p. 221, note 35; Mary A. Nourse, *The Four Hundred Million: A Short History of the Chinese* (Indianapolis: Bobbs-Merrill, 1935), p. 302.

46 Ida Belle Lewis, "Some Factors in the Evaluation of Christian Lower Primary Schools," booklet (Shanghai: Commercial Press, Ltd., 1921), p. 6; Mildred Test Young interview, p. 77, MCOHP, 1978, ELCA; William Nast Academy, Report, 1923, 79-16: 1459-4-3: 10, GBGM.

47 Caroline Johnson Memorial School, Principal's Report, 1911, p. 3, 79-16: 1459-4-2: 34, GBGM.

48 Elsie Reik to family, May 5, 1927, Elsie Reik Papers, RG 8, Box 163, YDSL; West China Union University, Vice-president's report, 1927–1928, 79-16: 1459-5-1: 40, GBGM.

49 Anna Moffett Jarvis interview, pp. 37–38, MCOHP, 1977, ELCA.

50 Chester Fuson, "Brief Report of Social Service in the Canton Christian College," *Chinese Recorder* 47(March 1916): 209–211.

51 Alice Reed to family, Dec. 12, 1920, Excerpts from Letters, p. 62, Alice Reed Papers, RG 8, Box 163, YDSL; Grace Boynton, "The Famine Refuge," n. d., Yenching University, UBCHEA, RG 11, Box 321, Folder 4904, YDSL; Matilda Thurston, "A Second Statement about Ginling Students," n. d., around 1922, Ginling College, UBCHEA, RG 11, Box 144, Folder 2856, YDSL; Fukien Christian College Catalogue, 1919, Fukien Christian College, UBCHEA, RG 11, Box 109, Folder 2397, YDSL.

52 Bertha St. Clair to family, November 10, 1918, Bertha St. Clair Papers, RG 8, Box 174, YDSL; "Social Service in Middle Schools," Report of the Special Committee to the Educational Commission, American Presbyterian Mission, n. d., probably early 1920s, Pommerenke Family Papers, RG 193, Box 2, Folder 37, PC (USA).

53 "Social Service in the Middle Schools," Pommerenke Family Papers, RG 193, Box 2, Folder 37, PC (USA). China's "boat people" were not refugees but a class of people, generally quite poor, who lived and worked on their boats. They were despised by most Chinese because they lacked the land-based "home" that was so significant in Chinese culture.

54 While many books mention and praise a few "heroines" for their individual contributions, the authors do not address the degree to which female students in the government school system participated in protest activities, whether their protests ever took different forms than those of the boys, or how well girls and young women were represented in the student leadership. See Chow, *The May Fourth Movement*, pp. 123, 129–130. In his first book, *Student Nationalism in China*, John Israel does not mention women; a more recent book does, but not in any detail. See John Israel and Donald W. Klein, *Rebels and Bureaucrats: China's December 9ers* (Berkeley: University of California Press, 1976). Hubert Freyn's *Prelude to War: The Chinese Student Rebellion of 1935–1936* (Shanghai: China Journal Publishing Co. Ltd., 1939) is similarly flawed. Works published since the late 1970s might be expected to incorporate gender analysis, but few of them do. See Yip Ka-che, *Religion, Nationalism and Chinese Students: The Anti-Christian Movement of 1922–1927* (Bellingham: Western Washington University Press, 1980), Jessie G. Lutz, *Chinese Politics and Christian Missions: The Anti-Christian Movements of 1920–1928* (Notre Dame: Cross Cultural Publications, 1988), Wen-hsin Yeh, *The Alienated Academy: Culture and Politics in Republican China, 1919–1937* (Cambridge: Council on East Asian Studies, Harvard University Press, 1990), and Lincoln Li, *Student Nationalism in China, 1924–1949* (Albany: State University of New York Press, 1994). Christina Gilmartin unveils some of the tensions between male and female communists in China before 1927, but her main point is to demonstrate how important women and women's issues were to the fledgling Chinese Communist Party. She thus overlooks the degree to which even Communist men and women played distinctly gendered roles, which is clear from her article. See Christina Gilmartin, "Gender, Politics, and Patriarchy in China: The Experience of Early Women Communists, 1920–1927," pp. 82–105 in Sonia Kruk, et. al., eds., *Promissory Notes: Women in the Transition to Socialism* (New York: Monthly Review Press, 1989). Ono Kazuko notes women's participation in student protest movements without noting whether they took on the same roles as men. Ono Kazuko, *Chinese Women in a Century of Revolution, 1850–1950* (Stanford: Stanford University Press, 1989). In his book, *Student Protests in Twentieth-Century China: The View from Shanghai* (Stanford: Stanford University Press, 1991), Jeffrey Wasserstrom does mention (p. 64) that while male students printed pamphlets, female students made special hats for

protesters. It is not clear how this division of labor was arrived at, nor how students of both sexes interacted with each other. Lee Feigon, on the other hand, describes the deep male chauvinism of the 1989 student movement in China. It is difficult for me to believe that similar patterns did not mark the earlier student movements. See Lee Feigon, "Gender and the Chinese Student Movement," pp. 165–176 in Jeffrey Wasserstrom and Elizabeth J. Perry, eds., *Popular Protest and Political Culture in Modern China: Learning from 1989* (Boulder, Colo.: Westview Press, 1992).

55 Chow, *The May Fourth Movement*, p. 123.

56 Mary Margaret Moninger to family, Jan. 13, 1920, Mary Margaret Moninger Papers, RG 230, Box 1, Folder 15, PC (USA).

57 Luella Miner, "A Pioneer College for Women in the East," n. d., Yenching University, Yenching Women's College, UBCHEA, RG 11, Box 313, Folder 4798, YDSL.

58 I-Chang Girls' Collegiate School, Changsha, Hunan, report, Aug. 1920, Pamphlet Collection, RG 31, Box 277, Folder 1966, YDSL; "Outstanding Days at Hwa Nan," Sept. 1922–June 1923, Elsie Reik Papers, UOSC.

59 George Barbour to family, May 17, 1925, George and Dorothy Barbour Papers, RG 8, Box 13, Folder 1925, YDSL; Luella Tappan diary, Oct. 10 and 11, 1923, David and Luella Tappan Papers, RG Ax 103, Box 1, UOSC.

60 Bertha St. Claire to family, May 9, 1925, Bertha St. Clair Papers, RG 8, Box 174, YDSL; Luella Tappan to family, Oct. 15, 1921, David and Luella Tappan Papers, RG Ax 103, Box 1, UOSC; Laura M. Wheeler, "Recollection of My Chinese Days, 1903–1948," printed pamphlet, Pasadena, CA., 1947 [*sic*], Laura Wheeler Papers, RG Ax 372, Box 1, UOSC.

61 Matilda Thurston to Miss Hodge, Sept. 6, 1928, Ginling College, Correspondence, UBCHEA, RG 11, Box 143, Folder 2845, YDSL.

62 Elsie Reik to family, June 26, 1926, Elsie Reik Papers, UOSC; Matilda Thurston, Typed Excerpts from Letters, Feb. 2, 1927, Ginling College, Correspondence, UBCHEA, RG 11, Box 142, Folder 2844, YDSL.

63 Elsie Reik to family, Aug. 20, 1925, Elsie Reik Papers, UOSC; Lois Young to family, June 21, 1925, Lois Young Papers, H85. 128491, BWM.

64 Abbie Sanderson to family, May 20, 1921, Abbie Sanderson Papers, RG 8, Box 178, YDSL; Elsie Reik to family, Nov. 26, 1925, Elsie Reik Papers, UOSC.

65 Olga Lang, *Chinese Family and Society* (New Haven: Yale University Press, 1946), p. 319.

66 *Ibid.*, p. 320. Girls in Presbyterian missionary Monona Cheney's school, for example, made soap, envelopes, linen hats and other articles "to take the place of Japanese goods on the market." Monona Cheney to family, June 15, 1919, Monona Cheney Papers, RG Ax 275, Box 1, UOSC.

67 Elsie Reik to family, June 12, 1927 and June 28, 1927, Elsie Reik Papers, UOSC; *Woman's Missionary Friend* 42 (November 1910): 403.

68 "Liz and Deb," letter fragment, Nov. 19, 1923, Frida Nilsen Papers, ELCA; Mali Lee, "The New Woman of China," *University of Nanking Magazine* (1930): 39, Nanking University, UBCHEA, RG 11, Box 236, Folder 3918, YDSL.

69 Elsie Reik to family, Sept. 25, 1925, Elsie Reik Papers, UOSC; Abbie Sanderson to family, July 13, 1925, Abbie Sanderson Papers, RG 8, Box 179, YDSL.

70 Liu En-lan, journal, June 16 and June 19, 1928, Ginling College, UBCHEA, RG 11, Box 144, Folder 2859, YDSL; Matilda Thurston, Typed Excerpts from Letters, May 27, 1928 and July 23, 1928, Ginling College, Correspondence, UBCHEA, RG 11, Box 144, Folder 2859, YDSL. This incident is described in greater detail in Gael Graham, "The *Cumberland* Incident of 1928: Gender, Nationalism, and Social Change in American Mission Schools in China," in the *Journal of Women's History* 6: 3 (Fall 1994): 35–61.

71 Matilda Thurston to Miss Hodge, Sept. 6, 1928, Ginling College, Correspondence, UBCHEA, RG 11, Box 143, Folder 2845, YDSL.

72 Ruth Chester to unknown recipient, July 23, 1928, Ginling College, Correspondence, UBCHEA, RG 11, Box 144, Folder 2859, YDSL; Matilda Thurston to Miss Hodge, Sept. 6, 1928, Ginling College, Correspondence, UBCHEA, RG 11, Box 143, Folder 2845, YDSL.

73 Lucy Wang to Mrs. Wallace, Sept. 25, 1929, Correspondence Between Hwa Nan and Fukien Christian University, UBCHEA, RG 11, Box 114, Folder 2476, YDSL.

74 Gladys Bundy to family, June 7, 1925, Bob and Gladys Bundy Papers, RG 8, Box 240, Folder 9, YDSL.

75 Frank D. Gamewell to Frank Mason North, Nov. 6, 1926, 73-43: 1041-1-1: 19, GBGM.

76 Lutz, *Chinese Politics and the Anti-Christian Movements*; Yeh, *Alienated Academy*; and Li, *Student Nationalism*.

77 Gladys Bundy to family, June 21, 1925, Bob and Gladys Bundy Papers, RG 8, Box 240, Folder 9, YDSL; William Cummings to home church, June 22, 1926, microfilm #102, BWM; see also Grace Manly, "The Present Problem in West China," *Woman's Missionary Friend* 59 (January 1927): 9–12.

78 "A History of the Peking Station of the North China Mission of the Woman's Foreign Missionary Society of the Methodist Episcopal Church," p. 207, RG 8, Box 73, YDSL; see also Minnie Vautrin, Diary, November 24, 1927, Ginling College, UBCHEA, RG 11, Box 144, Folder 2857, YDSL.

79 Alice Margaret Huggins, Nov. 7, 1925, Goodrich Girls' School report, Pamphlet Collection, RG 31, Box 276, Folder 1963, YDSL; George Barbour to family, May 30, 1925, George and Dorothy Barbour Papers, RG 8, Box 13, Folder 1925, YDSL; Luella Tappan to family, October 28, 1921, David and Luella Tappan Papers, RG Ax 103, Box 1, UOSC.

80 "Confidential, not for publication, A Review of the First Month," Ginling College, UBCHEA, RG 11, Box 138, Folder 2773, YDSL; Matilda Thurston, Typed Excerpts from Letters, May 13, 1928, Ginling College, UBCHEA, RG 11, Box 144, Folder 2859, YDSL; Alice Boring to family, March 28, 1926, Yenching University, Correspondence, UBCHEA, RG 11, Box 320, Folder 4893, YDSL; Reverend Beach to Frank North, November 6, 1926, 73-43: 1041-1-1: 19, GBGM; Minnie Vautrin, Diary, Nov. 15, 1927, Ginling College, UBCHEA, RG 11, Box 144, Folder 2857, YDSL; Elsie Reik to family, June 28, 1927, Elsie Reik Papers, UOSC.

81 "History of the Peking Station," RG 8, Box 73, YDSL; Luella Tappan to family, Oct. 15, 1921, David and Luella Tappan Papers, Ax 103 Box 1, UOSC.

82 Annual Reports, Han Mei Boys' School, 1920–1921, Harriet Stroh Papers, RG 187, Box 3, Folder 3, PC (USA).

83 Mary Margaret Moninger to family, Nov. 11, 1923 and November 18, 1823, Mary Margaret Moninger Papers, RG 230, Box 1, Folder 23, PC (USA); Rev. J. M. Wilson to home church, Jan. 27, 1921, microfilm #117, BWM.

84 Harriet Stroh to family, May 23, 1921, Harriet Stroh Papers, RG 187, Box 1, Folder 4, PC (USA); Mary Margaret Moninger to family, Jan. 13, 1924, Mary Margaret Moninger Papers, RG 230, Box 1, Folder 24, PC (USA); Luella Tappan to family, Oct. 6, 1921, David and Luella Tappan Papers, RG Ax 103, Box 1, UOSC.

85 *Ginling Bulletin*, 1915, p. 32, Ginling College, UBCHEA, RG 11, Box 128, Folder 2632, YDSL; Anglo-Chinese College of Foochow, Catalogue, 1898–1899, 79-16: 1459-4-2: 09, GBGM.

86 Mary Treudley, newsletter, July 15, 1927, Ginling College, Correspondence, UBCHEA, RG 11, Box 144, Folder 2863, YDSL; Henry Lacy to family, Feb. 19, 1928, Henry and Jessie Ankeny Lacy Papers, RG Ax 412, Box 1, UOSC.

87 Lida Ashmore to daughter Edith, April 25, 1926, William and Lida Ashmore Papers, RG Ax 564 Box 2, UOSC; Report of the United Lutheran Council and of the Committees Appointed by the United Lutheran Conference, Aug. 23–27, 1919, Lutheran Church of China, ELCA.

88 Mada McCutcheon to home church, April 20, 1922 and October 6, 1930, microfilm #108, BWM.
89 Frank D. Gamewell to John R. Edwards, June 18, 1925, 73-43: 1043-1-3: 18, GBGM; A. J. Bowen to Gamewell, June 12, 1925, 73-43: 1043-1-3: 18, GBGM.

Chapter 5:
"On the Top of a Volcano": American Protestants and the Attack on Christian Education

Chinese student nationalism did more than disrupt the missionary educational endeavor; it simultaneously challenged American Protestants to rethink their continuing role in China. Many came to agree with Alice Margaret Huggins, principal of the Goodrich Girls' School near Beijing that their work had been characterized by "too much of a feeling of white superiority" and excessive foreign control of Christian institutions. Having conceded this, however, few Americans were eager to make concrete concessions to Chinese nationalism. The Chinese were simply not ready, the missionaries argued, to replace foreigners in the administration of schools, churches, and hospitals.[1]

By the mid-1920s, however, Chinese Christians were no longer humbly requesting a larger role in the life of the church; rather, they asserted their right to greater control on both Christian and nationalistic grounds. Within the mission schools, demands by Chinese teachers for higher positions and greater responsibilities were matched by the insistence of the government that education in China be controlled by the Chinese. Government requirements became increasingly stringent during the 1920s, requiring mission schools to register with the Ministry of Education, to make religious studies voluntary, and to place Chinese in administrative and executive positions. Thus even as missionary educators were harassed by students' nationalistic activities, they were under attack from Chinese officials and teachers in their own schools.

Compounding their troubles, conservative and evangelical missionaries chose this moment to reopen the long-quiescent argument over the efficacy and value of mission schools. In the context of the well-known quarrel between fundamentalists and modernists that shook American Protestantism in the 1920s, conservative China missionaries seized on the turmoil within mission schools as evidence that these schools were lax in both discipline and theology. In a two-pronged attack, conservatives charged that education had been overemphasized in the missionary movement and that, due to the doctrinal weakness of liberal missionary teachers, modernism had taken root in the Christian schools.[2]

With the Chinese government, teachers, and students arrayed against them and fundamentalist Christians gloating at their discomfiture, American Protestant educators could feel the ground shifting treacherously under their feet. Believing, however, that nationalistic criticism was simply a phase based on jealousy of the Christian schools' financial support, superior discipline and modern facilities, few mission schools seriously prepared to register or to share administrative powers with Chinese Christians.[3] Then in March of 1927 the Nanjing Incident occurred. When radicals of the Guomindang [GMD] army attacked foreigners in Nanjing, American missionaries throughout China were evacuated from their posts. In their absence, the responsibility for running Christian educational institutions was necessarily handed over to Chinese subordinates. It proved impossible for missionaries to completely regain their old status once the crisis ended. Control of mission schools had effectively passed to the Chinese in most institutions; for the majority, registration with the government and compliance with its regulations were the next logical steps. Devolution of control and registration of the schools signaled the decline of foreign-dominated, autonomous Christian education in China.[4]

For Americans who returned to the schools after the Nanjing Incident, there followed a prickly period of adjustment. Those who felt they had been pushed from their positions had to overcome a sense of bitterness and betrayal to work alongside—and in many cases under—their former employees. Chinese Christians similarly struggled to carry the burden of new responsibilities, which, although long desired, had been abruptly thrust upon them by the emergency evacuation of the missionaries. In addition to working out a new relationship between American missionaries and Chinese Christians, three other issues had to be faced.

The first was the recurring dilemma of the identity and purpose of the Christian schools. When Christian teaching was severely limited by government regulations, should mission schools continue their work? American teaching missionaries, as we have seen, had collaborated in the dilution of religious education since they first opened their schools; they continued to do so now. Arguing that "Christian education" did not depend on the freedom to teach the doctrine and compel church attendance, they praised the "Christian atmosphere" that pervaded mission schools and prevented their total secularization. Evangelical missionaries were not impressed by this argument, but the majority of American teaching missionaries were willing to continue their schools under almost any circumstances.[5]

Money, the second issue, proved particularly problematic for missionaries and Chinese alike. Although the Chinese now held the seats of authority within most schools and some missions did permit the Chinese to handle the funds, neither the Chinese nor the missionaries in the field had control over the source of the money: mission boards and American church-goers. Some mission boards felt disinclined to support native churches and schools; a few missionaries endorsed this attitude, stating that if the Chinese wanted to be independent, they should not continue to take money from foreign sources. Other missionaries, however, thought this view unchristian and pleaded with the home boards not to cut off aid at this critical moment.[6]

The third problem related to gender, and the desire of American women to transfer control of their schools to Chinese women. Although missionaries had sought to end the traditional sexual segregation of Confucian China, missionary women wanted to retain a separate sphere for Chinese women. Chinese men did not share these women's concern to protect "woman's work," which led to some conflict between Chinese men and American women.

Besieged from several quarters, Christian education in China was forced by 1930 to give ground on nearly all fronts. Christian education and the American Protestant missionary presence continued in China until the early 1950s, but clearly an era ended in 1927. Before we examine the dynamics and difficulties of devolution, however, we must briefly review some of the key developments in American mission education between the turn of the century and 1927, especially the relationship of the mission schools and the Chinese government.

American Missionaries and the Modern Chinese Schools

In the late nineteenth century, the Chinese government opened a number of non-Confucian training schools, collectively known as "Self-

Strengthening Schools," in an effort to tap into what many Chinese reformers believed was the source of Western power: its technical know-how.[7] Pleased by this evidence of interest in Western knowledge, American missionaries assumed that the Chinese would welcome their advice on educational reform. Thus the Educational Association in China [EAC], a predominately American missionary body founded in 1890, often offered unsolicited advice to the Chinese government. In 1896, this organization appointed a committee to present a comprehensive plan for a system of public education to the Chinese government. Missionary motives were hardly disinterested, for as one missionary put it, the EAC sought to "exert a commanding influence" and keep the new education in China from being "dominated by such sentiments and influences as will be ruinous to the moral and spiritual welfare of the people." Ironically, in the light of later events, the EAC also recommended that the government establish a national Board of Education in Beijing and "place the whole control of education throughout the Empire in its hands."[8]

The Chinese paid no heed to missionary suggestions, but following the suppression of the Boxer Uprising in 1900, the Qing government undertook a more drastic overhaul of its educational system. The government ordered new schools to be established on the county, prefectural, and provincial levels, and in 1905 it created a Ministry of Education.[9] In 1907, the government ordered that public schools for Chinese girls be established although, with the exception of normal schools to produce badly-needed teachers, there were no government middle schools for girls at this time.[10]

The curriculum in the new schools attempted to balance Western academic subjects with Chinese values and traditions. Mathematics, science, geography, foreign language (usually English), music, group-singing and physical education were all introduced along with a continuing emphasis on the Confucian classics and ethics. Although the imperial examinations were finally abolished in 1905, an emphasis on the classics in government schools continued until the Republican revolution in 1911, and students were obliged to pay homage to Confucius.[11]

American teaching missionaries were pleased to see the Qing enacting these educational reforms and believed that at last the Chinese were moving in the right direction.[12] The fact that the government was now smashing idols and seizing temples to turn them into schools amazed many missionaries.[13] There were, however, aspects of the educational reform that caused the missionaries a degree of misgiving. Speaking at the China Centenary conference in 1907, Reverend F. L. Hawks Pott opened the session on education by criticizing, not praising, Chinese educational reform. He argued that the new education was too superficial. Students, he claimed, sought knowledge for utilitarian or mercenary considerations. Since missionaries, in spite of their more favorable attitude toward Confucius, still denied that the classics could impart genuine moral lessons, Pott stated that the curriculum in the government schools lacked an emphasis on moral training and was to some degree anti-Christian.[14]

Other American missionaries were not happy about the extent of Japanese influence in the new school system. Not only was the curriculum patterned after that of Japan, but Qing officials invited Japanese teachers and advisors to help establish the new school system, in the very positions missionaries had long coveted.[15] The government intended this to be an interim measure until there were sufficient Chinese teachers with modern training. Although a few American missionaries were employed in government schools as English teachers, the Japanese were culturally more akin to the Chinese and they were willing to work more cheaply than the missionaries.[16] The number of Japanese so employed was not tremendous; in the peak year of 1909 there were less than five hundred Japanese teachers and educational advisors in all of China. After the 1911 Revolution the number dropped to less than one hundred.[17]

Any Japanese influence, however slight, troubled American missionaries because just before the turn of the century the Japanese government had prohibited the establishment of Christian schools in Japan.[18] Missionaries thus feared that if they did not move swiftly, they would "lose the opportunity of leadership and to be compelled to take a secondary and inferior position" within Chinese education.[19] Therefore, American teaching missionaries debated whether they had "the ability and the obligation to help in Chinese schools." Besides building a bridge of trust between missionaries and the Chinese government, sending mission-trained teachers into the government schools might increase the range of Christian influence. The primary drawback of this plan was that the teaching of Christianity was not permitted in the government schools, which made some Christian mission school graduates feel that they could not in good conscience teach in the schools.[20]

Compulsory rites honoring Confucius in the government schools were a further impediment to missionary-government cooperation in education. Although these traditional ceremonies betokened respect and not worship to the Chinese, to American missionaries bowing to a tablet smacked of idolatry. At the same time, missionaries were blind to the fears of radicalism that prompted Chinese officials to insist on students honoring Confucius. Missionaries believed that this practice was deliberately designed to bar Christians from working in or attending government schools.[21] Worse yet, students in some government schools were required to sign a pledge that they would give service to the government after they finished their studies and, further, that they would not join any "depraved sect." Missionaries assumed that this referred to Christianity; in fact, it was more likely intended to prevent students from joining secret societies or revolutionary organizations.[22]

In addition to their disapproval of Japanese influence in the new schools and their hostility toward the ceremonial requirements, American missionaries for the first time began to consider the possibility that the Chinese government would now try to exert stronger control over the mission schools. In the first decade of the twentieth century, most missionaries agreed with F. L. Hawks Pott that if indeed enacted, government registration would be "only a temporary inconvenience to our work." Missionaries nonetheless began to circle defensively around "their rights in introducing into the regulations of the [mission] school attendance on divine worship, and courses in religious instruction," which were precisely the features of Christian education that the government did move to ban in the 1920s.[23]

At this early date, the Qing did not in fact attempt to control foreign education in China; efforts at achieving uniformity and control were instead focused on bringing the recalcitrant *sishu*, the traditional schools, which often resisted the transition to a modernized curriculum, into the educational fold. Before the 1911 Revolution, however, the government refused to recognize graduates of mission institutions, stating that to do so would "hinder the abolition of extraterritoriality." This meant that mission school graduates would not be eligible either to vote or to stand for election in the proposed constitutional government, which obviously had grave implications for the future of Christian education in China. American missionaries were not overly concerned about this policy, however, because enforcement was lax. Government institutions did hire mission school graduates, and these students were also made eligible for government scholarships to study abroad. The issue of government registration for the mission schools thus did not come to a crisis until 1927.[24]

The main anxiety for the missionaries after the establishment of the modern Chinese school system was their fear of competition. Mission and government schools were now offering parallel curricula, with the exception of Christian teaching in the former and a greater emphasis on Confucian teachings in the latter. In addition, many mission schools had already begun to charge tuition while government schools were initially comparatively inexpensive, if not free. Above the primary level, many government schools offered students a stipend, as had been done traditionally, in order to induce students to enroll in the new schools.[25]

By this time few Christian schools were still offering cash inducements, although the provision of free tuition, room, and board lingered to some degree, especially in the girls' schools. Believing that the Qing government had vast resources on which to draw for educational purposes, some missionaries feared that if they did not coordinate their own educational efforts they would "simply be squashed."[26] Missionaries were incorrect, however, in assuming that government education had a better financial basis. On local and national levels alike there was no fixed educational budget and schools were financed through a number of *ad hoc* means. Corruption was rife. This dismal situation plagued China into the Republican era. In the 1920s, because so much money was siphoned off into military spending, there was very little left over for education, and teachers' salaries were often months in arrears.[27]

What the central government had that the missionaries lacked was not so much money as cultural authority. The legitimacy of mission schools suffered not only from the government's power to withhold recognition and to deny perquisites such as voting from their students but also from their own tainted association in the public mind with foreigners, gunboats, extraterritoriality and imperialism. Government schools thus had an undeniable edge in commanding the loyalty of those Chinese who sought education for their children. Under these altered circumstances, missionaries wondered what Christian schools had to offer that government schools did not? What possible role could Christian education now play in China?

Christian Education in the Twentieth Century

Teaching missionaries had begun their work in China in order to educate their converts. When mission schools broadened their curricula in the 1880s, they justified this change by asserting that even a secular education could help to advance evangelical goals. As we have seen, they also articulated a specific rationale for each new subject introduced. After the emergence of the modern Chinese school system, the missionaries naturally had no intention of giving up teaching Christians; they regarded this work as undisputedly part of their missionary mandate. Educating children with no connection to the Chinese Christian community, however, was a different matter. With the government schools now offering a Westernized curriculum, missionaries could no longer claim to be the sole source of modern education. To diminish competition with government schools, some missionaries considered enrolling only students who were in some way affiliated with the Christian community and leaving the unconverted to the government schools. The majority rejected this possibility out of hand, not wanting to "unnecessarily restrict the field of [their] usefulness."[28]

Christian schools were still necessary, missionaries argued, as a means of helping young Chinese and their families to convert. Others asserted that the government schools themselves could be brought under the influence of Christianity through the provision of Christian teachers from the mission schools. Moreover, having non-Christians in mission schools gave the Christian students opportunities to engage in direct evangelism themselves; in addition, missionaries claimed that schools that ministered only to Christian students created an "unhealthy inbreeding" that was not good for the students.[29]

The most important justification missionaries put forward for continuing their educational work was that since Western education had received the government's imprimatur, students with a Western education were undoubtedly going to emerge as the leaders of the country, just as Confucian scholars had led in their day. American missionaries wanted a hand in the education of this elite for they had visions of being able to sway the course of Chinese history through ties to mission school graduates. The power of Christian influence, they argued, extended beyond promoting conversion; it could have an impact even on those who did not become Christians. Methodist Elizabeth Fisher Brewster described the purpose of her Guthrie Memorial High School: "Our aim was, as in other Christian schools, to pioneer in modern education, not only to prepare Christian boys for leadership, but to impart the Christian ideals to all non-Christian students who were to become leaders in the new China." Similarly, Lutheran missionary Katherine Ward claimed that Christian education affected the "value structure" of the students.[30]

If receiving a Western education was the *sine qua non* for joining the elite, then government schools were of course training leaders as well. Missionaries argued, however, that Christian schools emphasized moral training, which meant that they were preparing *better* leaders than the government schools. "A school without Christianity," asserted the *Missionary Review of the World* in 1925, "fails as a rule to prepare public-spirited, honest and efficient leaders."[31] Missionaries were fond of pointing out that in the years after the establishment of the Chinese school system, even government officials sometimes enrolled their own children in mission, rather than government, schools. "We had a big government school in Sinyang," recalled Lutheran missionary Frida Nilsen, "but the better people in town, even the wealthier non-Christians, preferred to send their girls to our school rather than to a government school. They said 'you teach them respect and manners.'"[32] In addition to enforcing strict discipline, missionaries alleged that Christian education built character as the government schools could not. The president of the Methodist Nanking University wrote to the home boards concerning the changing educational scene in China in 1909, stating: "The opportunity of demonstrating the advantage of character-building, as something different from and superior to mere mental and physical training, is unique."[33]

A final justification for mission schools continuing to operate after the development of a modern native school system was that there were simply not enough Chinese schools to accommodate all who wanted to attend. More than twenty years after the establishment of government schools, Methodist missionary Ida Belle Lewis described the lack of educational opportunity with powerful imagery, pointing out that a single-file line of college-educated Chinese men would stretch a mere twelve miles; college-educated women "would reach five city blocks." A line of Chinese youths with no hope of education would number many millions and straddle several continents. Lewis reported that in 1925 there were 6,201,622 boys and 418,170 girls in government schools, and 138,486 boys and 60,340 girls in the mission schools.[34] The serious shortage of schools was, in fact, one of the reasons the government was slow to seek control over the mission schools; schools of any sort were too badly needed.

Professionalization in Christian Education

Emphasis on Christian influence, training China's future leaders, and the moral teaching and character-building offered in Christian schools formed the core of missionaries' justification for continuing Christian education in China. Yet missionaries knew that if their schools were to appeal to non-Christian families, they would have not only to match but surpass the quality of education provided in the government schools. This competitive spirit fed an interest in professionalization that pre-dated the establishment of government schools.

The key event in professionalizing Christian education in China was the 1890 founding of the Educational Association of China (EAC), whose purpose was to "give unity to [the] work, to devise means for the discussion of matters of common interest, and to provide for the preparation and publication of suitable school and college material."[35] The EAC held triennial meetings in Shanghai and by 1912 membership jumped from the original thirty-six members to nearly five hundred. It had by then also published over two hundred works, primarily on non-religious topics such as mathematics, science, political economy, pedagogy, history, international law and other "Western" subjects that the missionaries believed were of interest to non-Christian Chinese.[36]

The EAC imparted a sense of group-consciousness to educational missionaries that was helpful in diminishing denominational narrowness and encouraging ecumenical cooperation in education. In 1902, the EAC launched a campaign to raise educational standards in Christian schools in China. The EAC's Executive Committee wrote an "Appeal to Foreign Mission Boards for Trained Educators in China" that was published in the

Chinese Recorder in December 1902. Arguing that education was "the most powerful subsidiary agency in evangelism," the EAC asserted that mission boards ought to send only highly trained educational missionaries to teach in China. While praising the efforts of pioneers in Christian education, the EAC made it clear that the day of the enthusiastic amateur was drawing to a close. "The modern educational system of China is now practically in the control of Christians," the Appeal continued, mendaciously. "By perfecting and strengthening this area of service, we increase the probability that the future governmental educational system of China will be largely influenced and moulded [*sic*] by such superior examples."[37] Mission boards responded in a polite but restrained manner. Methodist, Protestant Episcopal, and Presbyterian mission boards all sent letters to the *Chinese Recorder* agreeing that missionaries should be well trained for their positions and stating that for several years they had already been following such a policy.[38] This is probably true, but some evidence suggests that teaching missionaries in the field had higher standards than the home boards. In 1914, the Methodist Educational Secretary in China, Frank D. Gamewell, advised the boards that "a man who comes [to China] for work in a normal school should have graduated from one of our normal schools or teachers' colleges, or at least should have taken some courses in such excellent institutions as Teachers' College, Columbia."[39] Other educational workers were quick to admonish the boards for appointing missionaries with questionable credentials to work in their schools.[40]

After the 1890s, American missionaries were expected to have a Bachelor's degree. By the second decade of the twentieth century, increasing numbers had done some graduate work. According to missionary Monona Cheney, the Methodist mission board encouraged its missionaries to get more schooling while on furlough. Ida Belle Lewis recommended in 1925 that all missionaries utilize their first furlough in the United States to obtain, at the very least, the M.A. degree. Lewis held a doctorate in education herself; doubtless she would have approved more Ph.D.s among missionaries.[41]

American missionaries in the field took several steps to enhance the qualifications of newcomers. By 1900 and probably earlier, China missionaries were considered "probationers" until they had successfully completed two years of language study. This contrasts with missionaries of the earlier period who usually acquired their language skills on the job. By

1913, the training consisted of a four-year course. New missionaries were not permitted to vote in station meetings until they had passed their second-year examinations.[42] Missionaries established their own language training centers in China beginning in 1910. There were eight such institutions in 1916; according to Kenneth Latourette, the best of these were in Beijing and Nanjing.[43]

Professional organizations for missionary educators flourished in the early twentieth century. Not only did EAC membership increase, but missionaries established regional educational organizations: the Educational Association of Fukien (Fujian) in 1905; the West China Educational Union in 1907; and the Educational Association of Canton in 1909. The EAC was reorganized in 1909, changing its name to the China Christian Education Association (CCEA) and commencing publication of its own journal, the *Educational Review*.[44]

Educational missionaries also began to impose greater structure on Christian schools in China. In 1893, the EAC recommended systematizing the grading of mission schools. It pushed for uniform examinations in 1896, and for a uniform curriculum in 1898.[45] The West China Educational Union was the first to draw up a set of regulations for mission schools in 1906, and the other associations followed thereafter.[46] In 1914, the CCEA urged all Christian schools in China to adopt the Uniform Curriculum. With the exception of religious instruction, this curriculum conformed to that of the government schools. Although the mission schools were not registered with the government, Chinese patrons of mission schools preferred that the missionaries match the government's standards.[47]

Thus by 1915, most mission schools tried to abide by the Uniform Curriculum laid down by the educational associations, which roughly accorded with the government curriculum. This ended the days when mission schools were operated on a completely *ad hoc* basis, according to the whim and training of the missionaries in charge. It also gave the schools greater stability, for the institutionalization of the schools and their coursework meant that missionaries and Chinese teachers became interchangeable parts in a bureaucratic system. No longer did a Christian school grind to a halt when the missionary in charge left the field.

There was not, however, total adherence to the rules of the educational associations. In 1924, Methodist missionary Myrtle Smith wrote to her family that the curriculum for normal schools was "really impossible," so she and her colleague were going to continue to use the course they had worked out together the previous year.[48] The missionary educational associations had no power to enforce their decrees, but could only make suggestions and appeal to the professionalism of the teaching missionaries.

Along with the Uniform Curriculum, the EAC developed a system of Uniform Examinations. This helped to maintain common standards throughout the mission school system and to ensure that students could transfer between schools and that graduates of one school could proceed smoothly to the next level of education, whether in a government or mission school, without having to do remedial or preparatory work.[49] Like the now-defunct Chinese examination system, Uniform Examinations were taken anonymously, written in the classical language rather than in the vernacular, and were sent out to be corrected by specially appointed examiners.[50]

In addition to standardizing the coursework and the examinations, some American missionaries began to criticize the informal use of mission school students to teach in mission schools without having had any special training. Even before the turn of the century, some missionaries pointed out that it was "no boon" to the schools to have untrained teachers and urged that neophytes be directed by more experienced teachers until they had proven their competence.[51] To a limited extent, a rough and ready system of teacher recruitment among mission school students continued even into the 1920s and 1930s, particularly in primary day schools. For boarding schools and higher level schools, however, missionaries raised the standards required for their Chinese teachers and sought to instill a spirit of professionalism in them as well.[52]

American missionaries promoted normal training for Chinese teachers in three types of institutions. They established a few independent normal schools.[53] More commonly, they created normal training departments in existing high schools and colleges.[54] They also founded teachers' institutes. As in the United States, these institutes were held during the vacation months and were intended to supplement regular normal training rather than substitute for it. Missionaries expected that formal training for their Chinese teachers would yield both educational and evangelical benefits. In 1921, Ida Belle Lewis, who was conducting a study of Methodist education in China, praised the "splendid teachers' institute" held for eighty-five primary school teachers in central China. Lewis recommended that all teachers attend summer institutes.[55]

In addition to providing normal training for Chinese teachers, many mission schools set firm standards for employing Chinese teachers. Eva Sprunger reported in 1922 that the Gutian (Christian) Board of Education in Fujian decided not to hire primary school graduates as teachers until they had received some training beyond higher primary school. The board further stipulated that within five years all teachers must have two years' training beyond higher primary school.[56]

Rivalry with government schools was the main reason for enhancing the training of Chinese teachers in mission schools. Another reason was that by 1900, the graduates were younger than their counterparts of forty years earlier. This was particularly true of the girls' schools. Whereas in the nineteenth century few girls entered a mission school before the age of ten and thus were between eighteen and twenty-two years old before they completed higher primary school, in the 1920s these graduates were typically between fourteen and sixteen years old, which missionaries believed was too young to be put in charge of a classroom.[57]

Professional requirements and provisions for teachers' training did help to raise the standards of education in the mission schools. Since salaries were frequently tied to training, some Chinese teachers who had been hired when the requirements were less stringent resented their status as second-rate teachers. Myrtle Smith reported in dismay that one of her older teachers refused to help with the kindergarten work unless her salary was raised to the level of the younger, more highly trained teacher. "The scale for salaries is set by our Conference according to the years of training they have had," Smith wrote. "I could not raise her salary so she quit."[58]

Sally Borthwick has described "circular education" in the government schools: the phenomenon of teachers training students who in turn became teachers.[59] In the mission schools the problem of circular education was compounded by the very common practice of taking graduates to teach in their alma mater. The development of normal training courses helped to reduce this occurrence to some degree, but in the absence of deliberate efforts to hire outside the school and with the perennial shortage of teachers, progress was slow. In 1924, Presbyterian missionary Mada McCutcheon admitted that all three students who graduated that year had been retained to teach in her school; the following year, five of the six graduates stayed on to teach.[60]

This was a form of inbreeding that occurred in both mission and government schools. Unfortunately, Christian schools that were distant from the larger cities and treaty ports where the normal training schools were located found themselves more or less stuck with the practice. Even if there were government schools in the vicinity, Christian schools did not care to draw on them for teachers, if they could help it, because they preferred to employ Christian teachers. Furthermore, if a mission school decided to pay for one of its pupils to be sent to a normal school for more advanced training, this was nearly always done with the understanding that the student would work off the debt by returning to teach.[61]

The relationship between Chinese mission school teachers and their American principals and employers was tainted with racism and exploitation. Because missionaries regarded Christian work as "sacrificial," salaries for Chinese teachers in mission schools were shockingly low. Some missionaries recognized this as one reason why their pupils were sometimes unwilling to work for the mission. At the EAC meeting in 1896, one missionary noted pointedly, "Much has been said concerning the qualifications of teachers, but one very important qualification has not yet been mentioned, viz., a willingness to teach for a salary about one-third less than an ordinary coolie."[62] Whether Chinese teachers in mission schools earned less than coolies is not known. They did earn substantially less than teachers in government schools. Presbyterian missionary Andrew Sydenstricker reported unhappily in 1907 that mission school graduates preferred to work for between forty and sixty dollars a month in a government school than for the eight to ten dollars a mission school was willing to pay.[63]

Salaries increased over time, especially as the Chinese became more highly educated, but in regarding mission school teaching as a labor of love, American missionaries were not wholly committed to a professional ethic. Lois Young, principal of the Presbyterian Mary Thompson Memorial Girls' School in Suzhoufu, wanted to hire a Christian Chinese woman college graduate to teach science, even though the school would have to pay her forty dollars a month. She added, "I do not know if any of the girls will come for that money—the government school will pay them

$75-100 for English teachers [*sic*], so you see it is a sacrifice—but still they are Christians and ought to be willing to make some."[64]

Although missionaries were paid quite a bit more than they were willing to pay their Chinese assistants—in 1922 Methodist missionaries under the General Boards earned $1,800 [Mexican] a year and women under the Woman's Foreign Missionary Society earned $1,500—they regarded their presence in China, the health risks they believed life in China entailed, and their salaries as evidence of the sacrifices they had made.[65] But even in the Christian colleges where American missionaries and Chinese worked side by side in the same capacity, the salaries were not equal.[66] Some Chinese teachers may have accepted the idea of sacrifice as a way to show gratitude toward the missionaries who had educated them. Others, however, rejected the suggestion that they work for lower recompense. Speaking for herself and her friend Wu Yi-fang, Y. T. Zee, a Ginling alumna, stated, "They [missionaries] wanted us to accept a lower scale of salary because they said our work is from the heart....We did not think it was very fair to work on only a service level. Both of us had financial burdens to take care of."[67]

It was not only in the matter of salaries that inequities were revealed in the missionary relationship with the Chinese. Although the missionaries often proclaimed that their purpose was to make their schools and other institutions self-supporting and self-perpetuating, in fact they rarely welcomed the Chinese into positions of power or treated them as equals. This manifested itself in ways both petty and significant. American and Chinese teachers in the mission schools rarely ate together, nor did they eat the same food. The Chinese could not have afforded the meat-heavy diets of the missionaries.[68] Nor did missionaries and Chinese teachers usually live in the same residences.[69] Fifty years after her missionary service, it suddenly struck Mildred Test Young that she and her colleagues had never played tennis with the Chinese women connected with her school.[70] Moreover, American missionaries strongly disapproved of the rare love affairs and marriages between missionaries and Chinese.[71]

The most telling segregation was in the division of labor. In the United States, educational work divided along gender lines; women taught and men administered. In China, because mission schools were already sexually segregated, race was the factor that determined the ordering of the hierarchy. Except for private girls' schools and women's colleges, women in the United States had little opportunity to engage in administrative work until the 1920s.[72] In China, women missionaries administered girls' schools from the very beginning. This was due in part to the concept of "woman's work" that made female education the territory of women missionaries. It also stemmed from the stricter segregation of the sexes among the Chinese, because traditional Chinese found it improper for men to administer girls' schools. But in boys' and girls' schools alike, missionaries kept power from the hands of their Chinese associates.

Attacks on the Christian Schools

For the majority of American teaching missionaries, the desire to have their schools recognized by the Chinese government warred with their fear that this might mean a measure of government control over the schools. Beginning in the early twentieth century, these missionaries conformed to the government school curriculum to the degree that they felt they could.[73] The obstacle to complete conformity was religious education. Although the mission school curriculum had already been largely secularized to make room for the so-called "Western subjects," teaching missionaries continued to insist that religious teachings form part of their students' education and further, that attendance at church and chapel services be mandatory.[74]

Although missionary and historian Alice Gregg asserts that the first set of Chinese regulations for the registration of foreign schools was issued by the government in 1917, neither the government nor the Ministry of Education was stable in this era, so the regulations were unenforceable.[75] For this reason the first challenges to the autonomy of the Christian schools sprang from popular nationalism rather than government imperatives. During the May Fourth era, the pro-science, anti-superstition strains of that movement merged with Chinese nationalism to produce, in 1922, the Anti-Christian Movement (*Fan Jidu Jiao Yundong*).[76] Anti-Christian sentiments continued strongly throughout the decade, peaking in moments of intense nationalism in 1925 and 1927. American teaching missionaries comforted themselves by stating that the criticism would force Christianity to purify itself, and that anti-Christian agitation was, in fact, "one of the best testimonies of the remarkable progress of Christianity" in China.[77]

Nevertheless, they were shocked to discover that a number of mission school graduates were among "the most vehement Anti-Christian Movement leaders."[78]

Opposition to Christianity made mission schools a target of popular demonstrations, but foreign control of educational institutions also drew fire. The 1922 publication of the tactlessly titled mission survey, *The Christian Occupation of China*, alarmed many Chinese, for it not only detailed the degree to which foreign Christians had "occupied" China, but made clear that the foreigners planned for the further growth and coordination of their educational system to compete with government institutions. Moreover, many Chinese were "anxious to see that the education offered [in Christian schools] is wholly Chinese and that it is consistent with the ideals of the growing spirit of nationalism."[79]

Hardening attitudes toward Christianity, rising nationalism and pressure from a "Restore Educational Rights Movement" (*Xiuhui Jiaoyu Quanli Yundong*) led the Ministry of Education in Beijing to declare in 1925 that all schools, including mission schools, must register with the government. It further decreed that private schools must have Chinese vice-principals and that, although religious doctrine could be taught, "religious propaganda shall not be introduced into the teaching of other subjects."[80] Not to be outdone, the GMD, which in 1920 had established an opposition government in Guangzhou, promulgated its own set of regulations in 1926. In addition to limiting religious teaching, the GMD insisted that all schools have Chinese principals as well as vice-principals, and a Chinese-dominated local board of managers, with a Chinese chairman. Beijing said nothing about deadlines for registration while the GMD asserted the right to close any schools that had not met its requirements by April 1928.[81]

While a few missionaries understood that registration of one sort or another was inevitable and chose, therefore, to register under the less onerous Beijing rules, the majority correctly inferred that neither set of regulations was enforceable at the time, and ignored both.[82] Nevertheless, most American teaching missionaries knew that the problem could not be dodged forever. Both the Beijing and the GMD regulations touched on sensitive issues: the freedom of missionaries to teach religion any way they saw fit and to require that students attend worship services; and the role of Chinese teachers within the mission schools. Regarding the first issue,

American missionaries protested vehemently against efforts by the Chinese government to control religious proselytization in the schools. Presbyterian Mada McCutcheon argued that mission schools should take a united, militant stance against such rules. President of Ginling Women's College Matilda Thurston agreed, stating that "the state should not dictate to the private school." Some schools attempted to show their willingness to compromise by putting Chinese into administrative positions, while agitating "for the abolition of any condition that would interfere with religious liberties."[83]

The reluctance of teaching missionaries to submit to government rules limiting religious instruction in their schools is easy to understand since, notwithstanding the secularization that teaching missionaries themselves had fostered, the schools' purpose was still considered to be evangelism by missionaries and Chinese critics alike. Devolution of control to Chinese administrators was another matter. While American missionaries had long claimed to look forward to the day when they could transfer the responsibility for Christian institutions to Chinese Christians, they wanted to control when and under what circumstances they would relinquish their power. Most denied that their Chinese co-workers were ready to take over their positions.[84]

Prior to the 1911 Republican revolution, American missionaries spoke of devolution as an ultimate goal that was well in the future, and made no definite plans to turn their work over to Chinese Christians. After the revolution, Chinese Christians began to express interest in shouldering more responsibilities within their various churches. While some missionaries found this a reason for rejoicing, others expressed caution. "If independence means 'out with the foreigner,'" wrote one missionary in 1911, "it will prove just as insufficient for the ideal church as the 'dominant foreigner' policy has been and is."[85]

Although by the twentieth century the overwhelming majority of teachers in mission schools were Chinese, this numerical superiority did not translate into control over the schools or power within them. American Methodists, for example, had over eight hundred schools in China by the mid-1920s; 2,037 of the teachers were Chinese while only 246 were missionaries. Few of these schools had Chinese principals or vice-principals. Those that did highlighted this fact, making it clear that having Chinese administrators was unusual.[86] Even on the elementary school level, it was not until 1923 that the Eastern China Christian Educational Association (ECCEA) suggested that the Chinese could supervise these schools, and the Association made this recommendation primarily because there were not enough foreign missionaries to cover the field adequately.[87]

American missionaries defended the glacial pace of devolution by stating that "The missionaries are a good deal more ready to give responsibility than the Chinese are to receive it." They bolstered this argument by asserting that even when the Chinese were eager for greater responsibilities, few were sufficiently trained to undertake them. As the American Protestant educational mission increasingly defined itself as a professional enterprise and elevated its standards, it indeed narrowed the pool of Chinese workers whom missionaries regarded as eligible for administrative service. Thus when the ECCEA recommended using Chinese men to supervise the primary school system, it made clear that these men did not have to be college-trained; they should possess "horse sense," be among the best and most experienced teachers, and perhaps might be provided with a summer training course. Since most, if not all, American Protestant educational missionaries were college graduates by this era, the ECCEA's suggestion involved a lowering of missionary professional standards.[88]

Regardless of missionaries' qualms and foot-dragging, the issue of devolution was clearly coming to a head in the 1920s. Nationalism affected the Chinese who worked in the mission schools as much as it affected students. Like the students, Chinese teachers were encouraged by outsiders to criticize the missionaries, demand their rights, and quit if they were not granted satisfaction. At the same time, however, many nationalistic Chinese believed that the term "Chinese Christian" was an oxymoron; if one was Christian, one was *ipso facto* denationalized and unpatriotic. Moreover, American missionaries disapproved of nationalism among Chinese Christians, lending credence to the gibes of non-Christians that one could not be loyal to a foreign religion and one's nation simultaneously. In moments of tension between Chinese and missionaries, Chinese Christians, who dwelt in the interstices between Chinese and Western culture, found themselves precariously situated.[89]

Despite the mixed loyalties that many Chinese Christians undoubtedly felt, they began to push harder for an expanded role within the church. American Baptist missionaries in South China, for example, were stunned at the tenor of a 1924 meeting with their Christian constituents. Citing frank distrust of missionary motives in coming to China, the Chinese issued three demands: that Chinese Christians and Americans should have equal discretion over mission funds; that the Chinese and Americans be equal in all aspects of Christian work; and that the Chinese should have, at the very least, an advisory role in the placement of foreign missionaries. Reporting on the meeting to her parents, Abbie Sanderson noted that "a number of the Chinese here would like to see the foreigners ousted right off." She added that failing to agree to these demands would spell "our finish."[90] In the end, however, in the wider missionary movement, devolution occurred not because of negotiations between missionaries and Chinese Christians but because of political events within China.

Devolution by Default

On March 24, 1927, GMD soldiers attacked foreigners in Nanjing. Fearing, after three missionaries were killed, that the incident presaged another Boxer Uprising, five thousand missionaries left China, fifteen hundred were evacuated to the foreign concession in Shanghai, and another thousand fled to other treaty port cities. Only some five hundred missionaries remained at their stations in the interior.[91] The attack led to a sharp and decisive tilt in the balance of power away from the missionaries in favor of their Chinese co-workers. At Ginling Women's College in Nanjing, for example, students and Chinese teachers hid the foreigners and oversaw their evacuation to Shanghai two days later.[92] Then a hastily-formed Administrative Committee, consisting of students, faculty, and alumnae, took over the operation of the women's college. Seventy-one students and all of the Chinese faculty remained on the campus and reconvened classes less than three weeks after the Nanjing Incident.[93] A Chinese woman was elected chair of the Ginling Executive Committee, which, without consulting Matilda Thurston, the exiled president, voted to recommend replacing her with a Chinese graduate of the college, Wu Yi-fang.[94]

Accurately reading the temper of the times, some missionaries had anticipated being forced to leave their posts suddenly and had elected Chinese co-workers to run the schools while they were gone. Lois Young noted wryly: "I think they would be glad to have us go, they would like to have things in their own hands...."[95] Missionaries intended these emergency assignments to be temporary, but once they had relinquished command to their Chinese colleagues, it proved impossible, in most cases, for the missionaries to reclaim their previous positions when they returned. Devolution thus did not occur in the orderly fashion that American missionaries had vaguely envisioned for more than eighty years. Instead, responsibility descended on the Chinese willy-nilly, and in a manner that exacerbated existing friction between Americans and Chinese.

Once the immediate crisis had passed, missionaries began to return to their stations. But fewer than half were back in China by late 1928. Although the number of Protestant missionaries in China steadily increased until the outbreak of World War II in Europe, it never reached the level of the pre-Nanjing Incident days. Apparently, many disillusioned missionaries simply left the China field or gave up missionary work altogether. We may therefore infer that those missionaries who did return were those who were prepared, on some level, to accept an altered position in China.[96]

Returning teaching missionaries first had to adjust to having been sidelined in educational institutions which they were accustomed to thinking of as "theirs." Reflecting on Chinese agitation to gain control of the schools prior to the Nanjing Incident, Baptist Abbie Sanderson commented candidly: "We can't help feeling that they are trying to get rid of us as fast as they can, and while that has been the plan all the years I s'pose [sic] it hurts our feelings to be pushed out instead of being allowed to withdraw voluntarily and help plan the arrangements." Her use of the word "allow" is telling; while most American missionary educators angrily defended their "rights" in the mission schools, Sanderson seems to have been one of the few to perceive that the balance of power was shifting toward the Chinese. She did, however, worry about "getting the wrong attitude toward the Chinese."[97]

Aside from hurt feelings, one of the key conflicts between missionaries and Chinese in the Christian schools was money. Prior to the Nanjing Incident, few Chinese were apparently privy to the financial status of the schools or the missions which supported them. When Lois Young was forced to evacuate the Mary Stevens Memorial Girls' School in 1927, for example, the Chinese women left in charge wrote to her in perplexity, wondering how much money was allocated to the school, how it should be spent, and whether or not there would be funds enough to repair the school building. Clearly these women felt the weight of administrative and financial responsibility collapse upon their shoulders without having any previous notion of how the school was run.[98]

A greater problem was one that some missionaries had long foreseen: there were too many foreign Christian institutions and they were too expensive for Chinese Christians to maintain without help from abroad. Some missionaries had cited the financial burden as a reason to postpone devolution, but others correctly blamed themselves for having grafted an inappropriate structure onto the Chinese church.[99] Once devolution occurred, American missionaries had conflicting ideas about how to handle the problem of expenses. Most urged their mission boards to continue funding Christian institutions in China even if the missionaries no longer controlled them. They argued that devolution had brought about better relations between themselves and the Chinese and had in fact won more converts to Christianity. Many claimed that the Sinification of the Christian church denoted progress, and therefore American financial support should be continued.[100]

Not all missionaries agreed. Adam Groesbeck asserted that the foreign Christian institutional structure should be permitted to crumble so that the Chinese could rebuild a truly appropriate set of institutions themselves. Other American missionaries apparently resented the idea of continuing to support schools and churches that were now controlled by Chinese Christians, particularly since mission giving in the United States had been declining throughout the 1920s. Thus Frank Gamewell, the Methodist's Secretary for Education, recommended confidentially that the home boards cut back their appropriation for China. The Southern Presbyterian mission ruled that Chinese patrons of day schools now had to provide half of the funds needed to run the schools, which resulted in some school closings.[101]

Aware of these mixed feelings among the Americans, some new Chinese administrators, while asking for financial aid from mission boards, made clear that they would raise as much of the money as possible themselves. Others appealed to the religious and gender sensibilities of the Americans. Reminding the missionaries of their own gendered beliefs about character, Y. C. Yang, the new president of Soochow University, called upon them to demonstrate a "manly attitude" and be good sports, rather than saying "we will not play with you again." Likewise, Wu Yi-fang, the woman who replaced Matilda Thurston as head of Ginling College, played on missionary notions of feminine character when she coupled her request for mission funds with praise for "the great sacrifices the missions and missionaries have made" and the spirit the missionaries had shown in relinquishing their positions to Chinese Christians.[102] The fact that foreign mission societies still controlled the purse strings made the positions of the new Chinese administrators unenviable.

Another point of conflict was the question of "woman's work," the sexual division of labor in the mission field that provided American women with roles and tasks for which they regarded themselves as uniquely suited. One of the startling features of devolution within the mission school system was that American women were not invariably replaced by Chinese women; sometimes American "women's work" passed into the hands of Chinese men. Although exact numbers are impossible to determine, Chinese men frequently took over the headship of mission schools previously run by American women. Often a boys' and a girls' school would be combined into a single coeducational institution with a Chinese man acting as principal. Abbie Sanderson, for example, had been the principal of the Abigail Hart Memorial Girls' School in Shantou. After the Nanjing Incident, her school merged with the neighboring Baptist Boys' Academy and Sanderson became, in her words, "simply one of the corps of teachers" who worked for Mr. Ling, the new principal.[103] Some girls' schools did remain under the leadership of women. The Episcopalian St. Hilda's Girls' School, for instance, found a Chinese woman to serve as principal, but it is difficult to know how often this happened.

One possible reason why American women were replaced by Chinese men was that there were not enough single, educated, Christian Chinese women to fill the positions. One missionary report stated in 1926 that since there was only one Chinese Christian woman for every ten Chinese Christian men, it would take longer before "woman's work" could devolve into Chinese hands. Marriage interfered with the development of Chinese "women's work," too. The Keen School in Tianjin, for example, had tried for years to acquire a Chinese woman principal, but every time one was hired, she married soon after and left the school. Finally, the missionaries agreed to let a Chinese man, Dr. Liu Fang, divide his time between the Keen School and the Hui Wen Boys' School next door. A shortage of eligible Chinese women may also explain the anomalous situation at the Hangchow Union Girls' School, which had an American woman as principal but a Chinese man as dean in 1923. Given the tenacity with which missionary women defended their social space, it is difficult to imagine that they would have permitted themselves to be replaced by Chinese men except under the most extraordinary circumstances. The force of Chinese nationalism was obviously extraordinary.[104]

Here American missionary intentions to break down sexual segregation in China proved to be in conflict with missionary women's desire to create a protected sphere of "women's work" for Chinese women. Although Matilda Thurston was replaced by a Chinese woman, she was disturbed by the degree to which women's work was not being preserved. "I have serious misgivings about Chinese men getting control of girls' schools," she wrote, alluding to tales she had heard of "unhappy strain between foreign and Chinese workers."[105] Thurston hints at a level of strife that has largely disappeared from the written record. It is possible that she simply exaggerates the conflict, but it also seems likely that missionaries papered over disputes with Chinese co-workers so as to maintain the appearance of harmony. A sharp quarrel between Chinese men and American women in the Baptist Shantou mission reveals not only some of the tensions within the mission but also missionaries' hesitance in airing such events publicly. In a formal report to her home church, Abbie Sanderson described the contretemps as an "animated yet friendly debate."[106] Only to a member of the home mission board did she give a glimpse of what had really happened. A quarrel had broken out between a Miss Travers and Mr. Lo, the chairman of the mission's Executive Committee. Travers accused Lo of bad faith, for although he had agreed (under pressure from Travers and other missionary women) to create a special committee for Chinese women and to put Chinese women on other committees as well, there were no Chinese women on the Executive Committee. Lo retorted that he had not specifically promised to put Chinese women on the Executive Committee. He added that the Woman's Mission Board had agreed to hand over 5 per cent of its annual appropriation to the Chinese men in return for the representation of Chinese women on various committees, but had failed to do so. Finally, he accused the newly-formed Chinese women's committee of overstepping its bounds, for although it had been established to handle matters that the general committees felt were outside their purview, such as home-making and women's industrial work, the women had instead busied themselves with affairs that properly belonged to other committees. According to Sanderson, "He then read minutes of the committees to prove his statement."[107]

At this point, a missionary man named Speicher intervened to administer "a bit of a slap for both sides," admonishing Lo to speak courteously to the woman and reminding Travers that she was not in the United States and ought to try to understand the Chinese viewpoint. After considerable discussion, the Chinese men adopted Speicher's suggestion that the Executive Committee meet with the Woman's Board; if the latter had in fact cooperated with Chinese leadership, the men would then elect two Chinese women to the Executive Committee.

Sanderson believed that the conflict was about control. Noting the distrust on both sides, she stated that the Chinese men feared that American women only wanted Chinese women to be represented on mission committees because they wanted to be able to continue to exert influence over the Chinese Christian Church. Missionary women feared that Chinese men did not greatly care about "woman's work" and would "therefore let it slide," in Sanderson's words. Although she reported none of this in her formal report, Sanderson was both concerned with women's work and sympathetic to the views of the Chinese men. "The Chinese men were dead set against any kind of a woman's committee and the Chinese women were indifferent or fearful," she wrote. "We insisted, and so they compromised, but we are still insisting. *Can* we give in on some points?"[108]

Her question is revealing. Even after devolution had ostensibly occurred and the top administrative positions in Christian institutions had been turned over to Chinese, the money and therefore a good deal of power still remained in missionary hands. The problem could have been solved by turning over all monies unconditionally to the Chinese, but the missionaries did not do so. Instead, they continued to exert a certain amount of control over Christian institutions. In the mission schools, for example, a number of American missionaries left the daily administration in the hands of the Chinese and themselves joined committees devoted to overseeing the Christian school system as a whole. Others, like Matilda Thurston, refused to leave their school campuses and hung on as "advisors." In fact, one group of American missionaries formed the

Permanent Committee for the Coordination and Promotion of Christian Higher Education in China. At a December 1927 meeting, one person tentatively suggested that the Chinese might object to missionaries setting policies for the Christian colleges, now that these institutions were supposed to be under Chinese control. John Leighton Stuart dismissed this quibble as a "theoretical difficulty," and claimed that the Chinese did not mind if missionaries made policy. In any case, he argued, "this Committee or some other in this country should take the responsibility for stating the terms upon which the higher institutions should be supported." Stuart had managed to retain his power at Yenching University by agreeing to share leadership with Wu Leiquan, whose authority Stuart quickly usurped, turning the Chinese man into a mere figurehead. Devolution, then, was lopsided and incomplete; indeed, on the college level, it was something of a charade.[108]

The friction between American missionaries and Chinese over money and women's work exposes the missionaries' reluctance to relinquish their hold on Christian work in China. Frank Gamewell thought that the missionaries had "yielded much too easily" in the matter of devolution. Others feared that the Chinese were not ready for the responsibility. Reflecting on devolution forty years later, Methodist Katherine Ward stated that most missionaries were willing to try the experiment but "many of them felt that they would be right there to pick up the broken pieces if there was need."[109] Some American missionaries hovered anxiously, some sabotaged the new authority of Chinese Christians, while still others sullenly quit the field. A few, like Abbie Sanderson, genuinely tried to adjust. For teaching missionaries, devolution was complicated by the touchy issue of government registration of their schools.

Registration of Mission Schools

Following the Nanjing Incident, newly empowered Chinese administrators, with varying degrees of enthusiasm, pushed swiftly for government registration of mission schools. Although the GMD requirements were more stringent than those put forward by the Ministry of Education in Beijing, mission schools now had to adhere to the former for the GMD's military victories during the Northern Expedition put it in effective, although incomplete, control of the country. Missionaries were generally unable to resist the impetus toward registration; thus by 1930, three quarters of the mission schools had either registered or were in the process of doing so.[110]

Registration meant that religious courses and church attendance could no longer be mandatory, which heightened existing tensions between teaching missionaries and representatives of conservative Protestant missions. In 1920, fundamentalists established the Bible Union of China [BUC] and launched increasingly venomous attacks on theological modernism, which they saw as centered in the mission schools. Dorothy Barbour complained about conservative "agents" who came to Yenching University and its middle school to warn students away from modern biblical interpretations. She stated that many missionaries believed the fundamentalists would "set [Christianity] back five hundred years."[111]

The 1700 members of the BUC, however, believed that it was liberal missionaries who undermined the Christian cause. Conservatives had long argued that evangelism ought to take precedence over educational work; they supported the latter only if religious teaching was central to the schools' curriculum and purpose. The success of Christian schools in drawing students had muted late-nineteenth century objections to the educational mission, but patriotic upheavals in the mission school system in the twentieth century emboldened the evangelicals to renew their attack. Sophie Graham, a Presbyterian, spoke for many conservative missionaries when she reminded home supporters of her prediction that "if this craze for education continued and we did not keep abreast of it with the evangelism of the Chinese, it would be a perilous thing for China and for us."[112]

Educational missionaries were often annoyed by conservative attacks, but their schools felt little concrete impact. The Northern Baptist convention, to be sure, voted to investigate the theological orthodoxy of their missionaries, John Leighton Stuart was catechized by his sponsoring mission, the Southern Presbyterians, and Southern Baptists did withdraw from union educational institutions. Otherwise liberal missionaries and their institutions went on as they had before. Not only were the conservative Protestants greatly outnumbered in China, but most Chinese

Christians, according to Paul Hutchinson, linked liberalism with science and progress and thus were unsympathetic to the conservative position.[113]

Since mission schools continued to operate in China after registration requirements forced them to yield on the question of religious instruction and church attendance, it is clear that conservative Christians were correct, to some degree, in asserting that teaching Christian doctrine was not an overriding goal for educational missionaries. Missionary documents and correspondence, however, reveal that educational missionaries were greatly divided on the issue of how to respond not only to the GMD's ban on religious teaching but its parallel requirement that the political philosophy of Sun Yatsen be taught.[114]

Most American educational missionaries agreed that there was something distasteful in compelling students to study Christianity or attend worship services. As these missionaries pointed out, when only sincerely interested students attended chapel, there was no need to discipline individuals who expressed their boredom by reading newspapers and eating peanuts during services. Moreover, the participation of mission school students in the Anti-Christian movement convinced many that "compulsory religious training has borne but ill fruits in the past."[115] But some missionaries, while admitting the validity of these sentiments, objected to what they interpreted as the GMD's violation of religious and academic freedom, and argued that each school ought to be free to decide for itself how to handle religious instruction. In essence, these missionaries put a higher value on their own religious freedom than on Chinese national sovereignty.[116]

American missionaries and their Chinese associates were similarly divided by the GMD's demand that Sun Yatsen's "Three Principles of the People" [*San Min Zhuyi*] be taught by someone certified by the local party organization and that all schools hold a weekly memorial service before a picture of the late GMD leader. This paralleled, in some ways, the nineteenth-century necessity of teaching the Confucian classics in the mission schools. In both instances, missionaries were wary of the presence of an outsider, a non-Christian, whose teaching was in competition with Christian doctrine. Similarly, American missionaries objected to any posture of obeisance such as bowing the head or kneeling when not performed in a Christian context of worship. Thus some missionaries regarded honoring Sun Yatsen as idolatrous and argued that the GMD was attempting to turn all schools into centers for its own propaganda.[117] Other teaching missionaries believed that the ceremony was harmless, asserting that showing respect to Sun was no different from respecting American heroes, such as Washington and Lincoln.[118] Schools that outwardly complied with the requirements sometimes practiced a variety of evasions of the spirit, if not the letter, of the rule. At Ginling College, for example, the man who taught the *San Min Zhuyi* course was not a party member; schools officials hoped that GMD authorities would not object. In some schools, American missionaries compromised by agreeing to hold the memorial services while continuing to hold Christian services as well. To underscore the difference between the two services, missionaries often held them in separate rooms specifically set aside for that purpose.[119]

Just as some American teaching missionaries looked for ways around the GMD's regulations on party theory and memorials to Sun, so a number of missionaries sought to avoid government registration of their schools altogether, sometimes with the complicity of new Chinese Christian administrators. The key strategy was simply to delay registration in the hope that either the requirements would be changed or, that through a special relationship [*guanxi*] with a government official, a particular school might be exempted. The Chinese vice-president of West China Union University initially recommended postponing registration, while seeking to make friends with members of the Provincial Board of Education. In Hangzhou, missionaries at the Union Girls' School had prepared for registration in 1925, but after the GMD's more stringent rules were announced, they decided to put off registration "until the government can see new light and change this order, as we are not willing to give up the very thing for which the school was established, the spreading of the Gospel of Jesus Christ."[120]

Some teaching missionaries were more devious in evading registration. After Mary Margaret Moninger's Presbyterian school was forcibly closed for failing to register, Moninger and her colleagues rented the school buildings to the Chinese teachers, all of whom were Christian, in the belief that the school would not be harassed if the missionaries withdrew. It took another three years before the government responded with a new order to close, but since the proclamation mentioned only the boys' school by name, the missionaries took this as permission to continue to run the girls' school, although it was not registered either.[121] Since the government stated that no unregistered school could call itself "*xuexiao*" ("school") but had to take the name "institute" or some other equivalent, some teaching missionaries interpreted this to mean that if they changed the school's name, they could operate without registering. In some instances, Chinese officials permitted mission schools to slip through this loophole.[122]

One of the new government regulations was that no school could declare its purpose to be the propagation of religion. Many Christian schools found ways around this rule, too. The Hangchow Union Girls' School stated that its purpose was "to carry out the general educational aims of the Chinese government and in Christ's spirit of love, sacrifice and service to develop a noble character." GMD officials permitted it. Officials in Suzhou, however, were offended by Soochow University's statement that it aimed "to develop the highest type of Christian character," so the University changed this to read "to develop the highest type of character in accordance with the original purposes of the founders." The revision did not alter the meaning, but removing the word "Christian" made it acceptable. Not all teaching missionaries approved of the tactic. Matilda Thurston wrote that she would rather remove all references to religion than utilize any "watered down attempt to state a Christian purpose." She further noted: "Sacrifice and service are not essentially Christian; they are possible for the sake of Communism as well as for the Kingdom of God."[123]

Enforcement of mission school registration varied considerably. Some schools that defied the Ministry of Education were forced to close. Lutheran Thyra Lawson's school was one of these; she reopened it as an industrial school in 1929 since these schools were not required to pay homage to Sun Yatsen. Although she gradually reintroduced religious instruction in the new school, the government did not interfere. Other schools ignored registration requirements and simply waited to see what would happen. Lois Young wondered what action Chinese officials might take against her unregistered school. "It is possible that they will make it hard for us, it is also possible that they will not notice it for years."[124]

Students and Chinese parents sometimes lent their support to either the government or the missionaries in registration battles. At Shanghai Christian College, for example, student protests forced the school to register. On the other hand, girls in Caroline Lee's Presbyterian school blocked their ears with their fingers when a GMD official urged them to renounce Christianity, and missionaries at the Yenping Girls' School were following the wishes of local Chinese Christians when they defied the magistrate's order to register. [125]

Although not all mission schools were forced to register or shut down, by 1930 the majority of them were at least making a show of complying with governmental requirements. The administrative autonomy that these foreign schools had enjoyed prior to the Nanjing Incident was clearly dissipating; equally clearly, an era in the American missionary educational movement was drawing to a close.

ENDNOTES

1 Chapter heading comes from Frank D. Gamewell to Frank Mason North, Oct. 7, 1925, 73-43: 1041-1-1-:18, GBGM; see also Goodrich Girls' School, Alice Margaret Huggins to family, Nov. 7, 1925, Pamphlet Collection, RG 31, Box 276, Folder 1963, YDSL; Ida Belle Lewis to family, June 6, 1926, Ida Belle Lewis [Main] Papers, RG Ax 216, Box 1, UOSC.

2 Paul Hayes' papers contain a number of pamphlets and articles on this controversy, including Paul Hutchinson's "The Conservative Reaction in China," *Journal of Religion* 2:4 (July 1922): 337–361, reprints of letters to the *North China Daily* in 1924, and copies of *The China Fundamentalist and Anti-Bolshevik Bulletin* and *The Bulletin of the Bible Union of China*. Paul Hayes Papers, Folder 7, ELCA.

3 Minnie Vautrin, diary, Jan. 29, 1928, Ginling College, UBCHEA, RG 11, Box 144, Folder 2858, YDSL; Dr. Dyers to home church, quoting Dr. Newell, Feb. 1, 1927, Elizabeth Perkins Papers, RG 8, Box 159, Folder 49, YDSL.

4 Jessie G. Lutz, *China and the Christian Colleges, 1850–1950* (Ithaca: Cornell University Press, 1971), p. 269.

5 "Some Essential Characteristics and Problems of Christian Education," p. 34, from the Proceedings of the Second General Assembly of the Lutheran Church in China, March 30– April 2, 1924, ELCA.

6 Abbie Sanderson to Mabel McVeigh, Apr. 19, 1927, Abbie Sanderson Papers, RG 8, Box 183, YDSL; Edwin Lobenstine to Frank D. Gamewell, Sept. 3, 1927, 73-43:1115-5- 1:22, GBGM; memo from the Council of Higher Education, Aug. 31, 1927, 73-43: 1115- 3-2:12, GBGM.

7 Knight Biggerstaff, *The Earliest Modern Government Schools in China* (Ithaca: Cornell University Press, 1961).

8 *Records of the Second Triennial Meeting of the Educational Association of China* (Shanghai: American Presbyterian Mission Press, 1896), pp. 38, 42–45; *Records of the First Triennial Meeting of the Educational Association of China* (Shanghai: American Presbyterian Mission Press, 1893), pp. 24–25.

9 Sally Borthwick, *Education and Social Change in China: The Beginnings of the Modern Era* (Stanford: Hoover Institution Press, 1983), p. 87.

10 Lin Pao-ch'tuan, *L'Instruction Femenine en Chine (Apres la Revolution de 1911)* (Paris: Librairie Geuther, 1926), p. 16; Borthwick, *Education and Social Change*, p. 116.

11 Theodore Hsiao, *The History of Modern Education in China* (Peiping: Peking University Press, 1932), pp. 27–29, 37.

12 *China Centenary Missionary Conference* (Shanghai: Centenary Conference Committee, 1907), p. 481.

13 Chaoyang [Baptist mission station] Report, n.d., Adam and Clara Groesbeck Papers, RG Ax 818, Box 1, UOSC; Borthwick, *Education and Social Change*, p. 100.

14 *Centenary Conference*, pp. 60–72.

15 Hiroshi Abe, "Borrowing from Japan: China's First Modern Educational System" pp. 57–80, see p. 67, in Ruth Hayhoe and Marianne Bastid, eds., *China's Education and the Industrialized World: Studies in Cultural Transfer* (Armonk, N.Y.: M. E. Sharpe, 1987).

16 Alice Gregg, *China and Educational Autonomy: The Changing Role of the Protestant Educational Missionary in China, 1807–1937* (Syracuse, N.Y.: Syracuse University Press, 1946), p. 26; Adam Groesbeck to family, April 8, 1926, Adam and Clara Groesbeck Papers, RG Ax 818, Box 1, UOSC; Monona Cheney to family, Oct. 19, 1920, Monona Cheney Papers, RG Ax 275, Box 1, UOSC; Lois Young to family, April 17, 1921, Lois Young Papers, H85.128491, BWM.

17 Hiroshi Abe, "Borrowing from Japan," pp. 68–73.

18 Charles Iglehart, *A Century of Protestant Christianity in Japan* (Rutland, Vt.: Charles E. Tuttle, Co., 1959), pp. 110–111.

19 *World Missionary Conference, Report of Commission III: Education in Relation to National Life* (New York: Fleming H. Revell, Co., 1910), p. 110.

20 *Centenary Conference*, pp. 184–185.

21 *Chinese Recorder* 34 (May 1903): 230–235.

22 *Chinese Recorder* 34 (January 1903): 28.

23 *Centenary Conference*, p. 69.

24 Kenneth S. Latourette, *A History of Christian Missions in China* (New York: MacMillan Co., 1929), p. 644; Borthwick, *Education and Social Change*, p. 85.

25 Borthwick, *Education and Social Change,* p. 108. Borthwick points out that schools were not free for very long, with the result that although mission schools were the more expensive, government schools were not accessible to the poorest Chinese either.

26 *Centenary Conference*, p. 488.

27 W. Tchishin Tao and C. P. Chen, *Education in China, 1924* (Shanghai: Commercial Press Ltd., 1925), pp. 10, 29.

28 *Records of the Third Triennial Meeting of the Educational Association of China* (Shanghai: American Presbyterian Mission Press, 1899), p. 40.

29 Monona Cheney to family, Sept. 4, 1920, Monona Cheney Papers, RG Ax 275, Box 1, UOSC; *Centenary Conference*, p. 186; *Christian Education in China: A Study Made by an Educational Commission Representing the Mission Boards and Societies Conducting Work in China* (New York: Committee of Reference and Counsel of the Foreign Missions Conference of North America, 1922), p. 46.

30 Elizabeth Brewster, "Guthrie Memorial High School Historical Sketch," 1934, 79-16: 1459-4-2: 41, GBGM; Katherine Ward interview, p. 15, MCOHP, 1977, ELCA.

31 *Missionary Review of the World* (September 1925): 732.

32 Frida Nilsen interview, p. 221, MCOHP, 1976, ELCA.

33 Letter to to Mission Boards and Homes Churches, August 1909, Nanking University correspondence, 79-16: 1459-4-3: 25, GBGM.

34 Ida Belle Lewis, "The Need for Educational Missionaries in China," *Student Volunteer Movement Bulletin* 5: 12 (April 1925): 20–21, Ida Belle Lewis [Main] Papers, RG Ax 216, Box 1, UOSC.

35 D. McGillivray, ed., *A Century of Protestant Missions in China (1807–1907)* (Shanghai: American Presbyterian Mission Press, 1907), p. 582.

36 *Ibid.*, p. 584; Gregg, *China and Educational Autonomy*, ch. 4.

37 *Chinese Recorder* 33 (December 1902): 619–621.

38 *Chinese Recorder* 34 (November 1903): 558–560.

39 Frank D. Gamewell to Frank Mason North, March 26, 1914, 73-43: 1043-1-3: 16, GBGM.

40 Wu Yi-fang to the Methodist Board of Foreign Missions, Sept. 21, 1928, Ginling College, Correspondence, UBCHEA, RG 11, Box 147, Folder 2897, YDSL.

41 Monona Cheney to family, March 31, 1921, Monona Cheney Papers, RG Ax 275, Box 1, UOSC; *Student Volunteer Bulletin* 5: 12 (April 1925): 23, RG Ax 216, Box 1, Ida Belle Lewis [Main] Papers, UOSC. Around the turn of the century, the American Protestant mission boards were themselves adhering to a professional ethic. Patricia Hill, *The World Their Household: The American Woman's Foreign Mission Movement and Cultural Transformation, 1870–1920* (Ann Arbor: University of Michigan Press, 1985); and Valentin H. Rabe, *The Home Base of American China Missions, 1880–1920* (Cambridge: Harvard University Press, 1978).

42 Elsie Clark to family, Aug. 3, 1913, Elsie Clark [Krug] Papers, RG 8, Box 41, YDSL.

43 Latourette, *Christian Missions in China,* p. 757.

44 Gregg, *China and Educational Autonomy,* p. 81. There were 506 Chinese educational associations by 1908, and 723 the following year. Marianne Bastid, trans. Paul Bailey, *Educational Reform in Early Twentieth-Century China* (Ann Arbor: Center for Chinese Studies, 1988), p. 63.

45 *First Triennial of the EAC,* 1893, p. 10; *Second Triennial of the EAC,* 1896, p. 42; *Third Triennial of the EAC,* 1899, p. 41.

46 *World Atlas of Christian Missionaries,* 1911, p. 65. Adherence to the Uniform Curriculum and Uniform Examinations within the mission schools, however, was voluntary. See the *Chinese Recorder* 43 (April 1912): 226–229.

47 Lucius Eddy Ford, "The History of the Educational Work of the Methodist Episcopal Church in China: A Study of its Development and Present Trends" (Ph.D. diss., Northwestern University, 1936), p. 221; *Chinese Recorder* 45 (January 1914): 65.

48 Myrtle Smith to family, March 15, 1924, Myrtle Smith Papers, RG A 164, UOSC.

49 *Chinese Recorder* 43 (April 1912): 226–229.

50 Sheet of examination rules, 1915, Elizabeth Perkins Papers, RG 11, Box 154, YDSL.

51 *Chinese Recorder* 28 (January 1897): 3.

52 *Centenary Conference,* pp. 169, 580.

53 Annie E. Bradshaw, "Our Teacher Training Center in China: The Laura Haygood Normal," n. d., 79-16: 1459-4-1: 24, GBGM. Methodists established a normal school as early as 1903 in Fuzhou, which became a union institution in 1913 when the American Board joined in supporting the school. 79-16: 1459-4-2: 23, GBGM.

54 Sara Collins, "Presbyterian Schools in China," 1902, NT6.3 C692p, PC (USA) and Hangchow Union Girls' School catalogue, 1912, NT6.3 H193uc, PC (USA).

55 Mary Raleigh Anderson, *A Cycle in the Celestial Kingdom or Protestant Mission Schools for Girls in South China (1827 to the Japanese Invasion)* (Mobile, Ala.: Heiter-Starke Printing Co., 1943), p. 257; Ida Belle Lewis to family, Jan. 16, 1921, and "Some Factors in the Evaluation of Christian Lower Primary Schools," booklet (Shanghai: Commercial Press Ltd., 1921), p. 4, Ida Belle Lewis [Main] Papers, RG Ax 216, Box 1, UOSC.

56 Eva Sprunger, Report on Kutien, July 28, 1922, Myrtle Smith Papers, RG A 164, UOSC. A graduate of a higher primary school had the equivalent of an eighth-grade education in the United States.

57 District Conference Report, 1921, Myrtle Smith Papers, RG A 164, UOSC; Report of the Mary Stevens Memorial Girls' School, 1923, 79-16: 1459-5-2: 09, GBGM.

58 Myrtle Smith to family, Oct. 5, 1923, Myrtle Smith Papers, RG A 164, UOSC.

59 Borthwick, *Education and Social Change,* p. 121.

60 Mada McCutcheon to home church, June 30, 1924, and June 26, 1925, microfilm #108, BWM. In the Methodist Baldwin Girls' School, between 50 and 80 per cent of the faculty were Baldwin graduates in the 1920s. Lan-ching Chou Cheng, "Our History," n. d., 79-16: 1459-4-3: 11, GBGM.

61 Luella Tappan to family, May 20, 1922, David and Luella Tappan Papers, RG 103, UOSC; Myrtle Smith to family, Feb. 21, 1922, Myrtle Smith Papers, RG 164, UOSC.

62 *Second Triennial of the EAC*, 1896, p. 134.

63 Annual Report, Southern Presbyterian Mission, 1907, BWM.

64 Lois Young to family, Feb. 19, 1925, Lois Young Papers, H85.128491, BWM.

65 Myrtle Smith to family, April 2, 1922, Myrtle Smith Papers, RG A 164, UOSC; "The Kuling School Today—for Children of American Missionaries and Other Americans in China, Why?" pamphlet, 1934, Pamphlet Collection, RG 31, Box 297, Folder 1967, YDSL.

66 At Yenching University, for example, missionaries received their salaries in gold, which was worth twice as much as the Chinese money in which the Chinese faculty was paid. Alice Boring to Mr. Warner (Chair of Yenching's Board of Trustees), Nov. 17, 1930, Yenching University, Correspondence, UBCHEA, RG 11, Box 320, Folder 4893, YDSL.

67 Quoted in Jane Hunter, *The Gospel of Gentility: American Women Missionaries in Turn-of-the-Century China* (New Haven: Yale University Press, 1984), p. 254.

68 Elsie Reik to family, April 28, 1928, Elsie Reik Papers, UOSC; Hunter, *Gospel of Gentility*, pp. 134–135.

69 Abbie Sanderson to family, April 12, 1918, Abbie Sanderson Papers, RG 8, Box 177, YDSL.

70 Mildred Test Young interview, MCOHP, 1978, p. 37, ELCA.

71 Mary Margaret Moninger to family, Aug. 8, 1920, Mary Margaret Moninger Papers, RG 230, Box 1, Folder 16, PC (USA).

72 Joel Spring, *The American School, 1642–1985* (New York: Longman, 1986), pp. 113–124.

73 Gregg, *China and Educational Autonomy*, pp. 88–90, *Chinese Recorder* 42 (Jan. 1911): 43; *Chinese Recorder* 45 (Jan. 1914): 65.

74 *Chinese Recorder* 39 (Dec. 1908): 663–667; *Chinese Recorder* 45 (Jan. 1914): 2.

75. Gregg, *China and Educational Autonomy*, p. 92; Tao and Chen, *Education in China*, p. 3.

76 Chow Tse-tsung, *The May Fourth Movement: Intellectual Revolution in Modern China* (Cambridge: Harvard University Press, 1960), p. 59; Jessie G. Lutz, "Students and Politics, Revolution and Historical Continuity: The Chinese Anti-Christian Campaigns of the 1920s," pp. 191–217, in Jessie G. Lutz and Salah El-Shakhs, eds., *Tradition and Modernity: The Role of Traditionalism in the Modernization Process* (Washington, D. C.: University Press of America, 1982); Ka-che Yip, *Religion, Nationalism and Chinese Students: The Anti-Christian Movement of 1922–1927* (Bellingham: Western Washington University Press, 1980); Jessie G. Lutz, *Chinese Politics and Christian Missions: The Anti-Christian Movements of 1920–1928* (Notre Dame: Cross Cultural Publications, Inc., 1988).

77 Frank D. Gamewell to Rev. John R. Edwards, July 23, 1925, 73-43: 1043-1-3:18, GBGM; Grace Manly, "The Present Problem in West China," *Woman's Missionary Friend* (Jan. 1927): 12.

78 "A Gateway to Tientsin Hui Wen Academy," 1927, p. 7, 79-16:1459-5-1:13, GBGM.

79 Harold Balme to J. H. Oldham, Jan. 21, 1925, 73-43:1115-6-2:11, GBGM; Wu Chao-kwang, "The International Aspect of the Missionary Movement in China" (Ph.D. diss., Johns Hopkins University, 1930), p. 182.

80 Djung Lu-dzai, *A History of Democratic Education in Modern China* (1934; reprint, Taipei: Ch'eng Wen Publishing Co., 1974), pp. 174–175.

81 GMD power, however, was at this time limited to Guangdong and Hunan provinces. Gregg, *China and Educational Autonomy*, p. 139; Djung, *Democratic Education*, 175–176; Tsang Chih Sam, *Nationalism in School Education in China Since the Opening of the Twentieth Century* (Hong Kong: South China Morning Post, Ltd., 1933), pp. 206–208; "Tentative Regulations for Carrying Out Party Education," National Government, April 1927, UBCHEA, RG 11, Box 22, Folder 522, YDSL.

82 Frank D. Gamewell to Elizabeth Bender, Oct. 25, 1926, 73-43:1107-7-3:40, GBGM; Conference of Missionary Educators, report, April 22, 1927, 73-43:1115-5-1:22, GBGM.

83 Mada McCutcheon to home church, Jan. 29, 1926, microfilm # 108, BWM; Matilda Thurston, Jan. 3, 1926, Ginling College, Correspondence, UBCHEA, RG 11, Box 144, Folder 2857, YDSL; Report of the Council of the Lutheran Church in China, Hankow, President's Report, 1926, p. 15, ELCA.

84 Harriet Stroh to family, Aug. 1, 1922, Harriet Stroh Papers, RG 187, Box 1, Folder 5, PC (USA).

85 *Chinese Recorder* 42 (Aug. 1911): 470–471; *Chinese Recorder* 43 (March 1912): 125; *Chinese Recorder* 42 (May 1911): 248.

86 Ford, "History of the Educational Work," Table IV, "Methodist Schools in 1927," p, 217; "Marie Brown Davis Girls' Boarding School, "Ten Years Progress, 1905–1915," 79-16:1459-5-1:27, GBGM; "Minutes of the 6th Session of the Hinghua Mission Conference, Oct. 23–28, 1901, p. 41, Arthur and Mabel Billings Papers, RG Ax 652, Box 1, UOSC; Carolyn Johnson Memorial School, Principal's Report, 1911, 79-16: 1459-4-2:34, GBGM.

87 *Bulletin of the Eastern China Christian Educational Association*, May 30, 1923, 73-43:1043-1-3:17, GBGM.

88 *Ibid.*

89 "A Chinese Student Visits Japan," by Li Dze-djen, n.d., in the Emily Case Mills Papers, RG 8, Box 141, YDSL; Matilda Thurston, Jan. 3, 1926, Ginling College, Correspondence, UBCHEA, RG 11, Box 144, Folder 2857, YDSL; Abbie Sanderson to family, July 20, 1925, Abbie Sanderson Papers, RG 8, Box 179, YDSL; Ivy Chou interview, pp. 7–12, MCOHP, 1976, ELCA.

90 Abbie Sanderson to parents, June 10, 1925, Abbie Sanderson Papers, RG 8, Box 178, YDSL.

91 Latourette, *Christian Missions in China*, 820.

92 Matilda Thurston and Ruth Chester, *Ginling College* (New York: United Board for Christian Colleges in China, 1955), pp. 57–63.

93 "Gleanings from Ginling Letters," 1927, Ginling Women's College, Pamphlet Collection, RG 31, Box 275, Folder 1959, YDSL.

94 Report on the Nanking Incident, n.d., Ginling College, UBCHEA, RG 11, Box 144, Folder 2857, YDSL; Thurston and Chester, *Ginling College*, p. 64.

95 Lois Young to family, Feb. 9, 1927, Lois Young Papers, H85.128491, BWM; Florence Nickles, Letters About the Nanking Incident, n.d., Florence Nickles Papers, BWM.

96 William A. Brown, "The Protestant Rural Movement in China, 1920–1937," pp. 217–248, see p. 221, in Liu Kwang-ching, ed., *American Missionaries in China, Papers from Harvard Seminars* (Cambridge: East Asian Research Center, Harvard University Press, 1970).

97 Abbie Sanderson to parents, Aug. 9, 1925, Abbie Sanderson Papers, RG 8, Box 179, YDSL.

98 "The School Teachers" to Lois Young, Sept. 24, 1927, Lois Young Papers, H85.128491, BWM; Mary Margaret Moninger to family, Feb. 21, 1926, Mary Margaret Moninger Papers, RG 230, Box 1, Folder 30, PC (USA).

99 "Notes Taken on meeting of the Committee on China," Methodist mission, July 22, 1927, 73-43:1115-5-1:22, GBGM.

100 "Memo: The Missionary Situation in China, (2-14-27)," 73-43:1115-5-1:22, GBGM.

101 Adam Groesbeck to family, Mar. 3, 1927, Adam and Clara Groesbeck Papers, RG Ax 818, Box 1, UOSC; Frank Gamewell to Frank T. Cartwright, Apr. 16, 1929, 73-43:1043-1-3:22, GBGM; Ida Belle Lewis to family, Feb. 27, 1926, Ida Belle Lewis [Main] Papers, RG Ax 216, Box 1, UOSC; Lois Young to "Dear Partner," Dec. 19, 1928 and to Mrs. Woods, Feb. 13, 1930, Lois Young Papers, H85.128491, BWM.

102West China Union University Vice-President's Report, 1927–1928, 79-16:1459-5-1:40, GBGM; "The Place of Christian Education in New China," by Y. C. Yang, pamphlet, n. d., 73-43:1115-3-2:13, GBGM; Wu Yi-fang to Elizabeth Bender, May 29, 1928, 73-43:1109-1-1:38, GBGM.

103 Abbie Sanderson to family, Jan. 15, 1928 and Sept. 11, 1929, Abbie Sanderson Papers, RG 8, Box 183, YDSL; "Sinyang Girls' School, Before and Now," by Elsa Felland, pamphlet, n. d., in folder labeled "I Kwang/Lena Dahl," ELCA; 79-16:1459-4-2:28 and 2:29, GBGM; Station Annual Report, 1929–1930 in the Harriet Stroh Papers, RG 187, Box 3, Folder 3, PC (USA); Alice Reed, Excerpts From Letters, Sept. 7, 1930, p. 100, Alice Reed Papers, RG 8, Box 163, YDSL.

104 Report of the Woman's Unit, Shantung Christian College, 1926, Shantung Christian College, UBCHEA, RG 11, Box 244, Folder 3993, YDSL; "The Keen School I Remember," Ida K. Frantz, 1972, p. 7, 79-16:1459-5-1:12, GBGM; Hangchow Union Girls' School, report, 1923, NT6.3 H19ud, PC (USA).

105 Matilda Thurston, Typed Excerpts from Letters, Sept. 24, 1928, Ginling College, Correspondence, UBCHEA, RG 11, Box 144, Folder 2860, YDSL.

106 Abbie Sanderson, "Report on the Ling Tong Convention," Aug. 10, 1926, Abbie Sanderson Papers, RG 8, Box 179, YDSL.

107 Abbie Sanderson to Miss McVeigh, July 15, 1926, Abbie Sanderson Papers, RG 8, Box 179, YDSL.

108 *Ibid.* Emphasis in original.

109 Elizabeth Bender to Margaret Hodge, May 23, 1928, RG 11, Box 135, Folder 2710, YDSL; Minutes of the Meeting of the Permanent Committee for the Coordination and Promotion of Christian Higher Education in China, December 6, 1927, 73-43:1115-3-2:12, GBGM; W. B. Nance, *Soochow University* (New York: United Board of Christian Colleges in China, 1956), p. 103, Charles Corbett, *Lingnan University*, p. 107; Philip West, *Yenching University and Sino-Western Relations, 1916–1952* (Cambridge: Harvard University Press, 1976), p. 134, and Clarence Burton Day, *Hangchow University: A Brief History* (New York: United Board for Christian Colleges in China, 1955), p. 64.

110 Frank Gamewell to Rev. Edwards, May 31, 1929, 73-43:1043-1-3:22, GBGM; Katherine Ward interview, p. 8, MCOHP, 1977, ELCA.

111 Gregg, *China and Educational Autonomy*, p. 170; Djung, *History of Democratic Education*, p. 177.

112 Paul Hutchinson, "The Conservative Reaction in China," *Journal of Religion* 2:4 (July 1922): 337–361, in the Paul Hayes Papers, ELCA; Dorothy Barbour to family, Jan. 30, 1925, George and Dorothy Barbour Papers, RG 8, Box 13, Folder 1925, YDSL.

113 Sophie Graham to home church, July 13, 1927, Microfilm # 105, BWM; Paul Varg, *Missionaries, Chinese and Diplomats: The American Protestant Missionary Movement in China, 1890–1950* (Princeton: Princeton University Press, 1958), p. 213.

114 A. H. Page to the South China Mission, June 4, 1924, in the Abbie Sanderson Papers, RG 8, Box 179, YDSL; West, *Yenching University*, pp. 42–43; Hutchinson, "The Conservative Reaction," p. 380. 385, Paul Hayes Papers, ELCA.

115 Both issues were debated at the Conference of Missionary Educators, held in Shanghai on April 22, 1927, 73-43:1115-5-1:22, GBGM.

116 "A Gateway to the Tientsin Hui Wen Academy," pamphlet, 1927, p. 7, 79-16:1459-5-1:13, GBGM; Louise Ankeny to family, Nov. 9, 1925, Henry and Louise Ankeny Lacy Papers, RG Ax 412, Box 1, UOSC.

117 Conference of Missionary Educators, April 22, 1927, Shanghai, 73-43:1115-5-1:22, GBGM.

118 China Christian Educational Association to the Board of Foreign Missions of the Methodist Episcopal Church, May 2, 1927, 73-43:1115-5-1:22, GBGM.

119 Ethel Akins interview, pp. 19–20, MCOHP, 1976, ELCA; Paul Hayes interview, p. 23, MCOHP, 1977, ELCA; *Hainan Newsletter*, Fall 1926, 73-43:1115-5-1:22, GBGM.

120 Minnie Vautrin to Elizabeth Bender, Jan. 4, 1929, Ginling College, Correspondence, UBCHEA, RG 11, Box 145, Folder 2871, YDSL; Woman's Work, Foochow Conference, 1928, report of the Marguerite Stewart Girls' School, in the Ida Belle Lewis [Main] Papers, RG Ax 216, Box 2, UOSC; Annual Report of the Lutheran College, 1929–1930, Lutheran Church of China, ELCA.

121 West China Union University, Vice-president's report for 1927–1928, 79-16:1459-5-1:40, GBGM; Hangchow Union Girls' School, report, 1925, NT6.3 H193ud, PC (USA).

122 Mary Margaret Moninger to family, Feb. 27, 1927 and May 4, 1930, Mary Margaret Moninger Papers, RG 230, Box 1, Folders 32 and 33, PC (USA).

123 Abbie Sanderson to family, Sept. 11, 1929, Abbie Sanderson Papers, RG 8, Box 183, YDSL; Mada McCutcheon to home church, January 1930, microfilm #108, BWM.

124 Hangchow Union Girls' School, report, 1929–1230, NT6.3 H193ud, PC (USA); "Statement of Purpose in the Constitution of the Board of Directors," May 2, 1929, 79-16:1079-2-5:01, GBGM; Matilda Thurston to Elizabeth Bender, Aug. 16, 1928, 73-43:1109-1-1:38, GBGM.

125 Thyra Lawson interview, pp. 21–22, MCOHP, 1977, ELCA; Lois Young to family, Feb. 16, 1929, Lois Young Papers, H85. 128491, BWM.

126 "The Tang Pu's Attack on Shantung Christian University," pamphlet by "Eyewitnesses," 1928–1929, Shantung Christian College, UBCHEA, RG 11, Box 267, Folder 4272, YDSL; Caroline V. Lee to home church, April 13, 1929, microfilm #107, BWM; Yenping Pagoda Herald (November 1927), Mae Boucher Papers, RG Ax 262, UOSC.

EPILOGUE

American teaching missionaries were aware that with the passing of power into Chinese hands an era had ended, although another twenty years elapsed before the foreign missionary movement collapsed in China. They were not peaceful years. In 1931, Japan seized Manchuria and began exerting increasing pressure on China. In 1937, this pressure turned to full-scale warfare. Extraterritoriality, long despised by the Chinese, now came in handy, for many American missionaries remained in China with their schools operating under the protection of the American flag. After Pearl Harbor, most Americans left China, although some were interned in Shanghai and others fled to the interior, to "Free China." Most mission schools were forced to close then, but a number of Christian colleges packed up and moved to West China, out of the reach of the Japanese. After the war, American missionaries came back to China, and exiled schools returned to devastated campuses and began the process of rebuilding, only to be thrown into disorder once more as civil war raged across the country. After the Communist victory, there was again a mass exodus of missionaries, although a handful of Americans stayed on, believing that they could work with the new regime. The outbreak of the Korean War shattered that hope, however, and the few remaining missionaries either left voluntarily or were deported, some after having been imprisoned.[1]

Thus the years 1880 to 1930 were the high tide of American Protestant education in China. Before 1880, American mission schools were, on the whole, isolated and struggling institutions with no clear place either in American evangelism or Chinese education. After 1930, what had become an effective and organized system of education was largely in Chinese hands and subject to Chinese government control. Even during the fifty years in which American Christian schools enjoyed both popularity and autonomy, however, teaching missionaries found that many of their extracurricular goals eluded them. They had come to China in the late nineteenth century as harsh critics of traditional Chinese society: they disapproved of its educational system, its family organization, its religious beliefs and practices, its gender ideology, and its arrogant certitude that

China was the seat of all civilization. Chen Hengzhe [Sophia Chen], a Western-educated history professor at Beijing University, noted that those early missionaries could not conceive of Chinese culture as a rival to their own; instead, they stressed "the dark and savage" and set themselves to save China and the Chinese.[2] Mission schools were established to aid in this campaign.

The relationship between American Protestant missionaries and the Chinese, however, did not unfold in the way missionaries had envisioned. Missionaries had no authority to induce the Chinese to send their children to Christian schools and hence were compelled to compromise with some aspects of Chinese culture in order to attract pupils. The original missionary compromise was the agreement to teach the Chinese classics, even if they had to hire non-Christian men to teach this course. Girls' education succeeded initially only because the missionaries were willing to undertake the material support of poor girls. As time went on, missionaries made further compromises with the Chinese. In the late nineteenth century, they were persuaded to broaden the curriculum in their schools, making the Christian schools increasingly secular. Missionaries agreed to teach English, even though they could not develop any evangelistic justification for so doing. Finally, they compromised with the Chinese government by registering their schools, relinquishing (more or less) their positions as leaders in the Christian educational movement, and removing all compulsory features of Christian instruction within their schools.

Through these continuous compromises, the evangelical content of Protestant education in China steadily waned. The decline in evangelical emphasis was accompanied by a commensurate increase in the missionaries' devotion to educational and professional standards. Missionaries were determined that their schools in China would be as good as the missionaries could make them. This was both a function of missionary pride in their educational institutions as such and their desire to attract Chinese students. Once the Chinese government established a modern school system shortly after the turn of the century, missionaries wanted their schools to be able to compete successfully with the new government schools. By 1927, it was evident from the missionary response to devolution and government registration that they were willing to expunge nearly all religious elements from their schools if they were only allowed to continue to operate schools in China. After the mission schools were registered with the government, only "Christian influence" or "the Christian spirit" (and the presence of missionaries in various capacities) remained to define the difference between government and mission institutions. Missionaries insisted that although this Christian influence was "intangible" it was "real."[3] It is clear from this feeble assertion of a lingering evangelical purpose that missionaries were conscious of how far from their origins the Christian schools had strayed. Yet it was primarily missionaries who were not involved in education who suggested closing the schools and refocusing missionary energies on direct evangelism. For educational missionaries, education had acquired an imperative of its own.

Evangelism, however, had never been the sole concern of American educational missionaries. Besides seeking to educate and Christianize their students, missionaries had attempted to reform Chinese gender practices and attitudes, using their schools as vehicles for social change. Here, too, missionaries' efforts yielded mixed results. Originally, the Chinese had heeded the entreaties of the missionaries to treat their daughters and daughters-in-law in a "Christian" manner only when such entreaties were accompanied by some material incentive. After the turn of the century, as a result of long-existing strains within the Chinese family system and the various internal and external pressures that contributed to the disintegration of traditional society, Chinese gender practices likewise underwent rapid transformation. Missionaries suddenly found themselves attempting to stem a tide of social and sexual change that they believed they were responsible for setting in motion.

The way in which American missionary attitudes toward their own and Chinese culture changed over time is a phenomenon that has not been greatly heeded. Late-nineteenth-century American missionaries were unabashedly pro-American and pro-Western; they rarely had anything positive to say about Chinese culture; all of their efforts went into changing and reforming it. Shortly after 1900, however, missionary scorn for Chinese culture and pride in their own both began to shift. The "awakening" of China in the years following the Boxer Uprising and the Republican revolution unnerved the missionaries because they were not in control of events, nor were they serving as models or advisors to the Chinese in the changes that were taking place. The eruption of war in Europe and American participation in that war undermined the missionaries' confidence that the "Christian" nations of the West were any such thing. Worst of all, when the Chinese began to adopt certain external features of Western culture, missionaries were forced to do what they had denied was possible in the nineteenth century: to unbraid the Christian and Western elements of their culture and to distinguish among the beneficial, the neutral, and the downright harmful aspects of Western life.

But here, too, the missionaries had little success in forcing their outlook on the Chinese. For all of their alarmed attacks on Western fashions, hair styles, cigarettes, dancing, movies and manners, and in spite of their rear-guard defense of traditional Chinese society, the missionaries were powerless to reverse the sweep of change in China or to direct it into channels of their own choosing. From the perspective of American teaching missionaries, history had taken an ironic twist. In the late nineteenth century, they had attempted to convince the Chinese government to adopt a national Western-oriented system of education; when the government did so in the early twentieth century it ignored the missionaries' model and set up a system that ultimately rendered the mission schools vulnerable to state control. Missionaries had wanted to free Chinese women from Confucian contraints; in the twentieth century many Chinese women, in the Americans' view, had run amok, mistaking liberty for license and behaving in ways that were incompatible with missionary gender ideology. American missionaries had believed that students in their schools would be the future leaders of China and had sought to awaken a sense of national responsibility in these students; in the twentieth century Chinese students, young men in particular, developed a strong sense of social responsibility but rejected missionaries' controlling hand on how those responsibilities were to be worked out. Missionaries had also prayed for Chinese leadership to rise up within the Christian church and make the church indigenous; Chinese Christians ultimately had to wrench control away from the Americans in a manner that left both sides feeling hurt.

American Protestant missionaries played an important role in the Western pressure that compelled the Chinese to look beyond their own traditions to find ways to deal with the foreigners. Missionaries pressed for treaty provisions granting them access to potential converts to Christianity and defining their status as a privileged class within the Chinese realm. Through their schools, their translations of Western books, and their daily behavior, they taught the Chinese a good deal about Western ways, including alternative patterns of gender relations. Their purpose was to change China, and they pursued this goal tenaciously, in spite of the ambivalent reception they got from the Chinese. Missionaries must then bear some responsibility for sparking the very social changes they later detested. But although their schools undoubtedly had some impact on the students who had contact with them, the consequences were unpredictable. Some students became Christians while others became outspoken opponents of Christianity. Some adhered to Christian gender ideals in marriage and career while others far exceeded the bounds of propriety that missionaries had drawn. Probably the majority of students passed through the schools without embracing either extreme of attraction or repulsion toward missionary culture.

Joseph Esherick has demonstrated that many Chinese joined the Catholic church in order to utilize its temporal power, particularly its ability to protect them from the Chinese state and to permit them to dominate their non-Christian neighbors.[4] Much more research remains to be done before we understand why Chinese joined Protestant churches, which were less willing to intervene on behalf of their converts in civil affairs. It is not too much to suggest, however, that one strong motivation was the desire for education. For poor Chinese who could not afford to attend traditional schools in the nineteenth century or modern government schools in the twentieth century, Protestant missionaries provided access to education. Moreover, just as some Chinese used the Catholic Church to further their own ends, so other Chinese drew the Protestant mission schools into their cultural milieu and made them responsive to Chinese needs.

American teaching missionaries often exaggerated their influence on China, both when they laid claim to what they considered to be positive developments and when they blamed themselves for deleterious changes. Chinese nationalists likewise inflated the significance of the Christian schools when pointing out the harmful features of this foreign educational system. Interestingly, most Chinese commentators reluctantly praised the missionaries for the innovation that probably had the greatest impact on China—the introduction of schools for girls.[5] For different reasons, both American missionaries and Chinese critics chose to portray the Protestant missionary movement as a powerful cultural intrusion to which the Chinese responded relexively, not reflectively. This skewed version of Sino-American relations shaped American historiography on China until the

1980s and continues to affect the way contemporary Americans view China.[6] Even the terms used in this book have, in subtle ways, implied Western initiative and a more passive Chinese reaction; I have spoken of the "missionary movement," the "missionary enterprise" and the "missionary endeavor" as if movement, enterprise and endeavor were all on one side. It would be more accurate to speak of the "missionary encounter" *with* China (and vice versa), to suggest the reciprocal effects of this joint history, from which neither Americans nor Chinese emerged unchanged.

One hundred years after Elijah Bridgman and Henrietta Shuck founded their respective schools for Chinese boys and girls, Christian education had changed vastly. If Bridgman and Shuck could have strolled the grounds of Yenching University, laid out like an American college but boasting the finest Chinese architecture, what would they have thought? How would they have reacted to the Baptist's coeducational academy in Shantou, where American missionaries worked for a Chinese head? What would they have made of Ginling Women's College in Nanjing—a union institution backed by several American Protestant denominations and led by a Chinese woman with an American Ph.D.? Would they have recognized these institutions as the mature fruits of their own labors? It is difficult to know. Certainly there was nothing inevitable about the way that mission schools developed in China. They were the product of competition and collaboration, hostility and good-will, and the misunderstandings and shared vision of Americans and Chinese.

ENDNOTES

1 For information about the last twenty years of missionary activity (particularly educational work) in China, see Richard C. Bush, Jr., *Religion in Communist China* (Nashville: Abingdon Press, 1970), pp. 48–49, chapters two and three; Dwight W. Edwards, *Yenching University* (New York: United Board for Christian Higher Education in Asia, 1959), chapters 37 to 45; Reuben Holden, *Yale-in-China: The Mainland, 1901–1951* (New Haven: The Yale-in-China Association, 1964), chapters six and seven; Jessie G. Lutz, *China and the Christian Colleges, 1850–1950* (Ithaca: Cornell University Press, 1971), chapters eight to thirteen; and Philip West, *Yenching University and Sino-Western Relations, 1916–1952* (Cambridge: Harvard University Press, 1976), chapters six through eight.
2 Sophia Chen, "A Non-Christian Estimation of the Missionary Activities," p. 51, in "The Chinese Woman and Four Other Essays," Yenching University, UBCHEA, RG 11, Box 459, Folder 6107, YDSL.

3 "Some Essential Characteristics and Problems of Christian Education," the Second General Assembly of the Lutheran Church in China, March 30–April 2, 1924, p. 35, ELCA.

4 Joseph Esherick, *The Origins of the Boxer Uprising* (Berkeley: University of California Press, 1987).

5 Mali Lee, "New Woman of China," *Nanking University Magazine*, 1930, Nanking University, UBCHEA, RG 11, Box 236, Folder 3918, YDSL; Sophia Chen, "A Non-Christian Estimation," Yenching University, UBCHEA, RG 11, Box 459, Folder 6107, YDSL; Djung Lu-dzai, *A History of Democratic Education in Modern China* (1934; reprint, Taipei: Ch'eng Wen Publishing Co., 1974), p. 140; and Kiang Kang-hu, *On Chinese Studies* (Shanghai: Commercial Press, Ltd., 1934), p. 199.

6 Paul Cohen, *Discovering History in China: American Historical Writing on the Recent Chinese Past* (New York; Columbia University Press, 1984).

BIBLIOGRAPHY

Manuscripts

American Board of Commissioners for Foreign Missions. United Church Board for World Ministries (successor to the ABCFM). Houghton Library, Harvard University. Cambridge, Massachusetts.

Archives of the United Methodist Church. Drew University, Madison, New Jersey. Records of the General Board of Global Ministries, General Commission on Archives and History, United Methodist Church. Accession groups 73-43 and 79-16.

Board of World Missions, Presbyterian Church, U.S. Presbyterian Church (U.S.A.), Department of History. Montreat, North Carolina. Florence Nickles; Lois Young. Microfilms of letters from missionaries in the field to their home churches, #107, 108, 110, 116, and 117. Annual Reports of the Presbyterian Church, South, 1890-1912.

East Carolina Manuscript Collection, Special Collections. J. Y. Joyner Library. East Carolina University. Greenville, North Carolina. Venetia Cox; Ola V. Lee; Katie Murray.

Evangelical Lutheran Church in America, Region 3 Archives. St. Paul, Minnesota. Midwestern China Oral History Project: Viola Anderson; Ivy Chou; Daniel Chu; Ruth Gilbertson; Paul Hayes; Catherine Reynolds Hertz; Erwin Hertz; Thyra Lawson; Frida Nilsen; Olive Overholt; William Overholt; Henry Refo; Muriel Lockwood Refo; Maud Russell; Randolph Sailer; Arna Quello Sovik; Borghild Syrdel; Minnie Tack; Donalda Terhar; Ching Ching Wang; Katherine B. Ward; Wu Ming-chieh; Mildred Test Young. Personal Papers: Paul Hayes; Frida Nilsen. Miscellaneous: Lutheran Church in China, Minutes; Norwegian Lutheran Church of America, Reports. *White Unto Harvest— A Survey of the Lutheran United Mission: The China Mission of the Norwegian Lutheran Church of America*, by "Missionaries in the Field." (Minneapolis, MN.: Board of Foreign Missions, 1919). *Our First Decade in China, 1905–1915: The Augustana Mission in the Province of Honan* (China Mission Board of the Augustana Synod, 1915). *Our Second Decade in China, 1915–1925: Sketches and Reminiscences, by Missionaries of the*

Augustana Synod in the Province of Honan (Board of Foreign Missions of the Augustana Synod, 1925).

Hoover Institution Archives. Hoover Institution on War, Revolution and Peace. Stanford, California. Lucerne H. Knowlton.

Presbyterian Church (U.S.A.), Department of History of Records Management Services. Philadelphia, Pennsylvania. Mary Margaret Moninger; Pommerenke Family; Harriet Stroh; Gertrude Roe Bayless, "Diary Turned Narrative, 1923–1950;" Sara Collins, "Presbyterian Schools in China," 1902; Hangchow Union Girls' School, Catalogues and Minutes; Letterbooks (letters from missionaries in the field to the home boards, 1890–1900).

University of Oregon Special Collections. Eugene, Oregon. Arthur and Mabel Billings; Mae Boucher; Monona Cheney; Arthur and Ella Coole; Eliza Anne Hughes Davis; Murray S. and Alice Seymour Brown Frame; Adam and Clara Groesbeck; Henry V. and Jessie Ankeny Lacy; Bertha Magness; Ida Belle Lewis [Main]; Dorothy Walters Collection of Ida Belle Lewis [Main]; Elsie Reik; Myrtle Smith; David and Luella Tappan; Laura Maude Wheeler.

Yale Divinity School Library. Yale University, New Haven, Connecticut. United Board for Christian Higher Education in East Asia, Record Group 11: Ginling Women's College; Hangchow Christian College; Fukien Christian College; Lingnan University (Canton Christian College); Nanking University; Shantung Christian College (Cheeloo); West China Union University; Yenching University (including Yenching Women's College). China Records Project, Record Group 8, Personal Papers: George and Dorothy Barbour; Robert and Gladys Bundy; Ruth Chester; Elsie Clark [Krug]; Foster Family; Chester G. Fuson; Frank and Verna Garrett; Emily Susan Hartwell; Esther Kreps; Samuel Leger; Robert and Jeanie Sewell Graham McClure; Emma and Lizzie Martin; Fredericka Rutherford Mead; Emily Case Mills; Mabel Ruth Nowlin; Elizabeth Perkins; Alice Reed; Reuman Family; Bertha St. Claire; Abbie Sanderson; Martha Wiley; and Maynard Owen Williams. Pamphlet Collection, Record Group 31. "History of the North China Mission of the Women's Foreign Missionary Society of the Methodist Episcopal Church," journal begun in 1899 by Mary Porter Gamewell. Diary and Miscellaneous Papers of Lois Young.

Journals

Bulletins on Chinese Education, issued by the Chinese National Association for the Advancement of Education. Shanghai: Commercial Press, Ltd.,1923.

The China Yearbook, 1913–1916, H.T. Montague Bell and H.G. W. Woodhead. London: George Koutledge and Sons, Ltd.

The Chinese Recorder and Missionary Journal, 1876, 1890–1930. Shanghai: Presbyterian Mission Press.

The Missionary Review of the World, 1924–1930.

Conference Records

China Centenary Conference. Shanghai: Centenary Conference Committee, 1907.

Records of the First Triennial Meeting of the Educational Association of China. Shanghai: American Presbyterian Mission Press, 1893.

Records of the Second Triennial Meeting of the Educational Association of China. Shanghai: American Presbyterian Mission Press, 1896.

Records of the Third Triennial Meeting of the Educational Association of China. Shanghai: American Presbyterian Mission Press, 1899.

World Missionary Conference, 1910. Report of Commission III: Education in Relation to the Christianization of National Life. New York: Fleming H. Revell, 1910.

Secondary Sources

Anderson, Mary Raleigh. A Cycle in the Celestial Kingdom: Protestant Mission Schools for Girls in South China (1827 to the Japanese Invasion). Mobile, Ala.: Heiter-Starke Printing Co., 1943.

206

Bailey, Victoria W. Bailey's Activities in China: An Account of the Life and Work and Professor Joseph Bailey in and for China, 1890–1935. Palo Alto, Calif.: Pacific Books, 1964.

Baker, Frances J. The Story of the Woman's Foreign Missionary Society of the Methodist Episcopal Church, 1869–1895. Cincinnati: Cranston and Curtis, 1896.

Baker, Paula. "The Domestication of Politics: Women and American Political Society, 1789–1920," *American Historical Review* 89: 3 (June 1984): 620–647.

Barnett, Suzannne Wilson and John K. Fairbank, eds. Christianity in China: Early Protestant Writings. Cambridge: Harvard University Press, 1985.

Barrow, John. "American Institutions of Higher Learning in China, 1845–1925," *Higher Education* 4 (Feb. 1, 1948): 121–124.

Bartlett, Samuel Colcord. Historical Sketches of the Missions of the American Board. New York: American Board of Commissioners for Foreign Missions, 1872.

Barton, James. "The Modern Missionary," *Harvard Theological Review* VIII (January 1915): 1–17.

Bashford, James. China, An Interpretation. New York: Abingdon Press, 1919.

Bastid, Marianne. Educational Reform in Early-Twentieth-Century China. Translated by Paul J. Bailey. Ann Arbor: Center for Chinese Studies, 1988.

Beach, Harlan. Dawn on the Hills of T'ang, or Missions in China. New York: Student Volunteer Movement for Foreign Missions, 1898.

_____, ed. Student Volunteer Movement for Foreign Missions: World Atlas of Christian Missions. New York: Student Volunteer Movement for Foreign Missions, 1911.

Beach, Harlan and Charles H. Fahs, eds. World Missionary Atlas. New York: Institute of Social and Religious Research, 1925.

Beahan, Charolotte. "The Women's Movement and Nationalism in Late Ch'ing China" (Ph. D. diss., Columbia University, 1976).

Beaver, R. Pierce. American Protestant Women in World Mission: The History of the First Feminist Movement. Grand Rapids, Mich.: William B. Eerdmans Publishing Co., 1968.

Biggerstaff, Knight. The Earliest Modern Government Schools in China. Ithaca: Cornell University Press, 1961.

Boorman, Howard, ed. Biographical Dictionary of Republican China. New York: Columbia University Press, 1967.

Borthwick, Sally. Education and Social Change in China: The Beginnings of the Modern Era. Stanford: Hoover Institution Press, 1983.

Breslin, Thomas A. China, American Catholicism and the Missionary. University Park: Pennsylvania State University Press, 1980.

Brewster, William N. The Evolution of New China. Cincinnati: Jennings and Graham; New York: Eaton and Mains, 1907.

Brown, Arthur. New Forces in Old China: An Unwelcome but Inevitable Awakening. New York: Fleming H. Revell Co., 1906.

Brown, Anna and Oswald. The Life and Letters of Laura Askew Haygood. Nashville: Publishing House of the Methodist Episcopal Church, 1904.

Brumberg, Joan Jacobs. "Zenanas and Girlless Villages: The Ethnology of American Evangelical Women, 1870–1910" Journal of American History 69 (Sept. 1982): 347–371.

Burton, Margaret C. The Education of Women in China. New York: Fleming H. Revell Co., 1911.

_____. Women Workers in the Orient. West Medford, Mass.: Central Committee of the United Study of Foreign Missions, 1918.

Bush, Richard C., Jr. Religion in Communist China. Nashville: Abingdon Press, 1970.

Butler, Mrs. F. A. History of the Woman's Foreign Missionary Society, Methodist Episcopal Church, South. Nashville: Publishing House of the Methodist Episcopal Church, South, 1904.

Callahan, Paul E. "Christianity and Revolution as Seen by the National Christian Council of China" *Papers on China* 5: 75–106. Cambridge: East Asian Research Center, 1951.

Carlberg, Gustav. Thirty Years in China, 1905–1935, The Story of the Augustana Synod Mission in the Province of Honan as Told by the Missionaries. Board of Foreign Missions of the Augustana Synod, 1937.

Chamberlain, Mrs. W. I. (Mary E. A.). Fifty Years in Foreign Fields—China, Japan, India, Arabia: A History of Five Decades of the Woman's Board of Foreign Missions, Reformed Church in America. New York: Woman's Board of Foreign Missions, Reformed Church in America, 1925.

Chao, Yang Buwei. Autobiography of a Chinese Woman. Translated by Chao Yuanren. Westport, Conn.: Greenwood Press, 1947.

Chao, Celia Hwaguen. "The Life of Mali: An Ideal Biography of My Mother." MS, 1944, copy in the Harlan Hatcher Graduate Library, University of Michigan, Ann Arbor, Michigan.

Chapman, Owen H. The Chinese Revolution, 1926–1927: A Record of the Period Under Communist Control as Seen from the Nationalist Capital, Hankow. London: Constable and Co., Ltd., 1928.

Chow Tse-tsung. The May Fourth Movement: Intellectual Revolution in Modern China. Cambridge: Harvard University Press, 1960.

Christian Education in China: A Study Made by an Educational Commission Representing the Mission Boards and Societies Conducting Work in China. New York:

Committee of Reference and Counsel of the Foreign Mission Conference of North America, 1922.

Christiansen, Torben and William R. Hutchison, eds. Missionary Ideals in the Imperialistic Era: 1880–1920. Papers from the Durham Consultation. Denmark: Aros, 1982.

Chuang Chai-Hsuan. Tendencies Toward a Democratic System of Education in China. Shanghai: Commercial Press, Ltd., 1922.

Clifford, Nicholas. Shanghai, 1925: Urban Nationalism and the Defense of Foreign Privilege. Michigan Papers in Chinese Studies, #37. Ann Arbor: Center for Chinese Studies, University of Michigan Press, 1979.

Coe, John L. Huachung University. New York: United Board for Christian Higher Education in Asia, 1962.

Cohen, Paul A. China and Christianity: The Missionary Movement and the Growth of Chinese Anti-foreignism, 1860–1870. Cambridge: Harvard University Press, 1963.

_____. Discovering History in China: American Historical Writing and the Recent Chinese Past. Columbia: Columbia University Press, 1984.

Coleman, Michael C. "Presbyterian Missionary Attitudes Toward the Chinese, 1837–1900," Journal of Presbyterian History 56:3 (1978): 185–200.

Corbett, Charles Hodge. Lingnan University. New York: Board of Trustees for Lingnan University, 1963.

_____. Shantung Christian University (Cheeloo). New York: United Board for Christian Colleges in China, 1955.

Cott, Nancy F. The Grounding of Modern Feminism. New Haven: Yale University Press, 1987.

Cott, Nancy and Elizabeth Pleck, eds. A Heritage of Her Own. New York: Simon and Schuster, 1979.

Cressy, Earl Herbert. Christian Higher Education in China, A Study for the Year 1925–1926, China Christian Educational Bulletin Association, # 20. Shanghai: China Christian Educational Association, 1928.

Davin, Delia. Woman-Work: Women and the Party in Revolutionary China. Oxford: Oxford University Press, 1976.

Day, Clarence Burton. Hangchow University, A Brief History. New York: United Board for Christian Colleges in China, 1955.

Delamont, Sara and Lorna Duffin, eds. The Nineteenth-Century Woman: Her Cultural and Physical World. London: Croom Helm, 1978.

Dernberger, Robert, et. al. The Chinese: Adapting the Past, Building the Future. Ann Arbor: Center for Chinese Studies, 1986.

Diamond, Norma. "Women Under KMT Rule: Variations on the Feminine Mystique," *Modern China* 1:1 (January 1975): 3–45.

Djung Lu-dzai. A History of Democratic Education in Modern China. 1934. Reprint, Taipei: Ch'eng-Wen Publishing Co., 1974.

Edwards, Dwight W. Yenching University. New York: United Board for Christian Higher Education in Asia, 1959.

Esherick, Joseph. "1911: A Review," Symposium of the 1911 Revolution, *Modern China* 2: 2 (April 1976): 139–226.

_____.The Origins of the Boxer Uprising. Berkeley: University of California Press, 1987.

_____. Reform and Revolution: The 1911 Revolution in Hunan and Hubei. Berkeley: University of California Press, 1976.

Fairbank, John K., ed. The Missionary Enterprise in China and America. Cambridge: Harvard University Press, 1974.

Fairbank, John K. and Edwin O. Reischauer. China, Tradition and Transformation. Boston: George Allen and Unwin, 1979.

Fenn, William Purviance. Christian Higher Education in Changing China, 1880–1950. Grand Rapids, Mich: William B. Eerdmans Publishing Co., 1976.

Feuerwerker, Albert. The Foreign Establishment in China in the Early Twentieth Century. Ann Arbor: Center for Chinese Studies, 1976.

Field, Margaret. "The Chinese Boycott of 1905," *Papers on China* 11: 63–98. Cambridge: Harvard University, Center for Asian Studies, 1957.

Flemming, Leslie A., ed. Woman's Work for Woman. Boulder, Colo: Westview Press, 1989.

Ford, Eddy Lucius. "The History of the Educational Work of the Methodist Episcopal Church in China: A Study of its Development and Present Trends" (Ph. D. diss., Northwestern University, 1936).

Freedman, Estelle. "Separatism as Strategy: Female Institution Building and American Feminism, 1870–1930," *Feminist Studies* 5 (1979): 512–529.

Freyn, Hubert. Prelude to War: The Chinese Student Rebellion of 1935–1936. Shanghai: China Journal Publishing Co., Ltd., 1939.

Gamewell, Mary Ninde. Ming Kwong, "City of the Morning Light." West Medford, Mass.: The Central Committee on the United Study of Foreign Missions, 1924.

_____. New Life Currents in China. New York: Missionary Education Movement in the United States and Canada, Methodist Book Concern, 1919.

Goodsell, Willystine. Pioneers of Women's Education in the United States: Emma Willard, Catherine Beecher, Mary Lyon. New York: McGraw-Hill Book Co., 1931.

Graham, Gael. "The *Cumberland* Incident of 1928: Gender, Nationalism and Social Change in American Mission Schools in China," *Journal of Women's History* 6: 3 (Fall 1994): 35–61.

_____ "Exercising Control: Sports and Physical Education in American Protestant Mission Schools in China, 1880–1930." *Signs: Journal of Women in Culture and Society* 20: 1 (Autumn 1994): 23–48.

Green, Harvey. Fit for America, Health, Fitness, Sport and American Society. New York: Pantheon Books, 1986.

Gregg, Alice H. China and Educational Autonomy: The Changing Role of the Protestant Educational Missionary in China, 1807–1937. Syracuse: Syracuse University Press, 1946.

Grossberg, Michael. Governing the Hearth: Law and the Family in Nineteenth-Century America. Chapel Hill: University of North Carolina Press, 1985.

Guisso, Richard W. and Stanley Johannesen, eds. Women in China: Current Directions in Historical Scholarship. Youngstown, N.Y.: Philo Press, 1981.

Hackett, Roger F. "Chinese Students in Japan, 1900–1910," *Papers on China*, Vol. 3: 134–169. Cambridge: Harvard University Press, 1949.

Handy, Robert T. ed. The Social Gospel in America, 1870–1920. New York: Oxford University Press, 1966.

Hardesty, Nancy. Women Called to Witness: Evangelical Feminism in the Nineteenth Century. Nashville: Abingdon Press, 1984.

Hayden, Dolores. The Grand Domestic Revolution: A History of Feminist Designs for American Homes, Neighborhoods and Cities. Cambridge: Massachusetts Institute of Technology Press, 1981.

Hayhoe, Ruth and Marianne Bastid, eds. China's Education and the Industrialized World, Studies in Cultural Transfer. Armonk, N.Y.: M.E. Sharpe, Inc., 1987.

Hill, Patricia. The World Their Household: The American Woman's Foreign Mission Movement and Cultural Transformation, 1870–1920. Ann Arbor: University of Michigan Press, 1985.

Hocking, Ernest. Rethinking Missions: A Layman's Inquiry after One Hundred Years. New York: Harper and Bros. Publishers, 1932.

Hoh, Gunsun. Physical Education in China. Shanghai: Commercial Press, Ltd., 1926.

Holden, Reuben. Yale in China: The Mainland, 1901–1951. New Haven: Yale-in-China Association, 1964.

Hsiao, Theodore. The History of Modern Education in China. Peiping: Peking University Press, 1932.

Hsieh Ping Ying. Girl Rebel: The Autobiography of Hsieh Ping Ying. Translated by Adet and Anor Lin. New York: The John Day Co., 1940.

Hsu, Francis L. K. Under the Ancestors' Shadow: Kinship, Personality, and Social Mobility in China. Stanford: Stanford University Press, 1971.

Hunter, Jane. The Gospel of Gentility: American Women Missionaries in Turn-of-the-Century China. New Haven: Yale University Press, 1984.

Hutchison, William R. Errand to the World: American Protestant Thought and Foreign Missions. Chicago: University of Chicago Press, 1987.

_____. "A Moral Equivalent for Imperialism: Americans and the Promotion of 'Christian Civilization', 1880–1910," Indian Journal of American Studies 13: 1 (1983): 55–68.

Hyatt, Irwin T., Jr. Our Ordered Lives Confess: Three Nineteenth-Century American Missionaries in East Shantung. Cambridge: Harvard University Press, 1976.

Iglehart, Charles W. A Century of Protestant Christianity in Japan. Rutland, Vt.: Charles E. Tuttle Co., 1959.

Isham, Mary. Valorous Ventures: A Record of Sixty and Six Years of the Woman's Foreign Mission Society of the Methodist Episcopal Church. Boston: Woman's Foreign Missionary Society, Methodist Episcopal Church, 1936.

Israel, John. Student Nationalism in China, 1927–1937. Stanford: Stanford University Press, 1966.

Israel, John and Donald W. Klein. Rebels and Bureaucrats: China's December 9ers. Berkeley: University of California Press, 1976.

Jaschok, Maria and Suzanne Miers, eds. Women and Chinese Patriarchy: Submission, Servitude and Escape. Hong Kong: Hong Kong University Press, 1994.

Jeffreys, W. H. James Addison Ingle (Yin Teh-sen): First Bishop of the Missionary District of Hankow, China. 1913. Reprint, Taipei: Ch'eng-Wen Publishing Co., 1971.

Kaestle, Carl F. Pillars of the Republic: Common Schools and American Society, 1780–1860. New York: Hill and Wang, 1983.

Keenan, Barry C. The Dewey Experiment in China: Educational Reform and Political Power in the Early Republic. Cambridge: Council on East Asian Studies, Harvard University, 1977.

_____. "Educational Reform and Politics in Early Republican China," *Journal of Asian Studies* 33 (February 1974): 225–237.

Kelley, Mary, ed. Woman's Being, Woman's Place: Female Identity and Vocation in American History. Boston: G. K. Hall and Co., 1979.

Kerber, Linda. "Separate Spheres, Female Worlds, Woman's Place: The Rhetoric of Women's History," *Journal of American History* 75 (June 1988): 9–39.

_____. Women of the Republic: Intellect and Ideology in Revolutionary America. Chapel Hill: University of North Carolina Press, 1980.

Kiang Kang-hu. On Chinese Studies. Shanghai: Commercial Press, Ltd., 1934.

Kruk, Sonia, et. al., eds. Promissory Notes: Women in the Transition to Socialism. New York: Monthly Review Press, 1989.

Lamberton, Mary. St. John's University, Shanghai. New York: United Board for Christian Colleges in China, 1955.

Lang, Olga. Chinese Family and Society. 1946. Reprint, New York: Archon Books, 1968.

Latourette, Kenneth S. A History of Christian Missions in China. New York: The MacMillan Co., 1929.

Levy, Marion, Jr. The Family Revolution in Modern China. Cambridge: Harvard University Press in cooperation with the Institute of Pacific Relations, 1949.

Lewis, Ida Belle. The Education of Girls in China. New York: Teachers' College, Columbia University, 1919.

_____. Some Factors in the Evaluation of Christian Lower Primary Schools. Shanghai: Commercial Press, Ltd., 1921.

Li, Anthony C. The History of Privately Controlled Higher Education in the Republic of China. Washington D.C.: The Catholic University of America Press, 1951.

Li, Lincoln. Student Nationalism in China, 1924–1949. Albany: State University of New York Press, 1994.

Liao Kuang-sheng. Anti-Foreignism and Modernization in China, 1860–1980: Linkage Between Domestic Policies and Foreign Policy. Hong Kong: The Chinese University Press, 1984.

Lin Pao-ch'tuan. L'Instruction Feminine en Chine (Apres la Revolution de 1911). Paris: Librairie Geuther, 1926.

Lin Yutang, "Feminist Thought in Ancient China," T'ien Hsia Monthly 1: 2 (September 1933): 127–150.

Linden, Allen B. "Politics and Education in Nationalist China: The Case of the University Council, 1927–1928," *Journal of Asian Studies* 27 (August 1968): 763–776.

Liu Kwang-ching, ed. American Missionaries in China, Papers from Harvard Seminars. Cambridge: East Asian Research Center, Harvard University, 1970.

Livingston, Jon and Joe Moore and Felicia Oldfather. Imperial Japan, 1800–1945. New York: Pantheon Books, 1973.

Lutz, Jessie G. China and the Christian Colleges, 1850–1950. Ithaca: Cornell University Press, 1971.

_____. Chinese Politics and Christian Missions: The Anti-Christian Movements of 1920–1928. Notre Dame: Cross Cultural Publications, 1988.

_____. "Chinese Nationalism and the Anti-Christian Campaigns of the 1920s," *Modern Asian Studies* 10: 3 (1976): 395–416.

Lutz, Jessie G., ed. Christian Missions in China, Evangelists of What? Lexington, Mass., D. C. Heath and Co., 1965.

Lutz, Jessie G. and Salah El-Shakhs, eds. Tradition and Modernity: The Role of Traditionalism in the Modernization Process. Washington, D.C.: University Press of America, 1982.

Lyon, D. Willard, ed. The Evangelisation of China. National Committee of the College Y.M.C.A. of China: Tientsin Press, 1896.

McDowell, John Patrick. The Social Gospel in the South: The Woman's Mission Movement in the Methodist Episcopal Church, South, 1886–1939. Baton Rouge: Louisiana State University Press, 1982.

McGillivray, D., ed. A Century of Protestant Missions in China (1807–1907). China Centenary Conference, Historical Volume, Shanghai: American Presbyterian Mission Press, 1907.

McKee, Delber L. Chinese Exclusion vs. the Open Door Policy, 1900–1906: Clashes Over China Policy in the Roosevelt Era. Detroit: Wayne University Press, 1977.

Mangan, J. A. and Roberta J. Parks. From "Fair Sex" to Feminism: Sport and the Socialization of Women in the Industrial and Post-Industrial Eras. London: Frank Cass & Co., 1987.

Martin, W. A. P. The Awakening of China. New York: Doubleday, Page and Co., 1910.

Montgomery, Helen Barrett. Western Women in Eastern Lands: An Outline Study of Fifty Years of Woman's Work in Foreign Missions. New York: The MacMillan Co., 1910.

Nance, W.B. Soochow University. New York: United Board of Christian Colleges in China, 1956.

Naquin, Susan. Millenarian Rebellion in China: The Eight Trigrams Uprising of 1813. New Haven; Yale University Press, 1976.

Nash, Roderick. The Nervous Generation: American Thought, 1917–1930. Chicago: Rand McNally Publishing Co., 1970.

Neals, Patricia, ed. United States Attitudes and Politices Toward China: The Impact of American Missionaries. Armonk, N.Y.: M.E. Sharpe, 1990.

Nevius, Helen S. Coan. The Life of John Livingstone Nevius, Forty Years a Missionary in China. New York: Fleming H. Revell Co., 1895.

Nevius, John L. China and the Chinese: A General Description of the Country and its Inhabitants; its Civilization and Form of Government; its Religion and Social Institutions; its Intercourse with Other Nations and its Present Condition and Prospects. New York: Harper and Bros., 1869.

Nourse, Mary A. The Four Hundred Million: A Short History of the Chinese. Indianapolis: Bobbs-Merrill, 1935.

Oldfield, W. H. Pioneering in Kwangsi: The Story of the Alliance Missionaries in South China. Harrisburg, Pa.: Christian Publications, Inc., 1936.

Ono, Kazuko. Chinese Women in a Century of Revolution, 1850–1950. Stanford: Stanford University Press, 1989.

Park, Roberta J. "'Embodied Selves': The Rise and Development of Concern for Physical Education, Active Games, and Recreation for American Women, 1776–1865," *Journal of Sports History* 5: 2 (Summer 1978): 5–41.

Peake, Cyrus H. Nationalism and Education in Modern China. New York: Columbia University Press, 1932.

Petty, Orvilla A., ed. Laymen's Foreign Mission Inquiry, Regional Reports of the Commission of Appraisal—China. New York: Harper and Bros., 1933.

Phillips, Clifton Jackson. Protestant America and the Pagan World: The First Half-Century of the ABCFM, 1810–1860. Cambridge: East Asian Research Center, Harvard University, 1969.

Rabe, Valentin. The Home Base of American China Missions, 1880–1920. Cambridge: Harvard University Press, 1978.

Rawski, Evelyn Sakakida. Education and Popular Literacy in Ch'ing China. Ann Arbor: University of Michigan Press, 1979.

Rhoads, Edward. "Nationalism and Xenophobia in Kwangtung (1905–1906): The Canton Anti-American Boycott and the Lenchow Anti-Missionary Uprising," Papers on China 16: 154–197. Cambridge: East Asian Research Center, Harvard University, 1962.

Rozman, Gilbert, ed. The Modernization of China. New York: The Free Press, 1981.

Sandeen, Ernest R. The Roots of Fundamentalism, British and American Millenialism, 1800–1930. Chicago: University of Chicago Press, 1970.

Schurman, Franz and Orville Schell, eds. The China Reader, vol. 2, Nationalism, War, and the Rise of Communism, 1911–1949. New York: Vintage Books, 1967.

Schwartz, Benjamin I. Reflections on the May Fourth Movement: A Symposium. Cambridge: East Asia Research Center, Harvard University, 1972.

Siu, Bobby. Women in China: Imperialism and Women's Resistance, 1900–1949. London: Zed Press, 1982.

Smith, Samuel F. Missionary Sketches: A Concise History of the Work of the American Baptist Missionary Union. Boston: W. G. Corthell, 1879.

Smith-Rosenberg, Carroll. Disorderly Conduct: Visions of Gender in Victorian America. Oxford: Oxford University Press, 1985.

Snow, Helen. China Builds for Democracy: A Story of Cooperative Industry. New York: New Age Books, 1941.

Solomon, Barbara. In the Company of Educated Women: A History of Women and Higher Education in America. New Haven: Yale University Press, 1985.

Speer, Mrs. Robert and Constance M. Hallock. Christian Homemaking. New York: Round Table Press, Inc., 1939.

Spring, Joel. The American School, 1642–1985. New York: Longman, 1986.

Stockard, Janice E. Daughters of the Canton Delta: Marriage Patterns and Economic Strategies in South China, 1860–1930. Stanford: Stanford University Press, 1989.

Tao, W. Tchishin and C. P. Chen. Education in China, 1924 . Published under the joint auspices of the National Federation of Provincial Educational Associations and the National Association for the Advancement of Education. Shanghai: Commercial Press, Ltd., 1925.

Teng Ssu-yu. The Taiping Rebellion and the Western Powers—A Comprehensive Survey. Oxford: Clarendon Press, 1971.

Teng Ssu-yu and John K. Fairbank, eds. China's Response to the West: A Documentary Survey, 1839–1923. Cambridge: Harvard University Press, 1961.

Thomson, James C., Jr. While China Faced West: American Reformers in Nationalist China, 1928–1938. Cambridge: Harvard University Press, 1969.

Thomson, James C., Jr., et. al. Sentimental Imperialists: The American Experience in East Asia. New York: Harper and Row, 1981.

Thurston, Mrs. Lawrence (Matilda S. Calder) and Ruth M. Chester. Ginling College. New York: United Board for Christian Colleges in China, 1955.

Torbet, Robert G. Venture of Faith: The Story of the American Baptist Foreign Mission Society and the Woman's American Baptist Foreign Mission Society, 1814–1954 . Philadelphia: The Judson Press, 1955.

Tsang Chih-sam. Nationalism in School Education in China Since the Opening of the Twentieth Century. Hong Kong: South China Morning Press, Ltd., 1933.

Tucker, Ruth. Guardians of the Great Commission: The Story of Women in Modern Missions. Grand Rapids, Mich: Zonderven Publishing House, 1988.

van der Valk, Marc. An Outline of Modern Chinese Family Law. Peking: Henry Vetch, 1939.

Varg, Paul. Missionaries, Chinese and Diplomats: The American Protestant Missionary Movement in China, 1890–1950. Princeton: Princeton University Press, 1958.

Verbrugge, Martha H. Able-Bodied Womanhood: Personal Health and Social Change in Nineteenth-Century Boston. Oxford: Oxford University Press, 1988.

Wakeman, Frederic, Jr. The Fall of Imperial China. New York: Free Press, 1975.

Wallace, L. Ethel. Hwa Nan College, The Woman's College of South China. New York: United Board for Christian Colleges in China, 1956.

Wang, Y. C. Chinese Intellectuals and the West, 1872–1949. Chapel Hill: University of North Carolina Press, 1966.

Wasserstrom, Jeffrey. Student Protests in Twentieth-Century China: The View from Shanghai. Stanford: Stanford University Press, 1991.

Wasserstrom, Jeffrey and Elizabeth J. Perry, eds. Popular Protest and Political Culture in Modern China: Learning from 1989. Boulder, Colo.: Westview Press, 1992.

Webster, James B. Christian Education and the National Consciousness in China. New York: E. P. Dutton and Co., 1923.

West, Philip. Yenching University and Sino-Western Relations, 1916–1952. Cambridge: Harvard University Press, 1976.

White, Ronald C. and C. Howard Hopkins. The Social Gospel: Religion and Reform in Changing America. Philadelphia: Temple University Press, 1976.

Wolf, Arthur and Chieh-shan Huang. Marriage and Adoption in China, 1845–1945. Stanford: Stanford University Press, 1980.

Wolf, Margery and Roxane Witke, eds. Women in Chinese Society. Stanford: Stanford University Press, 1975.

Woody, Thomas. A History of Women's Education in the United States, vols. I and II. New York: Octagon Books, 1966.

Wu Chao-kwang, "The International Aspect of the Missionary Movement in China" (Ph. D. diss., Johns Hopkins University, 1930).

Yang, C. K. The Chinese Family in the Communist Revolution. Cambridge: Massachusetts Institute of Technology Press, 1959.

Yang, Martin. A Chinese Village: Taitou, Shantung Province. New York: Columbia University Press, 1945.

222

Yeh, Wen-hsin. The Alienated Academy: Culture and Politics in Republican China, 1919–1937. Cambridge: Council on East Asian Studies, Harvard University Press, 1990.

Yip Ka-che. Religion, Nationalism and Chinese Students: The Anti-Christian Movement of 1922–1927. Bellingham: Western Washington University Press, 1980.

Yung Wing. My Life in China and America. New York: Henry Holt and Co., 1909.

Index

\

DATE DUE